Not for Sale

Not for Sale

DECOMMODIFYING PUBLIC LIFE

EDITED BY GORDON LAXER & DENNIS SORON

broadview press

Garamond Press

Copyright © 2006 Gordon Laxer and Dennis Soron

All rights reserved. The use of any part of this publication reproduced, transmitted in any form or by any means, electronic, mechanical, photocopying, recording, or otherwise, or stored in a retrieval system, without prior written consent of the publisher—or in the case of photocopying, a licence from *Access Copyright* (Canadian Copyright Licensing Agency), One Yonge Street, Suite 1900, Toronto, Ontario M5E 1E5—is an infringement of the copyright law.

LIBRARY AND ARCHIVES CANADA CATALOGUING IN PUBLICATION

Not for sale : decommodifying public life / edited by Gordon Laxer & Dennis Soron.

Includes bibliographical references and index.
ISBN 1-55111-752-5

1. Municipal services—Economic aspects. 2. Privatization. I. Laxer, Gordon, 1944-
II. Soron, Dennis, 1968-

HD3850.N67 2006   338.9'25   C2006-901399-3

BROADVIEW PRESS is an independent, international publishing house, incorporated in 1985. Broadview believes in shared ownership, both with its employees and with the general public; since the year 2000 Broadview shares have traded publicly on the Toronto Venture Exchange under the symbol BDP.

We welcome comments and suggestions regarding any aspect of our publications—please feel free to contact us at the addresses below or at broadview@broadviewpress.com/www.broadviewpress.com.

North America
Post Office Box 1243,
Peterborough, Ontario, Canada K9J 7H5

Post Office Box 1015,
3576 California Road,
Orchard Park, New York, USA 14127
TEL: (705) 743-8990; FAX: (705) 743-8353

customerservice@broadviewpress.com

UK, Ireland and continental Europe
NBN International
Estover Road, Plymouth PL6 7PY, UK
TEL: 44 (0) 1752 202300;
FAX: 44 (0) 1752 202330;
enquiries@nbninternational.com

Australia and New Zealand
UNIREPS University of New South Wales
Sydney, NSW 2052 Australia
TEL: 61 2 96640999; FAX: 61 2 96645420
infopress@unsw.edu.au

Broadview Press gratefully acknowledges the financial support of the Government of Canada through the Book Publishing Industry Development Program for our publishing activities.

Cover & Interior by Liz Broes, Black Eye Design.

Printed in Canada

10 9 8 7 6 5 4 3 2 1

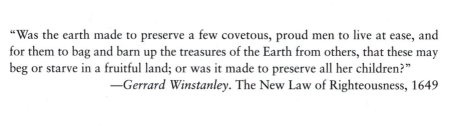

"Was the earth made to preserve a few covetous, proud men to live at ease, and for them to bag and barn up the treasures of the Earth from others, that these may beg or starve in a fruitful land; or was it made to preserve all her children?"
—*Gerrard Winstanley*. The New Law of Righteousness, 1649

"Earth provides enough to satisfy every man's need but not for every man's greed."
—*Mohandas Gandhi* n.d.

"Water is a shared right, and that right is not for sale."
—*Oscar Olivera*, Cochabamba Federation of Factory Workers/
The Coalition for the Defense of Water and Life, 2000

CONTENTS

Part Three: Democratic Struggles for Decommodification

LIST OF TABLES AND FIGURES

ACKNOWLEDGEMENTS

The editors wish to thank the chapter authors for the fine quality of their work and their readiness to make revisions. We thank the anonymous reviewer of this book for helpful comments. We are grateful for the fine work that Goze Dogu did in checking and formatting the amalgamated references. We also wish to thank Kate Nunn for her consistent support throughout the publishing process, and our other colleagues at the Globalism and its Challengers project, who patiently listened to and gave helpful comments on various versions of chapters in this book. Finally, we would like to recognize the Social Sciences and Humanities Research Council of Canada for generously supporting the networking and the conferences, which made this book possible.

Gordon Laxer thanks Judith Beirs for putting up with his verbal enthusiasms on the book, and for her emotional support and love. He also thanks Steve McBride for a trenchant, yet surprisingly gentle critique of an early draft of his chapter in Mexico City and Ineke Lock for doing such creative research work. Dennis Soron extends thanks in particular to Sandra Starmans for her kindness, patience and support, and to the many friends and colleagues in the Globalism Project and the Parkland Institute who helped to make his time in Edmonton as a postdoc a particularly stimulating and fulfilling one.

part one
FRAMING THE ISSUES

CHAPTER ONE

Thematic Introduction
Decommodification, Democracy, and the Battle for the Commons

DENNIS SORON & GORDON LAXER

In the early 1990s, coin-operated "oxygen booths" began to appear in smog-choked cities such as Tokyo, Mexico City, and Beijing, offering the overtaxed lungs of urbanites a brief respite from car exhaust, dust, and other pollutants. The fledgling field of consumer breath delivery was born. As inadequate as these booths may have been as a response to contaminated air, they promised to be at least as effective as Beijing's earlier experiment in adding rose-scented air freshener to water sprayed onto city streets.

Following the debut of the O2 *Spa Bar* in Toronto in 1996, upscale "oxygen bars" appealing to a health-conscious, yuppie clientele opened in New York, Chicago, Los Angeles, Reno, Bombay, and other cities. Customers pay one or two dollars per minute to "gas up" on pure oxygen, often infused with patented aroma blends like "Cloud Lime," "Eclipse," and "Revitalize." As oxygen treatments grew more popular in health resorts and spas, tie-in products were spawned: oxygen pills; oxygenated face creams and fruit drinks; oxygenating liquid supplements such as "Oxy-Up"; even portable oxygen canisters, designed like bottled spring water for on-the-go personal use. One on-line entrepreneur gushes about the "way-cool" business opportunities offered by oxygen-related products and services, promising investors up to 500 per cent profit margins (A Way-Cool Profit Center).

Passed over in this chirpy sales pitch is whether these products benefit people worried about deteriorating air quality. What is striking is the cheerful lack of concern for the conditions that generate demand for commodified oxygen. Only the narrowest concern for private gain could construe the relentless poisoning of the earth's atmosphere as a "way-cool" opportunity. Others might conclude that there is something seriously wrong when people feel compelled to pay for oxygen, which people have always had free access to by simply breathing the atmosphere, which is a common gift for all.

Though marginal, the "oxygen industry" illustrates the stark incompatibility between maximizing opportunities for private profit and ensuring human and ecological well-being. It draws attention to the irrationality of an economic system in which the evisceration of the social and environmental commons is seen as a by-product of progress or an "opportunity" for more profitable commodities, rather than an urgent collective problem. Today, commodities proliferate while meaningful democratic options shrink. Frivolous consumer choices multiply, but a sense of political impotence sets in about our capacity to confront effectively mounting social and environmental problems: global South poverty, global warming, deteriorating essential public services.

THE BATTLE FOR THE COMMONS

Challenging the prevailing sense of political pessimism, this book develops the twin notions of commodification and decommodification as means to understand many contemporary democratic struggles. It builds upon both previous academic discussions and "the promising critique of commodification that is developing within the anti-globalization movement" (McNally, 2002, p. 232). While the chapters take up a variety of specific issues—body parts, water, land, labour, public services, consumer culture, the knowledge economy, and beyond—from diverse perspectives, the book has two main goals. First, it examines central dimensions of the assault waged on "the commons" by the commodifying and privatizing thrust of global capitalism. Second, it engages with alternatives to *neoliberal globalism* from both the work of progressive intellectuals and a range of contemporary struggles to defend and democratically reinvent the commons by "decommodifying" much of collective life.

By "neoliberal globalism," we mean an ideology that attempts to create a seamless link amongst recent technological innovations, current trends towards greater global integration, and pro-capitalist governance. Neoliberal globalism mandates that all countries encourage foreign ownership and control of their economies, remove foreign exchange protections, cut public services, and balance budgets while cutting corporate taxes. Government-owned enterprises must be sold. The neoliberal globalism regime includes the norms, institutions, and laws that support corporate profitability along neoliberal lines. Governments turn away from citizens' concerns, and, outside imperial USA itself, the sovereignty of political communities. Instead, they focus on exports and on enshrining transnational corporate rights, often acting as junior partners to the US Empire. Countries are currently locked into neoliberal principles by structural adjustment programs in the South and by neoliberal agreements such as NAFTA in the North.

Recently, the notion of "the commons" has gained renewed currency in scholarly and popular works critical of both "neoliberal globalism" and US imperialism. Generally, the commons refers to those areas of social and natural life that are under communal stewardship, comprising collective resources and rights for all, by virtue of citizenship, irrespective of capacity to pay. As Maude Barlow and Tony Clarke (2001) argue, the decisive impetus of global capitalism today is "the commodification of the commons—areas like seeds and genes, culture and heritage, health and education, even air and water—access to which was once considered a fundamental right" (p. 4). Similarly, Naomi Klein (2001) suggests that a war on the commons is being waged through many changes "whose common thread might broadly be described as the privatization of every aspect of life, and the transformation of every activity and value into a commodity"(p. 4). The commodification identified by these authors involves the transformation of *collective goods*, whose use and allocation are determined, at least in principle, through democratic decisions and common rights, into *privately owned goods*, produced for profit rather than use value. As the oxygen industry case suggests, opportunities for profit expand when the commons shrink and people are deprived of common rights and adequate access to viable non-commodified sources of clean air, water, food, shelter, land, transportation, health care, and education.

In view of this predicament, struggles to reinvent the commons and deepen democracy today require confronting the capitalist drive to commodify nearly all aspects of existence and defending collective life from private appropriation and capitalist market regulation. As Ralph Miliband (1995) argues, restoring democratic control over our fate requires us "to extend the areas of 'decommodification' from which market forces are excluded" (p. 117). Barlow and Clarke (2001) take a minimalist position and call for "drawing a line around the commons" and insisting that key collective goods and services like health care and education remain uncommodified and under public control (p. 182). More radically, Ellen Meiksins Wood (1999b) argues that liberating collective life from capital's dominance will require struggling for "the decommodification of as many spheres of life as possible and their democratization" (p. 25).

"Decommodification" is not simply an abstract possibility pointed to by intellectuals. As David McNally (2002) argues, "if there is one thing that links together the wide range of social justice struggles occurring around the globe, it is opposition to commodification" (p. 232). Thus, when landless peasants in Brazil occupy land, indigenous people in India mobilize against giant dam projects, workers in Bolivia oppose water privatization, or unemployed Argentinians demand public spending and job creation, they all insist that social justice and collective welfare should not be subordinate to private profit-making. They demand that these aspects of the commons be shielded from commodification and market regulation. Thus, "decommodification" offers a useful umbrella concept for drawing together otherwise dispersed and localized struggles against capitalist globalization.

RETHINKING "COMMODIFICATION"

What do we mean by "commodification," and what are the grounds for opposing it? Commodification is the production of a good or service for a profit. GDP measures the profitable portions of the economy including positive ones like producing necessities for everyday living and negative ones like an oil spill in the ocean, which also adds to the GDP (Cobb, Halsead, & Rowe, 1995). GDP measures the visible market transactions, mainly the profitable portions or commodified parts, of the economy.[1] But it ignores enormous economic portions like unpaid work. If work or nature is not commodified, it cannot bring a profit.

Many things are bought and sold in capitalist markets, things not created for these purposes. The most notable examples are what Karl Polanyi (1957) called "fictitious commodities"—land, labour, and money—pivotal elements that, while bought and sold, are not strictly commodities:

> Labour is only another name for a human activity which goes with life itself, which in its turn is not produced for sale but for entirely different reasons, nor can that activity be detached from the rest of life, be stored or mobilized; land is only another name for nature, which is not produced by man [sic]; actual money, finally, is merely a token of purchasing power which, as a rule, is not produced at all, but comes into being through the mechanism of banking or state finance. None of them is produced for sale. The commodity of description of labour, land and money is entirely fictitious. (p. 72)

However "fictitious," such "commodities" are the basis of an economic system in which all elements of production are brought into the market and regulated primarily by commercial imperatives. Today, the commercial patenting of gene sequences in traditional medicinal plants and human genes indicating susceptibility to certain types of disease are the new commodity fictions. In these instances, profits derive not from "producing" something new, but simply by extending private property rights to domains previously outside capitalist markets.

Free market enthusiasts wonder why anyone would oppose commodification because, in their view, commodities are the lifeblood of capitalist market economies—the proud outcome of its sophisticated social and technical division of labour; the incarnation of value in exchange, the source of profit, and hence the catalyst for endless innovation and growth; the means of transforming dormant nature and other non-market spheres into objects of human use and enjoyment. To remove public authorities from allocating social goods is hardly to be deplored, for the market is a coordinating mechanism, acutely responsive to the revealed preferences of "sovereign consumers" and thus the very embodiment of democracy. In this view, paring back the public sector and allowing the market to provide for most human needs liberates productive resources from the arbitrary and wasteful hands of the state. What invariably results, it is assumed, is increased efficiency, reduced costs, and a greater range of goods and services. If private profit, as opposed to "the common good," is the impetus for delivering diverse commodities to the market, it is also what, via the "invisible hand," spurs continual growth, innovation, and technological development that benefit all.

In contrast to this rose-tinted conception, criticisms of commodification hinge on two considerations: first, from principled objections to the inappropriate treatment of some particular thing, being, or activity as a "commodity"; second, from practical concerns about how commodification and capitalist market regulation restrict the range of collective and individual choice and leave key social needs unsatisfied.

How do we determine what can properly be regarded as a commodity? This question carries us into a range of complex moral debates. Commodities are most commonly regarded as "things" that can be used, exchanged, altered, withheld, or destroyed according to their owner's desire, without regard to intrusive notions of moral responsibility or intrinsic value. Thus, to regard an object as a "commodity" is to assume that its primary "value" resides in its monetary worth and that markets are the most appropriate means to regulate its production, exchange, and enjoyment. As Elizabeth S. Anderson (1990) has argued, "to the extent that moral principles or ethical ideals preclude the application of market norms to a good, we may say that the good is not a (proper) commodity" (p. 72). For many social "goods," she suggests, allowing market norms to override moral considerations can result in a failure to value such goods appropriately. For example, slavery is condemned because it enables some people to treat others inappropriately, as simply objects of use or gain.

Arguments against slavery can be extended to many other "goods" that are devalued when treated as mere commodities. As Margaret Jane Radin (1996) argues, today's expansion of global capitalism means that "the contemporary arena of moral and political debate is full of painful and puzzling controversies about what things can properly be bought and sold: babies? sexual services? kidneys and corneas? environmental pollution permits?" (p. xiii). Radin's moral concern with "contested commodities" is echoed and extended in this book, particularly in Harrison's discussion of selling human body parts, Bakker's analysis of struggles over commodifying water, and Sumner's discussion of commodifying knowledge. The growing number of "contested commodities" challenges us to re-examine continually our assumptions about the appropriate scope of capitalist markets. As novel as they may seem, however, these conundrums return us to long-familiar debates over the "fictitious commodities" of labour and land (or, more broadly, the natural environment). Indeed, as McNally and Müller's chapters make clear, the fact that labour and the environment are seldom seen currently as "contested commodities" reveals today's political predicament. Why? What are the consequences of valuing these "goods" primarily as "commodities"?

A key moral issue in commodifying labour is the abandonment of collective responsibility for individual welfare and subordinating subsistence rights to the capricious whims of the market. As Gosta Esping-Andersen (1990) asserts, "in the Middle Ages it was not the labour contract, but the family, the church, or the lord that decided a person's capacity for survival" (p. 37). Stripped of "pre-commodified" social protections and rendered entirely dependent upon the "cash nexus" for survival, workers in capitalist society, he argues, become dehumanized commodities, "captive to powers beyond their control ... [and] easily destroyed by even minor social contingencies, such as illness, and by macro-events, such as the business cycle" (p. 37). In contrast to other commodities, labour-power is not an object that can be manipulated at will or withheld from the market, but is inseparable from the physically vulnerable and emotionally complex person who owns it. As Polanyi (1957) suggests, "the alleged commodity 'labour power' cannot be shoved about, indiscriminately, or left unused, without affecting also the human individual who happens to be the bearer of this particular commodity"(p. 73). Thus, as Esping-Andersen emphasizes, society's responsibility to at least partially "decommodify" labour has been the mainspring of social policy in capitalist societies from the Speenhamland system of poor relief in the 1790s in England, to contemporary welfare states.

When a good or service is commodified, access to it depends on one's ability to pay. In contrast to public goods supplied freely by the "commons" or the state, commodities have capitalist market prices, set not to ensure access but to yield maximum profits. High profit rates are compatible with situations where large numbers have no ability to buy goods, regardless of their importance to individual well-being, social participation, or self-development. We see this logic in the US today, where private insurance companies reap vast profits even as millions have little or no access to adequate health care. Indeed, when a commodity is needed or desired by large numbers, prices rise, which systematically restricts its availability. Hence, for many goods today—basic foodstuffs in Eastern Europe, AIDS drugs in Africa, electricity and water in Johannesburg's shanty-towns—capitalist markets tolerate massive exclusion. In such cases, the market's profit logic conflicts with egalitarian traditions of universal public services and collective commitments to meet human needs.

Once a good or service is commodified, Colin Leys (2001) argues, it becomes "liable to constant transformation under the logic of capitalist competition" (p. 90)—entailing competition in price, advertising, innovations in packaging and design, and so on. The outcome may not be diversification of supply and lower prices, but market-control by large suppliers, monopolistic pricing, and a stark uniformity of goods. Attempts to lower costs can include changing the composition of a good to make its production and delivery cheaper, standardizing components to achieve economies of scale, using lower-grade materials, minimizing labour-intensive services, or off-loading some production work to consumers. These measures can alter the quality or even safety of various goods, producing such things as chemically-laced food, dumbed-down television programming, substandard rental housing, contaminated drinking water, or online education services. Cost-minimizing imperatives also require continual efforts to raise productivity and increase surpluses wrung from workers by introducing labour-saving technologies, changing the pace and organization of work, lowering wages, reducing benefits, and undermining safety. As anti-sweatshop and fair-trade activists today underline, such exploitation is a vital, but largely hidden, dimension of the commodities we buy daily. Rosemary Hennessy (2001) reminds us that commodification "invariably depends on the lives and labour of invisible others" (p. 142). As Jennifer Sumner also emphasizes, we must continually strive to reconnect the commodity form with the underlying relationships and social processes it tends to obscure.

Similarly, certain forms of ecological thought—as Birgit Müller and Anita Krajnc's chapters powerfully remind us—hold that treating the environment as a commodity fails to value nature appropriately. As the precondition for all life, and as a complex, intricate, and interdependent system with its own requirements for self-reproduction, nature's value is immeasurable. Recognizing this, many non-capitalist societies accorded nature a supreme spiritual value, acknowledged human dependence, offered rituals of gratitude for its countless gifts, and remained acutely attuned to the inexhaustible wonder of its many beauties and sensual delights. This approach contrasts markedly with the crass, utilitarian mindset in today's capitalism, in which, as Richard Swift (2002) puts it, the planet's diverse gifts are merely disenchanted objects of use, raw materials for the treadmill of production, "nature's free inputs into the creation of commodities" (p. 110). As Andrew Bard Schmookler argues, "in the grip of a system that breaks everything down into commodity form ... [t]he living planet is dismembered, as land becomes real estate, forests become lumber, oceans become fisheries and sinks" (quoted in Foster, 2002; p. 55).

Our failure to confront mounting environmental crises shows how pervasive commodification leads to democratic incapacity. As Polanyi (1957) argues, commodifying land, labour, and other dimensions of collective life means subordinating "the substance of society itself to the laws of the market" (p. 71). Recognizing this, most communities have striven to ensure that the use of human labour and nature's resources remains determined by *extra-economic* criteria: custom, religion, hereditary duty, reciprocal obligation, and political direction. In contrast to historical situations in which economic life was largely embedded in and guided by broad societal norms, however inegalitarian and unjust, capitalist regulation means that the allocation of goods, services, labour, and investment is largely determined by the impersonal will of the market. As Ellen Meiksins Wood (2002) puts it, "all aspects of life that become market commodities are removed from the sphere of democratic accountability, answering not to the will of the people but to the demands of the markets and profit" (para. 11). Capitalist regulation means that many decisions of broad collective significance are removed from the public, political sphere. Thus, commodifying the commons depoliticizes and "economizes" areas of life that would otherwise fall under conscious collective deliberation. The outcome depletes the scope and content of popular democracy.

CAPITALISM VERSUS DEMOCRACY—THE DOUBLE MOVEMENT

Capitalists' intense pressure to commodify everything sounds like a new phenomenon associated with the most recent phase of global integration. However, the issue of commodification has long been central to critiques of capitalism as exploitive and destructive. Marx begins his book *Capital* with a discussion of commodified social relationships as destroyers of "idyllic," patriarchal community relations, leaving the cash nexus as the only remaining social bond. Karl Polanyi described how commodification separated labour from other activities, subjecting it to the market and thereby annihilating non-contractual forms of kinship, neighbourhood, and other organic forms of existence. Kees van der Pijl (1998, p. 12) notes that early twentieth-century art often focused on commodification—depicting an atomized society of disoriented, dehumanized individuals. Cubist paintings, such as Fernand Leger's *Soldiers Playing at Cards*, show humans composed of machine-like body parts, from which all organic life has been removed.

The drive to commodify has usually met resistance, sometimes to slow it down, at other times in robustly reversing the trend. Karl Polanyi (1957) famously called such reactions a "double movement":

> Social history of the nineteenth century was thus the result of a double movement: the extension of the market organization in respect to genuine commodities was accompanied by its restriction in respect to fictitious ones. While on the one hand markets spread all over the face of the globe ... on the other hand a network of measures and policies was integrated into powerful institutions designed to check the action of the market relative to labour, land, and money. (p. 76)

Over the past two centuries, democracy and capitalism have been in contention, now in open battle, now in uneasy compromise. The Greeks, who invented the term democracy, understood its radical meaning. "The real difference between democracy and oligarchy is poverty and wealth," wrote Aristotle (1908). "The rich are few and the poor many ... where the poor rule, that is a democracy" (p. 116). Aristotle's version was the way democracy was understood in the main tradition of Western political thought down through the nineteenth century. It is essentially the same radical conception that citizen activists mean today by "democracy from below" or "deep democracy." We use the term in this radical sense. Democracy was seen by the upper classes as dangerous because it meant "rule by the poor, the ignorant, and incompetent, at the expense of the leisured, civilized, propertied classes." It signalled "class rule, rule by the wrong class" (Macpherson, 1977, pp. 9–10). In other words, rule by the people.

John Ball, a leader of the 1381 English Peasants Revolt was said to have declared, "Things cannot go well in England, nor ever will, until all goods are held in common, and until there will be neither serfs nor gentlemen, and we shall all be equal" (Beer, 1929, p. 28). Ball's statement shows that contests over equality and democracy have been historically based, and are not debates dreamed up by political philosophers.

Attempts to expand capitalism have engaged pro-business forces versus their democratic adversaries over the extent to which people, nature, and essential services can be bought and sold for profit. The contest has been based on contradictions between two expansionary ethics—capitalism versus democracy. Capitalism is a revolutionary system, continually attempting to remake society by relentlessly pursuing profits. Success often depends on destroying bonds of community—aboriginals, farm families tied to the land, associations of workers—on narrowing the "public" sphere over which the ethic of democracy applies. The bonds of community are necessary for the functioning of democracies. When a good or service is commodified for profit, the opportunity to make collective, deliberative decisions is replaced by the capitalist market. In contrast, struggles to win bottom-up democracy involve enabling people to determine their social, political, and economic lives as collectivities.

The principles underlying capitalism and democracy are opposed. Capitalism is based on individual greed and inequality, while democracy is premised on the common good and equality. Economic privilege based on property rights produces vast inequalities between those with lots of capital and those with little or none. In contrast, democracy is about achieving equality amongst citizens, securing personal rights, and making collective decisions about the common good. When expanded beyond a limited sphere, democracy "may challenge, indiscriminately and irreverently, all forms of privilege" and encroach on the capacity of capital to invest profitably and discipline its work force (Bowles & Gintis, 1986, p. 5). This possibility is why the Trilateral Commission, founded in 1973 by David Rockefeller and others to bring corporate and political leaders in North America, Western Europe, and Japan together to fend off attacks on capitalism, identified an "excess of democracy" as a major threat. "The democratic spirit is egalitarian, individualistic, populist, and impatient with the distinctions of class and rank," the Trilateralists' first book stated. "The spread of that spirit ... may pose an intrinsic threat" (Crozier et al., 1975, p. 162).

Of the two expansionary systems, capitalism has more often been on top. But impulses for deep democracy kept capitalists from commodifying much of what they wanted to. In the global North, extensions of the franchise from property holding males, to male workers, to women, and then to racial minorities and immigrants brought great demands for the state to bring into the commons parts that had been alienated, privatized, and commodified or to offer new public services with access on the basis of citizenship. The result was that "labour" became citizens with rights to a social wage and a degree of freedom from total dependence on the capitalist labour market. Some "resources" reverted to nature through the creation and expansion of national parks, and services such as education and health care were removed from the for-profit sphere and largely decommodified. In the 1950s to 1970s, popular-democratic movements in the global South achieved victories for decolonization, "inwardly directed development," and the deglobalizing of transnational corporations in a massive wave of nationalizations. Sometimes there were gains in decommodifying land. After Mexico's 1910 revolution, for instance, the state recognized *ejidos*, communal ownership of land expropriated from large landowners and returned to the peasants. These gains were reversed in conjunction with NAFTA.

Expansionary democracy and expansionary capitalism have both engaged with other forces: pre-capitalist societies and traditional conservatives who often opposed both commodification and popular sovereignty. Traditional conservatives opposed free market capitalism because they thought it would undermine stability, class harmony, loyalty, and productivity. German Historical School proponents such as Friedrich List and Adolph Wagner advocated patriarchal families, a paternalistic welfare state, and absolutism as guarantors of discipline, efficiency, and stability (Esping-Andersen, 1990, p. 10). It was conservatives who, in the 1880s, brought in the first modern welfare state to undercut the appeal of socialism. As Bismarck stated, "If Social Democracy did not exist ... then the moderate advances which we have managed to push through in the area of social reform would not yet exist" (quoted in Therborn, 1984, p. 15). Bismarck's reforms included sickness, accident, and old age protections based on a conservative social insurance model that created distinct sets of rights and privileges amongst status groups. Their effect was to decommodify labour partially.

Thus an historical explanation that sees contentions as largely between capitalism and democracy is not sufficient. The direction of change resulted from contestations amongst three main forces, with traditional conservatives playing an important part. In the three actor contestations, there were shifting pairings between two of them against the third. Currently, traditional conservatives generally ally with neoliberals in Thatcherism, Reaganism, and their successors. But in welfare state formation and important struggles for decommodification, Red-Tory couplings [socialists with conservatives], either as tacit alliances or in symbiotic contention with each other, as in Bismarck's Germany, have been crucial.

Bowles and Gintis (1986) argue that the contradictory logics of democracy and capitalism were able to coexist only through a succession of compromises that involved broad collective understandings about proper spheres for business, governments, workers, and citizens. The Keynesian welfare state, or Great Compromise, "represented some form of accommodation between the demands for political and economic democracy from below and the needs of capital" (Gamble, 1988, p. 24). The compromise recognized that business had exclusive rights to private property, including management rights to determine unilaterally an enterprise's strategic direction. But the sphere for private property rights steadily shrank, as the public sphere in the global North grew from about 10 per cent of the economy in the late 1800s to about half the economy by the 1970s (Desai, 2000).[2] While the public sphere bought commodified goods and services, the overall effect of public sphere growth was to remove a rising share of the economy from profit making. Global expenditures on education now exceed US $2 trillion. In health care, they are over US $3.5 trillion (Barlow & Clarke, 2001, p. 84).

While popular with voters, the growth of public services was unpopular with capitalists because it removed a rising share of the economy from capitalist profitability, squeezed investment opportunities, and partially decommodified people. The ethic of equality and citizenship covered a growing set of services, offsetting much of the social authority of capitalist markets. The public sphere's expansion contributed powerfully to the 1970s crisis in corporate profitability. Capitalism's logic of "who has the most money can buy the best services" was replaced with "equal rights regardless of ability to pay." Thus, the balance of class forces shifted, and workers were partially freed from having to depend wholly on capitalist employment to survive. As well, workers gained collective bargaining rights and came to expect rising real wages. A private sphere of the "personal" was reserved for the family, gender relations, and the voluntary sector. The system worked with considerable consensus, if not always harmoniously or fairly, as long as each stuck to its own recognized sector.

This uneasy compromise fell apart in the late 1960s and early 1970s, when the Left led powerful movements for decommodification, autocentric development, and deglobalizing transnational corporations. This sparked a capitalist counter-reaction—the current wave of neoliberal globalism. The Trilateral Commission challenged not only democracy, but also the economic nationalism that underpinned a wave of government takeovers of transnational corporations in the early 1970s. Their neoliberal agenda intended to throw back expansionary movements for popular and national sovereignty and recommodify much of what had been moved to non-profit sectors. Current negotiations on the General Agreement on Trade in Services (the GATS) in Geneva, which Ellen Gould discusses in chapter five, are attempting to reverse this.

THE NEOLIBERAL COUNTER-REVOLUTION AND THE "NEW ENCLOSURES"

Even zealous proponents of neoliberal globalism deny its essentially *political* nature. Thus, we are continually assured by media, corporate, and government elites that neoliberal globalism has not been politically shaped, but instead is "an inevitable destiny thrust upon us by economic progress and technological change" (Singer, 1999, p. 186). Critics have been suspicious of the claim that neoliberal restructuring is simply adapting to unavoidable exigencies of the global market and see it as "a *political* enterprise based upon the wish to widen the scope of the private sector, to weaken government's capacity to direct economic life according to criteria determined by democratic deliberation and decision" (Miliband, 1995, p. 107). Critics depict today's drive to commodify or "recommodify" extensive areas of social and natural life as both perennial expansive impulses of capitalism and part of a political struggle to overcome the "crisis of accumulation" associated with the end of the long post-war economic boom.

The neoliberal counter-revolution reversed long-standing trends in the global North, in which organized labour, social democratic parties, and citizens groups had deployed liberal-democratic institutions to regulate business, achieve new rights and material benefits for ordinary citizens, and press the state to remain at least partially independent of corporate interests. Practically, the reversal has involved attempts to pare back the welfare state's regulative and redistributive activities while intensifying its disciplinary ones. As well, it removed restrictions and obligations on corporations that had been in place since the inception of mass democracy. A key part of this process has been the creation of binding international agreements and supra-governmental institutions (NAFTA, the WTO, etc.) whose express purpose is to safeguard corporate capital's investment and trade rights against popular-democratic control.

A central aspect of the neoliberal offensive has been the attack on state regulations, policies, and collective provisioning that had partially shielded people from direct market pressures and limited the spheres of public life and the commons that could be commodified. Thus, as Miliband (1995) argues, the neoliberal project is a concerted assault upon those, "decommodified areas [which] already exist in capitalist economies, and are largely the product of pressure from below in the decades following World II to ensure that access to health, education and other services should be viewed as rights inherent in citizenship, without any regard to ability to pay" (p. 117).

Capitalists attack "decommodified areas" because they exclude key domains of collective life, and much of the economy, from profit making. They also create disincentives for wage work and private consumption, extend government reach into economic life, and increase taxes. Worse, they provide an everyday alternative to capitalism, in which services are provided to each citizen according to her need, rather than according to her ability to pay. Historically, powerful workers movements in the North overcame corporate animosity by mobilizing the votes of the many to establish government-guaranteed social citizenship rights and by union power to wrest concessions from capital. Thus, the balance of class forces shifted and workers were partially freed from capitalist market dependency in earning a living.

Esping-Andersen (1990, 1999) calls the neoliberal rollbacks of Keynesian welfare states "recommodification." This process radically reduces the "decommodified" goods and services available to citizens as a matter of right and increases the number of human needs that must rely on markets to be met. Recommodification requires abrogating regulations and social rights that have offset the commodity status of labour and that shield workers from extreme exploitation and vulnerability. Neoliberal states recommodify workers by compelling them into labour markets on terms beneficial to employers—by restricting eligibility for income supports and social benefits, attacking collective bargaining rights, introducing punitive "workfare" schemes, relaxing labour standards, and bringing in low wage workers from abroad. As well, states have increasingly disciplined people and enforced social order in conditions of growing inequality and social insecurity—cracking down stiffly on protest and dissent; enlarging prison, policing, and surveillance systems; spearheading "law and order" campaigns; curtailing civil rights; and so on.

In much of the global South, neoliberal recommodification of labour has been accompanied by measures that strip communities of self-determination. The global South has been increasingly seen simply as a repository of cheap labour and natural resources. Taking advantage of the South's debt crisis and vulnerabilities to financial collapse and capital flight, Northern-dominated institutions such as the IMF and World Bank have pushed countries to adopt neoliberal measures called "structural adjustment programs." These mandate the neoliberal globalism policies outlined earlier. Despite pledges to reduce poverty, the main purpose of these programs is to ensure loan repayments to Northern bankers and to enable transnationals [TNCs] the right to enter and do as they please. In many places, the result has been increased poverty and suffering, extreme environmental damage, and undermining of the preconditions for genuine democracy and economic development (Bello, 2003). A key dimension has been the "proletarianization" of peasants, driven from the land by debt, foreclosures, and expanding corporate agribusinesses. Dispossessed peasants form huge pools of cheap, disposable labour for TNCs, and add to exploitable migrant workers heading to the North.

Under strict control by Northern-dominated financial institutions and unilateral US power, foreign corporations and banks increasingly limit the options of impoverished countries. Locked into debt-repayments and unequal economic exchange, Southern countries today largely experience "the market" not as a liberating force, but as a source of compulsion and domination. It strips them of control over their collective resources, deprives them of state subsidies and protections, which are common in the North, and undermines their ability to protect their social and environmental commons.

Taking advantage of scientific breakthroughs and new "intellectual" property rights for TNCs, corporations have patented and privatized growing segments of the environmental commons. We now witness the rising private monopolization of biology and chemical goods—seeds, plants, life-saving pharmaceutical goods and medical treatments, foodstuffs, fertilizers, industrial materials, and the genetic make-up of life. Similarly, by struggling against public services and public provision, corporations have colonized new domains of the public sector—education, health care, hydro power, welfare case management, water purification services. The corporate-backed GATs initiative threatens to open up much more. These attempts are politically contested and may be reversed.

As well, speculation with the "fictitious commodity" of money in deregulated international financial markets has destabilized national currencies, devastated local economies and created intense insecurities. Commodification extends its global reach through the spread of consumer culture, which entices us to construct our identities and social bonds out of the commodities we consume. This superficially diverse, but ultimately homogenizing, culture threatens to erode the rich plurality of world cultures and immobilize genuinely creative and transformative energies with endless waves of pre-packaged gratification.

As Patrick Bond (2000) argues, neoliberalism has steered us dangerously towards a free market utopia, whose lodestars are "the universal rule of property, and the commodification of all aspects of daily life everywhere." As Bond and McNally emphasize, such developments are not novel excesses of "globalization" or "corporate rule." They are better seen as continuations of private appropriation, as the "enclosures" of communal property and resources that accompanied capitalism from its inception. The "new enclosures" of the neoliberal era, while perhaps unprecedented in their extremity, draw attention to historical conflicts between capitalist property rights and universal citizenship rights, between imperialism and popular sovereignty, between private economic power and collective democracy. In this context, we present a "decommodification" strategy as both a useful guiding principle and a practical possibility for people struggling to assert control over their lives.

DECOMMODIFICATION AND THE STRUGGLE TO RECLAIM THE COMMONS

"Decommodification" appears to be an ambiguous goal, negating commodification rather than creating positive alternatives. In this light, it is understandable why critics such as Radin have mistakenly equated this goal with a thoroughgoing rejection of commodities, consumption, and markets. However, as David McNally (1993) has argued, the chief moral and political issue at stake here is not the simple existence of commodities and markets per se, but *market regulation* of social and economic life. Accordingly, "decommodification" is meant to overcome the radical extension of the scope and authority of the market, emancipating extensive areas of life from demands for private profit and recreating a public, not-for-profit sphere. It is about fulfilling the radical promise of genuine popular democracy by "breaking down the fences that prohibit the will of the majority from intruding upon economic property arrangements" (McNally, 2002, p. 234).

The goals of radical transformative decommodification are not to dismantle all markets, but to remove *capitalist markets*, extend democratic authority, and reorient society away from producing commodities for profit as dominant collective activities. Decommodification is a process that transforms activities away from production for profit for the purpose of meeting a social need, meeting a use value, or restoring nature. Decommodification pertains both to production of an economic good or service and to the removal from production of something of nature that had been used to generate profits. Decommodification is a process and a continuum. It is not an "either/or" issue of having a society that has been wholly commodified or one that is fully decommodified. It is variable, and a matter of degree (Wright, 2005, p. 2). Thus we can speak of the degree to which labour has been decommodified into a worker with rights, or the extent to which resources have been decommodified and turned back into nature, or the extent to which services like education and health care are provided on the basis of citizenship rather than ability to pay. In reality, all current societies are hybrids in which commodification and decommodification live side by side, if not always amicably. But, the predominance of commodification or decommodification in a country or community matters a great deal and has huge implications. This book explores many of them.

As we have seen, Karl Polanyi famously portrayed commodification as a negative process, from which society needed protection. But it was Gosta Esping-Andersen (1985, 1990) who first proposed decommodification as a positive goal, one that described the vision socialists and trade unionists had long tried to achieve. As he sees it, decommodification is central to the historical practice of traditional social democracy and trade unionism, part of incremental gains by which newly-enfranchised workers used political power to overcome their vulnerabilities in labour markets and establish secure claims on the state for wide-ranging social citizenship rights. Extending the franchise created demands for governments in the global North to protect wage earners in times of unemployment, injury, sickness, and old age. Sometimes called a "social wage," such public supports gave all households some security from the dangers of total market dependency. The decommodifying effects of welfare state regimes can be assessed by the "degree to which individuals, or families, can uphold a socially acceptable standard of living independently of market participation" (p. 37).

In pre-capitalist societies, most workers were coerced in non-economic ways, did not have citizenship or individual rights, and usually lived in precarious subsistence. But few were treated as commodities. Workers were embedded in societies where there were mutual, if unequal, obligations, and their survival did not depend on selling their labour power. As capitalist labour markets spread, however, institutional guarantees outside labour contracts were stripped away. The livelihoods of unpropertied workers came to depend entirely on selling their labour power. Families could starve if breadwinners became sick, injured, or old. The winning of modern social rights partially reversed labour's pure commodity status. According to Esping-Andersen (1990), labour is decommodified when "citizens can freely, and without potential loss of job, income or general welfare, opt out of work when they themselves consider it necessary" (p. 23). A service is decommodified when it is rendered as a matter of right, such as during sickness, retirement, maternity leave, parental leave, educational leave, and unemployment.

These supports have political consequences. The less their labour market dependence, Esping-Andersen (1990) argues, the less that wage-earners can be frightened by the economic blackmail threats of corporations moving elsewhere if governments enact policies corporations dislike. For unions, decommodification has always been a priority. "When workers are completely market-dependent, they are difficult to mobilize for solidaristic action" (p. 22). Divisions emerge between workers who are the "ins" and those who are the "outs." Solidaristic action happens when highly paid workers support the interests of low paid workers and the unemployed. Labour market inequalities make the formation of solidaristic labour movements more difficult.

For Esping-Andersen (1985, pp. 3–38), decommodifying goes far beyond alleviating the worst excesses of capitalism. It is a strategy to replace capitalism gradually, one that grew out of the "Austro-Swedish" social democratic route to economic citizenship. This route rejected Lenin's revolutionary authoritarianism and moderate Social Democracy's co-optation by capitalism. The Austro-Swedish strategy envisaged a process of expanding citizenship in progressive stages, along lines paralleling those of T.H. Marshall (1950).[3] In stage one, newly-enfranchised, nationally-based workers used *political citizenship* [i.e., gaining the vote] to overcome their labour market vulnerabilities by electing left-wing governments committed to establishing universal public services and income supports for those unable to get paid work. The long process of setting up wide-ranging *social citizenship* rights is stage two. If completed fully, proponents argue, social citizenship emancipates workers from fears of losing work and income through corporate threats of pulling out, so they may be willing to take the risk of challenging corporate power. Wage earners are then ready to move to stage three—*economic citizenship*—in which they partake effectively in democratically running the economy. The latter is about socializing the economy, but not necessarily by a centralized state.

The struggle to decommodify is part of an incremental process of building wage earners' capacities for democratic participation in the short term, creating institutional bases for expanding non-market values and activities, and laying the ground for achieving genuine economic democracy in the long term. Esping-Andersen (1985) characterizes this radical evolutionary strategy as "salami tactics, slicing away at traditional capitalist prerogatives and replacing them with democratic forms of control" (p. 23). This process is similar to what Andre Gorz (1967) famously referred to as "non-reformist reforms," which aim to "restrict or dislocate the power of capital" while giving radical anti-capitalist forces some practicable means of controlling and planning the development of existing society (pp. 6–8).

The problem for the three-stage strategy to economic citizenship is that neoliberal forces have rolled back some of the gains of stage two, in part to keep wage earners insecure and off balance. While insecure, they are less likely to demand as much pay and more likely to accept commodified labour conditions—such as longer hours, fewer rights—so that corporations can make higher profits. With some reverses in stage two, many workers in most Northern countries do not feel secure enough to move to the third and highest stage of citizenship, where, as voters, they not only choose governments and public services, but, as workers, also determine what is produced, how it is produced, and for what purpose.

Since Esping-Andersen's first writings on the issue, the concept of decommodification as a positive goal has been broadened to include changes in economic life and nature. Williams and Windebank (2003) have done path-breaking work on the non-commodified activities of economic life in the household and the community. For them commodification is a process whereby "goods and services are increasingly produced for monetized exchange under profit-motivated market-orientated conditions" (p. 251). In contrast, decommodification includes "firstly, non-exchanged work, secondly, non-monetized exchange and, third and finally, monetary exchange where the profit motive is absent" (p. 251). Non-exchanged work is unpaid work like preparing meals, child rearing or repairing your house. It involves self-provisioning or production for use value. Such work never enters the market or economists' measurements of the size of the economy. Non-monetized exchange includes barter or doing an exchange of mutual aid. I scratch your back, you scratch mine. Finally, monetary exchange where the profit motive is absent includes such things as consumers paying for municipal water through metering from a public utility that provides a service to all, but does not earn a profit. Williams and Windebank (2003, p. 252) calculate that only about 50 per cent of the economies of the advanced countries are commodified. Moreover, their data challenge the work of those who claim that commodification is increasing continually by showing that that level has not increased in the past 30 years. They attribute the lack of increase to "strong cultures of resistance" (p. 260).

In addition, the decommodification of land or nature involves removing from production some part of nature that had been used to make profit. Thus, in the broadest sense, progressive decommodification is a positive vision of how society could be transformed for the better in the areas of 1) citizens' security in receiving social income for non-work purposes such as retirement, sickness, periods of unemployment, or education; 2) removing exploitation and hierarchy from economic life and making work more meaningful by moving towards employee-run co-operatives, self-provisioning, bartering, and volunteering; and 3) reclaiming nature by reversing much of its commodification into for-profit resources.

However, as Esping-Andersen acknowledges, decommodification can also take conservative or reactionary forms. Indeed, traditional conservatives[4] historically spearheaded the most systematic attacks on the corrosive social effects of commodification. In their own way, traditional conservatives have consistently recognized that capitalism is a revolutionary system, continually undermining traditional forms of communal life and remaking society by relentlessly pursuing profits. Where commodification holds sway and the "cash nexus" serves as the primary mediator of social relations, they erode tradition, deference, obligation, and non-contractual bonds, on which social order and cohesion depend. Thus, as Esping-Andersen (1999) suggests, a "conservative politics against the market" is one version of decommodification, struggling to reproduce pre-capitalist institutions and life-ways, defending traditional authority and hierarchy, and upholding non-marketized domains like church and patriarchal families (p. 44). As he argues, resistance to reducing human social relations to the narrow cash nexus brings conservatism into strange alliances with socialism and other radical traditions.

Claus Offe (1984) also emphasizes the politically ambivalent or "conservative" character of decommodification, arguing that certain decommodified areas of life represent not a progressive counterbalance or alternative to capitalism but a means to stabilize and preserve it. Capitalism's private economic sphere, organized through ostensibly spontaneous market processes, survives only through the "decommodifying" activities of the state and domestic spheres. Indeed, as Offe insists, capitalist states systematically enable "free markets" to thrive by providing social and physical infrastructures essential for private profit-making—building roads, educating and disciplining workers, enforcing contracts, maintaining social order and cohesion, subsidizing businesses, assuming the negative social and ecological costs of private production. The "free market" as a regulator of social life is thus not a substitute for the state. Capitalism is saved from its own anarchic self-destruction by the state's decommodifying and market-enabling activities. If so, the decommodifying activities of the welfare state are contradictory. Some offset the worst effects of private production and foster some social equality, while others systematically preserve the power of capital. Still others may take the form of what

Andre Gorz (1967) has deemed "revolutionary reforms," such as not-for-profit medicare, which may encourage an expansion of progressive decommodification.

Similarly, few could deny the importance of uncommodified activities in the domestic sphere, largely women's unpaid and undervalued labour, in ensuring capitalist reproduction. Production in formal "economic" spheres traditionally rested on the reproductive, nurturing, and caring activities of women in families. Thus, we need to be wary of how a politics of "decommodification" could be regressive and misogynist, harkening back sentimentally to patriarchy and the soothing benefactions of women's non-commodified labour. In this vein, feminists have criticized Esping-Andersen for failing to appreciate the extent to which women have been institutionally constrained by their "decommodified" familial roles or the ways that gendered welfare states perpetuate women's dependence on men, undermine their capacity to secure the relative financial autonomy of paid work, and thus structurally confine them to the domestic sphere. Ann Shola Orloff (1993) argues that decommodification must be supplemented with women's rights for access to paid work—"the right to be commodified" (p. 318). She adds that "if decommodification is important because it frees wage earners from the compulsion of participating in the market, a parallel dimension is needed to indicate the ability of those who do most of the domestic and caring work—almost all women—to form and maintain autonomous households, that is, to survive and support their children without having to marry to gain access to breadwinners' income" (p. 319).

Esping-Andersen (1999) accepted the challenge from Orloff and others and broadened his concepts. In his later formulation, he states that although women are increasingly inserted into wage relationships, "the functional equivalent of market dependency for many women is family dependency" (p. 45). Female independence necessitates "de-familialization," he argued. De-familialization does not mean the destruction of families, but refers to state policies that lessen individuals' financial reliance on the family. In their chapter, Ray Broomhill and Rhonda Sharp also argue that a programme of decommodification needs to be complemented by a simultaneous commitment to "defamilialization." Defamilialization need not supplant decommodification; instead, a simultaneous commitment to "defamilialization" would help free women from both patriarchal domestic domination and capitalist exploitation, enabling them to participate more fully and equally in all areas of economic and political life.

Such caveats do not invalidate decommodification as a goal. Rather, they show the need to develop thoroughly egalitarian and democratic forms of it, which seriously challenge patriarchy and other forms of social domination, as well as capitalist economic power. In any case, focusing on the many preconditions of social reproduction becomes increasingly important now that capitalism is colonizing more areas of existence and straining the remaining areas of the commons—democratic political institutions, the public sector, family and kinship networks, affective communal relationships, aquifers, soil, food systems, oxygen, the biosphere—which sustain and protect human life. As Polanyi argued, efforts to implement liberal utopias engender counter-forces committed to protecting society and nature from unbridled markets and to re-establishing collective control over economic life.

We can see that the neoliberal drive to "commodify the commons" is leading to contradictions, such as the Asian financial crisis of 1997–98, that threaten its continued legitimacy. It has created openings for transformative struggle such as World Social Forum process (Gret & Sintomer, 2005) and struggles over popular national sovereignty against the US Empire. Current conjunctural changes may be more conducive to progressive decommodification campaigns. Laxer, for instance, argues in his chapter that we may be entering a renewed cycle of the renationalization of economies.

Is the contest between commodification and decommodification just the struggle over public ownership and privatization dressed up in new clothing? No. There is much overlap, but important differences too. Privatization often leads to greater commodification, and it almost always prevents moving toward decommodification. But public ownership does not always decommodify, especially when neoliberals successfully demand that government-owned economic institutions such as crown corporations, which have not already been privatized, operate strictly along for-profit principles and drop non-market, public policy goals such as serving remote communities or protecting environments.

There can be public ownership in name only. For example, governments may own public or crown lands and charge royalties for the use of renewable resources such as forests or for depleting the public's non-renewable resources, such as oil or minerals, but stumpage or royalty rates may be so low that the commons are virtually being given away. Thus, having public or crown-owned land or bringing land back under formal public control is not sufficient to bring it into the commons or decommodify it. Further, state reclamation of land from private owners may not decommodify any aspect of its use. It is difficult to return areas despoiled for resources to a state of nature. Thus, public ownership is usually a necessary but not a sufficient condition for decommodification.

Non-profit, communal control is possible without state control. We have already mentioned the *ejido* and indigenous communities' systems of communal land control in Mexico and contemporary struggles to prevent their privatization and commodification. (See the chapters by Guttiérez-Haces and Otero & Jugenitz). Other examples are various forms of communal control by aboriginal peoples in other countries, and co-operatively owned enterprises. Having land and labour controlled by non-state communal bodies fits well with Marx's vision of socialism, which he called "a free association of producers." Today's Lefts are rightly suspicious of state bureaucracies and believe in bottom-up control.

If public ownership is not the same as decommodification, neither is privatization wholly coincident with commodification. Land can be privatized, but this does not necessarily lead to commodification. Families or larger communities could own land, but work it for their own use-value. Their labour may not be commodified. To a great extent, Hutterite colonies have decommodified their labour and provided services to themselves. Much of what they produce is for their own use value rather than for external markets. But there is a danger in such private ownership. It can be sold at any time, likely resulting in multiple, commodified effects.

In the short term, efforts to resist commodification and reclaim the commons will likely primarily be localized struggles to contest the capitalist logic on specific fronts and secure reliable collective access to shelter, food, water, education, income support, and so on. A diversity of political struggles now underway can be brought together under the broad banner of progressive decommodification. These struggles range from opposing sweat-shop labour on US university campuses, trying to recommunalize land in Latin America and India, opposing commodifying sewage and water services in Ireland, fighting for radical forms of union democracy in East Asia, and struggling against commercial logging of old-growth forests in British Columbia. They also include resisting deregulating electricity in California and Ontario, challenging biopiracy in the global South, supporting native and non-native efforts to widen title over aboriginal lands, workers taking over and running factories in Argentina in a wave of "*fabrica ocupada*," and privatizing water management services in Ontario. While such struggles are dispersed and lack overall coherence, their victories may be cumulative, pointing to alternative models of society where non-monetary values are reaffirmed and popular democracies are given new depth and substance, emancipating the rich possibilities of democratic life from the compulsions of capitalist markets and the US Empire.

In the long term, there will be much debate and contention over how best to advance a radical project of decommodification and create practical democratic alternatives to the neoliberal model. For some, the main path to a decommodified future is to be found in the self-emancipatory potential of popular movements from below, which can challenge bureaucratic and top-down state structures, create strategic beachheads of strong and participatory democratic life, and mount effective mass opposition to the economic and political powers sustaining the capitalist commodity economies. Such movements can slow down, stop, and, in some cases, reverse powerful pressures for commodification.

However, if governments also implacably oppose decommodification, it will be difficult to make substantial progress. For this reason, others argue that the most compelling way forward lies in creating citizen-oriented states, severing their current alliances with transnational corporations, and getting them to reclaim the social and environmental commons. History shows that the problem for such progressive governments is that, in the absence of substantial, continual mobilization from below and effective alliances of like-minded states, they tend to bow to enormous economic blackmail pressures. Such pressures come from threats of corporate flight, withdrawal of short-term financial capital, and IMF/World Bank sanctions and corporate lawsuits alleging the loss of "future profits" under investment rights clauses in agreements such as the World Trade Organization and NAFTA.

Given the histories of most governments elected on progressive platforms backing down under such pressures, perhaps the most fruitful paths are multi-scale—

working at local, national and inter-national levels—and multi-pronged— synergistically combining the strengths of transformative governments and citizens movements. Historically, some of the greatest strides in decommodifying collective life and nature came when progressive and determined citizens' movements worked with change-oriented governments: Chile under Allende, Nicaragua under the Sandinistas, Nordic countries in the 1960s and 1970s, and the state of Kerala, India since the 1950s. The problem for all of the above cases, except the Nordic ones, is that, as peripheries, they lacked the effective sovereignty to challenge capitalist commodification substantially. The Bolivarian revolution in Venezuela under Hugo Chávez's Presidency today faces similar challenges, but so far the government has fended off an attempted coup and economic blackmail techniques waged by the US government in conjunction with the small, but rich, Venezuelan elite. One way to prevent attempts to overthrow radical, democratically elected governments is to create strong bonds of solidarity with like-minded states and foreign citizens' movements. Venezuela is trying to create such a *sovereign nations community*, a "Bolivarian Alternative for Americas" in which Latin America would create a continental region to gain independence from the United States. It would pursue alternatives to neoliberal policies (Moncton, 2005).

There are also debates amongst advocates of decommodification and the commons about whether the long-term goal is to create a "global civil commons" ruled by global citizens, which would weaken or, in the extreme case, wipe out existing national borders, or, on the other hand, to create many sovereign commons, each with its own programme of decommodification. In the global South, and sometimes in in-between countries like Canada, critics tend to conceive of neoliberal globalism as *re-colonization* and its opposite as *sovereignty*. Indigenous peoples are unlikely to give up their land to an abstraction called the "global commons," no matter how generously conceived. Neither are peasant communities rooted in their local commons nor local communities with strong roots likely to give up claims to "their" commons. Even in a post-corporate era, sovereign control over their own commons will likely be a continuing demand of such countries and nations.

Tensions about competing conceptions of the commons can be partially, but not fully, resolved by separating levels and resources. The ozone layer and global climate need the responsibility of a global commons, while land, fresh water, sub-surface resources, and bottom-up democracy could come under the purview of smaller, sovereign commons. Debates and tensions about the scale of democratic control in post-neoliberal settings and the tensions between global solidarity and the sovereignty of political communities such as nations are sure to remain. This is healthy.

CONCLUSION

Whatever strategy one favours, it is clear that "political" action in the narrow sense is not enough. Indeed, decommodification also necessarily implies a profound cultural and moral revolution—a reassertion of the authority of non-economic values, a rejection of consumerism, a renewed capacity to value and engage with nature, other people, and life's possibilities in a non-commodified manner. Ultimately, the goal of progressive decommodification is to liberate democratic life from enslavement to capitalist market imperatives, namely, to broaden the space for the free expression of our needs, preferences, and capacities, for those autonomous activities and engagements that are valued as ends in themselves rather than for their commercial potential.

We believe that current decommodification struggles to claim new commons and reclaim old ones are central to the ongoing contestation between deep democracy and capitalism. Progressive forms of decommodification are about enlarging the social and natural spheres over which the egalitarian and collective ethic of democracy applies and reducing the spheres under which the greed of capitalist profits applies. Indeed, as Ellen Meiksins Wood (1999b) emphasizes, achieving meaningful democracy today will require striving to decommodify broad new areas of social life:

> That means not just their subjection to the political rule of formal democracy but their removal from the direct control of capital and from the impersonal control of market imperatives, which subordinate every human need and practice to the requirements of accumulation and profit maximization. (p. 25)

Such varied and ongoing struggles to emancipate our lives from capitalist market imperatives will involve action in state and extra-parliamentary arenas and will need to take place locally, nationally, and through the international coordination of both people's movements from below and their progressive governments working together. In the past, struggles in the North managed to push back the sphere of capitalist markets dramatically by pressing governments to bring into the commons some parts that had been alienated and privatized and to bring new areas into commons control. The result was that people, nature, and services such as education, health care, and national park areas were substantially decommodified. In the mid-1900s, popular-democratic movements in the South achieved victories for decolonization and inwardly directed development, sometimes decommodifying land and deglobalizing transnational corporations. The various struggles being waged against neoliberal globalism today continue historical efforts to reclaim the commons from private appropriation and transcend limits exerted by capital over the practice and potential of democratic life.

Notes

1. GDP measures all recorded market exchanges. These include not-for-profit transactions in the public sector, but exclude the informal, under the table economy and all unpaid work and the value of nature.
2. In addition to the state sphere, we can add a voluntary, not-for-profit sector and a parapublic sector, which is non-profit and non-state. Parapublic institutions may run state-sanctioned services, such as child protection, not-for-profit hospitals, or public universities.
3. There are differences, however. Marshall saw social citizenship as the goal, whereas the Austro-Swedish model saw it as a means to achieve the final goal—economic citizenship.
4. Traditional conservatives are not "neo-conservatives." See Nisbet (1986).

CHAPTER TWO

The Commodity Status of Labour
The Secret of Commodified Life

DAVID MCNALLY

While a powerful critique of commodification has recently entered the public realm, thanks in no small measure to the new global justice movement, one particular commodity has generally been absent from this critique: human labour. And this absence, as I argue below, is replete with consequences, both theoretical and political.[1]

It is of tremendous import, of course, that as social movements contest the privatization and marketization of public goods like water and electricity, they have directed withering criticism at the neoliberal myth of the market as efficient allocator of all goods and services. It is now possible, at conferences and rallies and in numerous books and articles, to find the commodification of goods such as water, plant seeds, electricity, health care, and education regularly challenged, with critics insisting that such goods should be exempted from private ownership and market allocation.

Building on these arguments, Maude Barlow and Tony Clarke (2001) assert that there are four categories of things that ought not to be commodified: pernicious goods such as nuclear arms and toxic waste; life-building blocks such as bulk water, air, and genes; common inheritance goods such as plants, seeds, and animals (which should not be patented); and democratic rights including health care and education (pp. 182–83). The buying and selling of such goods on open markets and their patenting as the property of private owners is, they urge, contrary to the public interest. Consistent with this, important legal theorists are criticizing the bias of Western law in favour of market (rather than public) regulation. In *Contested Commodities* (1996), for instance, Margaret Jane Radin takes on what she calls "inappropriate commodification," arguing that sex, children, and body parts in particular ought not to be market goods (p. 8).

These eloquent pleas to limit and constrain commodification represent a significant challenge to neoliberal dogma, to the myth that market regulation of virtually everything on the planet (and beyond) will usher in the best of all possible worlds. One of the most insidious features of the globalization agenda of multinational corporations and agencies such as the International Monetary Fund (IMF) and the World Bank, after all, is the commitment to what I have elsewhere (McNally, 2002) called "global commodification": the idea that every conceivable good and service under the sun should be turned into a marketable item. For writers aligned with the global justice movement to have challenged the logic of global commodification is an accomplishment of no small import.

Yet, despite the power of these attacks on commodification, the existence of a global market in which billions of people sell their labour typically goes unmentioned. And this has significant consequences, both theoretical and political, because, as I argue below, the logic of global commodification cannot be uprooted without confronting its inner secret: the commodification of human labour.

THE BUSINESS OF BODIES

There is a certain irony to the general silence surrounding the commodification of labour since the buying and selling of human bodies and body parts generally provokes widespread revulsion. A sensational headline in the *Toronto Sun* in the fall of 2002, for instance, screamed, "Body Parts Pedlar." Below, a subheading elaborated details of the story: "He stole human brains, hand and foot from University of Toronto, then sold them to antique dealer" ("Body Parts," 2002). Even when pitched in a less sensationalistic vein, the buying and selling of human body parts still evokes deep anxieties. A year earlier, for instance, the *New York Times Magazine* ran an anguished article describing a global market in which poor people in the Third World sell their kidneys for less than $1,000 (Finkel, 2001a).[2]

As Trevor Harrison's chapter in this book further underlines, dramatic stories such as these barely touch on the true dimensions of the contemporary body business. A variety of scholarly studies—bearing titles like *The Human Body Shop* (Kimbrell, 1993), *Body Bazaar* (Andrews & Nelkin, 2001), and *Spare Parts* (Fox & Swazey, 1992)—inform us that more than 1,300 biotechnology firms now compete in a $17 billion (US) industry that trades genetic data, tissue samples, umbilical cords, eggs, sperm, blood, and more. One biotech company, deCODE Genetics, has a 12-year monopoly on investigating, storing, and selling the genetic data of the entire population of Iceland. A rival corporation, Autogen Ltd., has purchased the right to conduct genetic research on the people of Tonga, the results of which it can patent and sell (Senituli, 2002; "Pirates," 2002). Another firm, Myriad Genetics, has filed patents on two genes that indicate susceptibility to breast cancer. Claiming ownership of these genes, it is suing hospitals and laboratories around the world that conduct breast cancer tests on them, insisting that only Myriad's labs can be used for this purpose (McNally, 2002, p. 79). Unsettling as developments such as these are to many people, this commercialization of human life is entirely in accord with a 1980 decision of the US Supreme Court, which defined living forms as "machines or manufactures," thereby upholding the principle that living beings can be patented and their life forms owned (Pigem, 2002).

The US Supreme Court notwithstanding, dramatic newspaper headlines suggest that few things are so shocking as the idea that human body parts (and the human genome itself) might be bought and sold. What is deeply disturbing about this trade—be it in organs, blood, eggs, or tissue—is that human identities are inextricably bound up with our bodies. Take away the personal histories that we carry around with our bodies—our births, the places our bodies have dwelled, our experiences of pleasure and pain, illness and health, celebration and loss, labour and love—and you take away our very being. To attack the integrity of our bodies is thus, in the deepest and most profound sense, to attack our selves. This is why "body snatchers" occupy a central place in horror films: to invade our bodies is to assault an integral part of what makes us who we are. Indeed, most people recoil from the commercialized language of property rights, supply and demand, trade, contract and profits that permeates the body business. In the jargon of the industry, "body parts are extracted like a mineral, harvested like a crop, or mined like a resource." Such language suggests that, rather than being inviolable sites of personhood and individual identity, our bodies are merely a collection of parts that "can be pulled from their context, isolated, and abstracted from real people." When this happens, "the body has become commodified, reduced to an object, not a person" (Andrews & Nelkin, 2001, pp. 5–6). Responding to deep ethical concerns about such developments, governments in many countries are undertaking to constrain, regulate or ban the trade in human body parts. In 1984, for instance, then-US Congressman Al Gore pronounced: "It is against our system of values to buy and sell parts of human beings" (US House Committee on Energy and Commerce, 1984, p. 128). That a mainstream politician (who subsequently became US Vice-President and systematically favoured business interests) could voice such sentiments speaks to widespread qualms about the body business and strong, abiding beliefs that certain aspects of life should be strictly excluded from the sphere of commerce.

This concern for non-commercial values is central to debates over bio-ethics, the ethical issues associated with buying, selling, patenting, researching, and commercializing parts of the human body and its genetic makeup. In an effort to protect social values from the effects of commerce, critics have advocated limiting or preventing such commodification by "sequestering the body from the market."[3] There is great merit in such proposals. But in an important sense, they do not address the deepest roots of the commodification they resist. After all, trade in the human body is hardly something new. In fact, such trade utterly saturates modern life in the form of the mass market in human labour. And such a market is the space in which people sell bits and pieces of their bodily talents, skills, creativity, strength, and energies—in short, integral aspects of their embodied personhood. Without addressing this issue, attempts to limit the commodification of the body, and with it, as I shall argue, the commodification of most of our planet, are likely to be futile.

PERSONS, BODIES, AND THINGS

The resistance of many people to the idea of selling parts of the body is rooted in long-standing cultural meanings and traditions. One modern source of this resistance is the opposition to the enslavement of persons that has figured prominently in much liberal political thought. A staple of such liberalism is its sharp distinction between persons and things. Persons, it is held, can own things but not other persons. This imperative exists because these two kinds of entities are radically different by virtue of the freedom and autonomy that pertain to persons.

The German philosopher Immanuel Kant (1724–1804) mobilized this distinction to argue that humans could not sell themselves: "Man cannot dispose over himself because he is not a thing; he is not his own property ... if he were his own property, he would be a thing over which he could have ownership. But a person cannot be a property and so cannot be a thing which can be owned" (Kant, 1979, p. 165). The next great German philosopher, G.W.F. Hegel (1770–1831), deepened and extended this argument by claiming that the human body—and not just an abstraction called the human will or personality—cannot be treated like an object. Because humans are embodied beings, violation of our bodies constitutes violation of our freedom. "My body is the embodiment of my freedom," Hegel (1952) wrote. "Because I am alive as a free entity in my body," he added, my body "ought not to be misused by being made a beast of burden" (p. 43).[4] In short, the body is not a thing that can be separated from personhood; it is integral to that personhood itself.

The philosophical approach developed by Kant and extended by Hegel suggests, therefore, that to treat persons and their bodies as things is to violate human freedom and, in so doing, to deprive people of a fundamental component of their humanity. This claim is powerful—and sits uneasily with the dominant institution of modern capitalist society, the labour market. Although capitalism was only minimally developed in the Germany of his day, Kant was aware of the dilemma. Troubled by the implications of wage-labour for personhood, he proposed that, while selling goods was unobjectionable, selling one's labour ought to disqualify one from citizenship. In cases where an individual "must earn his living from others," he wrote, "he must earn it only by selling that which is his [i.e., goods], and not by allowing others to make use of him." Those who make their living as "merely labourers"—i.e., sellers of their labour—would be "unqualified to be citizens" (Kant, 1991, p. 78).

With this argument, Kant identified wage-labour—the selling of one's labour, energy, and skill for a wage—as a threat to the freedom and autonomy that are integral to personhood. By selling their labour, wage-labourers treat intrinsic parts of themselves as things—and this violates the very distinction between persons and things upon which human freedom (and morality) rest for Kant. Of course, Kant's "solution" is an anti-democratic one: rather than challenge the institution of wage-labour, he sought instead to disqualify labourers from citizenship.

In his major work of political philosophy, Hegel tried to find a way out of this dilemma by distinguishing between selling "the use of my abilities for a restricted period" and "alienating the whole of my time." By alienating the whole of my time, he claims, "I would be making into another's property the substance of my being" and, with it, "my personality"(Hegel, 1952, p. 54). Yet, this distinction is not nearly so secure as Hegel would like. At what point, for instance, would selling parts of my body qualify as violating my bodily integrity? And at what point would selling some parts of my life energies and time—"the substance of my being"—constitute my transformation into a beast of burden? After all, if I spend a huge part of my life treating my energies, talents, and bodily powers as things, commodities for sale, mustn't this in some significant way imperil that which makes me free, my differentiation from thinghood? Is it not probable that the systematic and persistent commodification of my labouring energies and skills will affect my personhood in some fundamental way? If my body is "the embodiment of my freedom," then are not the continual commodification of my embodied abilities and my regular treatment as a beast of burden contrary to the personal (and bodily) autonomy that is integral to human freedom?

Hegel is not alone in his blindness to the force of these questions. After all, while the sale of body parts makes sensational headlines today, the sale of human labour is not in the least newsworthy. So imbued is modern society with the commodification of labour, so normalized even "naturalized" has it become, that few bother to question it. While selling body parts still appears offensive, selling parts of our life's labouring energies seems entirely reasonable and acceptable. Yet this very fact speaks to just how thoroughgoing commodification has become. After all, wage-labour was once considered to be similar in kind to selling part of one's body; indeed, as I point out following, in some parts of the world today it is still associated with diabolical forces. How this deeply disturbing arrangement came to be considered normal speaks to one of the most momentous transformations in human history.

DEMONIC MONEY AND WAGE-LABOUR

The classic analysis of wage-labour is, of course, that developed by Karl Marx. No one before Marx had systematically probed the purchase and sale of labour in all its human dimensions. For Marx, this transaction involves much more than just an economic exchange; it also shapes the very identities and life experiences of the human agents involved. Declaring that to be human is to engage in creative work with others, Marx (1952) argued that wage-labour involves a loss of control over a fundamental human life-activity. Invariably, it entails the alienation of the worker's essential life-energies:

> [In] ... the exercise of labour-power, labour is the worker's own life-activity, the manifestation of his own life. And this life-activity he sells to another per-

son in order to secure the necessary means of subsistence. Thus his life-activity is for him only a means to enable him to exist. He works in order to live. He does not even reckon labour as part of his life; it is rather a sacrifice of his life. It is a commodity which he has made over to another ... life begins for him where this activity ceases, at table, in the public house, in bed. (p. 20)

In wage-labour, human creative energies are no longer an expression of one's life, but a denial of it; they are transformed into things (commodities) that are sold like any other thing. And this process of turning labour into a commodity to be "made over to another" is not an isolated event, but an experience that is repeated over and over throughout a lifetime. Thus, while not sold in their entirety, as is a slave, the wage-labourer nonetheless "sells himself and, indeed, sells himself piecemeal. He sells at auction eight, ten, twelve, fifteen hours of his life, day after day, to the highest bidder ... to the capitalist. The worker [unlike a slave or a serf] belongs neither to the owner nor to the land, but eight, ten, twelve, fifteen hours of his daily life belong to him who buys them" (Marx, 1952, p. 21).

The capitalist who buys this unique commodity (labour-power), does so with one intention alone: to turn a profit on it. One of the great secrets of capitalism is that work performed under the direction of the employer produces substantially more than the value of the wages paid. Capital thus lives by exploiting labour, by appropriating a surplus beyond the value of the costs of labour. For this reason, capitalism has devoted extraordinary attention to studying the labour process, breaking it down into the smallest possible physical motions, and using machinery to speed up each and every one of these movements.[5] The more they can intensify labour, however alienating it may be, the more profit capitalists can accrue. As a result, the exchange of money for labour, by a process that appears obscure and mysterious, breeds ever more money for the buyer of labour. And this money is turned into ever more means of production—machines, factories, and the like—for the further exploitation of labour.

A whole system of exploitation is thus erected in which workers produce the very instruments of production that are used to further exploit them. And this system of exploitation rests upon a Frankenstein-like inversion in which workers are dominated by their own creations, in which workers themselves produce the elements of capital (machines, factories, and so on) that are used to exploit them. Capital, therefore, is at root the alienated labour of workers that has accumulated in the hands of the employing class. So, the more labour is intensified, the more gigantic the stock of capital. Drawing on folklore, Marx dramatically expresses this process with the image of the vampire. "Capital," he writes, "is dead labor which, vampire-like, lives only by sucking living labor, and lives the more, the more labor it sucks" (Marx, 1976, p. 342).

Marx could not possibly have known just how resonant this imagery would prove to be. Yet, the depiction of capitalists as diabolical creatures who suck human blood and consume human bodies has been one of the most enduring in the popular imagination in many parts of the world.

In many societies of the global South, where fully modern capitalism has not been as deeply entrenched as it has in Europe and North America, the intensification and extension of capitalist relations is frequently associated with devils and demons. This is particularly so when these societies are subjected to intensified commodification. In parts of Colombia during the nineteenth century, for instance, black and indigenous peasants typically resisted entry into the labour market, clinging tenaciously to small plots of land. Wage-labour, as Michael Taussig (1980) has suggested, was construed as an evil and barbaric arrangement; indeed, people often believed that "success" on its terms involved contracts with the devil, contracts that ultimately entailed the sacrifice of one's life powers.[6]

More recently, in African countries such as Ghana and Nigeria, which have been subjected to the intense commodification demanded under Structural Adjustment Programs imposed by the likes of the International Monetary Fund and the World Bank, images of capitalist wealth as derived from ritual murder and the theft of body parts have proliferated in films, novels, folklore, and the media.[7] The brilliant Nigerian novelist Ben Okri has captured these cultural meanings to great effect in a series of novels, particularly *The Famished Road* (1992). The central capitalist figure in that novel, Madame Koto, grows physically huge as she becomes rich. Okri draws upon the vampiric image of the capitalist with great literary effect: "At night, when she slept, she stole the people's energies. (She was not the only one; they were legion.) ... Madame Koto sucked in the powers of our area. Her dreams gave the children nightmares. Her colossal form took wings at night and flew over our city, drawing power from our sleeping bodies" (p. 495).

The imagery of capital "drawing power" from the bodies of the poor is a widespread one in societies where commodification is experienced as a shock. Rather than "primitive" understandings, these images ought to be seen as dramatic metaphors through which people struggle to make sense of the unnaturalness of capitalism, particularly its accumulation of immense wealth through the commodification of labour, through the piecemeal purchases of people's bodily energies—purchases that enable the employing class to grow extraordinarily rich. The people "captured" by capitalist demons are depicted in many of these popular images as money-spewing zombies or "human ATMs" whose mouths spew out currency.

These ostensibly "fantastic" notions capture key elements of what Marx described as the "phantasmagoria" of commodities, the swirling images that allow capital to depict itself, and not human labour, as the self-generating basis of wealth. That people in "advanced" capitalist societies now experience these arrangements based upon the buying and selling of labour as normal and natural speaks to their cultural impoverishment, to the loss of rich systems of meaning that problematize capitalism's reduction of every aspect of life—most centrally human labour—to just another thing to be bought and sold.

It wasn't always this way, of course. Even in the birthplace of capitalism, Britain, capitalism did not conquer without a centuries-long battle to subjugate the poor, break down long-standing socio-cultural traditions, and deprive the subaltern population of every other alternative but wage-labour.

COMMODIFYING HUMAN LABOUR: THE SECRET HISTORY OF THE RISE OF CAPITALISM

"Never before our own time were markets more than accessories of economic life," wrote the economic historian Karl Polanyi in *The Great Transformation* (1957, p. 68). Prior to the rise of capitalism, markets operated at the periphery of social life; most of the goods people consumed were produced directly by themselves and their immediate social group (family, tribe, clan, village community). While exchange might take place for unique sorts of items, the idea of the systematic buying and selling of virtually every good and service necessary for human comfort would have struck people as utterly bizarre.

In particular, the selling of one's labour was a deeply offensive idea. This had to do with the fabric of social-economic relations in most pre-capitalist societies. Prior to capitalism, a large part of economic life was communally organized and regulated according to the principles of reciprocity and redistribution. The principle of reciprocity holds that all individuals are organically interconnected and have responsibilities for and duties toward one another. Linked to this is the redistributive principle, the notion that the community provides a transfer of wealth to those who have too little. The desire of individuals to accumulate as much personal wealth as they could would have struck most people in pre-capitalist societies—certainly those outside the elites—as a thoroughly repulsive sort of anti-social behaviour. Society was organized to insure the collective well-being of its members. As one anthropologist has pointed out, in most human societies prior to our own "the objective of gathering of wealth ... is often that of giving it away" (Sahlins, 1972, p. 213). As a result, no individual faced the threat of starvation so long as society had enough to support its members. In such circumstances, noted Polanyi (1968), "the individual is not in danger of starving unless the community as a whole is in a like predicament" (p. 66).

Even in class-dominated societies, such as feudal Europe, where lords exploited the labour of peasants, the poor still maintained important means for looking after themselves and their communities. Crucial in this respect were the common lands and a whole battery of common rights that applied to them. It was typical in feudal Europe for every village, dominated as it was by the lord's estate, also to have a mix of personal plots worked by peasant households and vast expanses of forests and fields that "belonged" to all. On these common lands, peasants could hunt, fish, graze animals, and gather wood for fuel in the winter.[8] Without the millions of acres of land that were held in common—and the fish, game, wood, and grazing land they provided—a huge proportion of the European peasantry could not have survived.

It was not just Europe that knew such arrangements. Well into the twentieth century, common lands were widespread among peasants in many parts of the world. In Colombia, for instance, such lands were known as *indivisos* among other terms. One Colombian peasant describes them as follows:

They also called these lands communeros; that was the land where you and I, and he, and someone else and someone else, and so on, had the right to have our animals ... no bit of land was divided by fences. There were some communeros with eighty families. They were lands where you place yourself as an equal with everybody else. Here almost all the land used to be like that. But after the War of One Thousand Days [which ended in 1902], the rich came along and closed off the land with barbed wire. (quoted in Taussig, 1980, pp. 73–74)

The modern history of Colombia is, among other things, a story of violent appropriation of the lands of the poor by the rich. In this respect, for all their marked differences, histories of the rise of capitalism almost invariably involve the privatization of land and the dispossession of the bulk of the rural poor. Britain was just the first case. When vast social and economic changes in the sixteenth and seventeenth centuries pushed British landlords toward new forms of capitalist farming (based on hiring out large tracts of lands to rich farmers who employed wage-labourers), a class war over the common lands became the decisive contest of the age. By driving up rents, foreclosing on debts, and disputing peasant ownership in the courts, landlords drove hundreds of thousands of peasants off their lands. These lands, now centralized in the hands of landowners, were then rented as large farms to wealthy capitalist tenant farmers who hired propertyless wage-labourers (many of them former peasant farmers).

Relentlessly, then, landlords were forcing millions of the rural poor off the land and into the labour market. Valiantly, peasants resisted this process. They tore down fences ("enclosures") barring them from the common lands; they rioted and invaded the forests, erecting cottages and "poaching" fish and game that had previously been available to all. A guerrilla war of localized resistance raged across the decades. Through violence, extortion, and intrigue, however, the landlords won battle after battle, enclosing perhaps 30 per cent of all English lands between 1600 and 1760. Then, having seized the momentum, the landlords turned to the political institution they thoroughly dominated, Parliament, to put the seal on the whole process. In the seventy years after 1760, landowners introduced "enclosure acts" that privatized at least six million acres of common lands, turning them into their own private property.[9] As these acts were put into effect, new waves of rebellion and resistance were again met by troops and weapons. With the violent subjugation of the rural poor, the new capitalist order emerged, as Marx (1976) put it, "dripping from head to toe, from every pore, with blood and dirt" (p. 926).

Over the course of two centuries or more, English society was utterly remade. A village-based system that, however much it rested on the exploitation of peasant labour by lords, guaranteed peasants access to the resources provided by communal lands was transformed into a system based upon a capitalist labour market.[10] The key development here is what Ellen Meiksins Wood (1999a) has appropriately dubbed "market dependence" (pp. 70–71). Prior to enclosure of the common lands, peasants had non-market access to basic means of life. But the

TABLE 2.1	Proportion of English Peasants Employed as Wage-Labourers, 1066-1688

Date	% of peasants employed as wage-labourers
1086	6
1279	10
1380	12
1540–59	11
1550–67	12
1600–10	35
1620–40	40
1688	56

Source: Lachman (1987, p. 17).

privatization of the common lands involved the separation of peasants from their communal means of production, and this meant that huge numbers could no longer support themselves without going to the market. There, they had to sell a commodity in order to acquire the money with which to buy the necessities of life. Prior to the loss of the commons, peasants could directly procure most of what they needed to survive without entering the sphere of market exchange. Henceforth, they no longer had that option. As a result, they now found their social-economic existence marketized in two fundamental ways. First, they could only procure basic means of subsistence through buying on the market. And, secondly, on the market they typically had to sell their labouring ability ("labour-power") in order to obtain the wage-money with which to purchase basic goods, foodstuffs in particular. The daily lives of the rural poor had thus become completely reliant upon the market; wage-labour now governed their existence.

The shift to market dependence represented a massive rupture in the fabric of everyday life. In closing off non-market forms of life, the loss of communal rights and properties was catastrophic. Even before the landlords used Parliament to enclose millions of acres, a majority of peasants had already been driven onto the labour market, as Table 2.1 indicates.

Even if these figures are not entirely precise, they certainly capture the basic trends. For nearly 500 years, around 10 per cent of the rural population engaged in wage-labour. Then came the upheavals of the seventeenth century. Before it was out, a majority of peasants has been forced by economic circumstances to turn to wage-labour. Capitalism's first war against the poor had been won. Yet, these wars were far from over. They would soon spread to more and more parts of the globe, as capitalism became the dominant system on the planet. And they continue to rage today as part of the battle over globalization. In fact, James Petras and Henry Veltmeyer (2001) calculate that the number of propertyless wage-labourers on the planet has risen dramatically as neoliberal policies displace peasants, encourage export-oriented agriculture, and cater to Western agri-businesses. They suggest that the global pool of wage-labourers has increased from 1.9 billion in 1980 to roughly three billion as of 1995, an increase of over 50 per cent during the globalization era (p. 24).[11]

WAGE-LABOUR AND GLOBAL COMMODIFICATION

It is often forgotten that the commodification of one's productive time and creative energies, their transformation into things for sale on the market, has dramatic effects upon an individual's sense of self, body, nature, and others. The systematic, regularized sale of "the very substance" of one's being, to use Hegel's formulation, deeply affects the individual's experience of life, time, persons, and things.

Central to the commodification of labour, argued Marx (1976), is that the capitalist "treats living labour power as a thing" (p. 989). More than this, however, as the Hungarian philosopher Georg Lukacs (1971) pointed out, labour commodification also imposes its stamp upon the very subjectivities of workers themselves. Rather than just a specific way of organizing the allocation of goods and services, commodification also reorganizes the very forms of human experience, the ways in which we perceive and understand ourselves and our capacities. Commodification is thus a thoroughly two-sided process, one that reshapes the world around us and penetrates into the psyche of the human individuals involved: "Objectively a world of objects and relations between things springs into being (a world of commodities and their movements on the market). Subjectively—where the market economy has been fully developed—a man's activity becomes estranged from himself" (Lukacs, 1971, p. 87). As a result, labour commodification "stamps its imprint upon the whole consciousness of man; his qualities and abilities are no longer an organic part of his personality, they are things which he can 'own' or 'dispose of' like the various objects of the external world" (p. 100).

Thus, when critics today object to the way the body business employs "a set of cultural assumptions," which treat the body as a package of "units" that "can be pulled from their context, isolated and abstracted from real people," they are also unwittingly describing exactly what happens with the commodification of human labour (Andrews & Nelkin, 2001, p. 6). Of course, people do not easily submit to this thingification (reification) of their selves. At first, as already noted briefly, commodification is experienced as unnatural, as involving non-human and demonic forces that are invading social life. But once alternative systems of meaning have been decisively uprooted, once people have learned to accept wage-labour as normal and natural, once alternative ways of organizing social life are no longer part of their waking conscious life, then commodified understandings of self and other become the norm.[12]

In "developed" capitalist societies today, for example, how to "sell yourself" has become a regular subject of advice columns and talk shows, with individuals being encouraged to package their "assets," their looks, aptitudes, skills, strength, smile, personality, and so on for life in a market society. Commodification thus involves the reification of parts of the self—their isolation as abstractable components of the human being that can be put on the market. In this vein, two American economists have recently argued that individuals should begin to imagine themselves as corporations and sell shares in themselves (Church, 1998). This sort of self-commodification is an inevitable part of the logic of a commodified society. We should not be surprised, then, that people who have grown accustomed to commodifying themselves would similarly consider all the elements of the natural environment—minerals, trees, fossil fuels, water, and air—to be commodifiable, or that they might be susceptible to seeing education, health care, wombs, or human organs in these terms. In a society in which essential elements of our being, such as time, skill, energy, and creativity, are regularly put up for sale, why should we expect people to look at other parts of the world around them differently? Why should we expect people who are compelled to sell themselves on labour markets to automatically find the commercialization of water or education objectionable?[13]

DECOMMODIFYING HUMAN LABOUR

At the heart of my argument is the claim that commodification of one of our fundamental life-activities—labour—generates what has been called "commodification as a worldview," an outlook in which commodification is seen as the only possible way of organizing the allocation of every conceivable good or service. For this reason, those who wish to decommodify a whole range of goods and services—from water and wombs to education and health care—need to grapple with the deep structures of commodification that have made the commodity-basis of socio-economic life seem normal and natural. A number of critics have argued eloquently for overturning "commodification as a worldview" without giving serious consideration to the effects of the market organization of our working lives. Yet, since commodification shapes the very subjectivities of people in a capitalist society, so long as human labour is organized as a market commodity, the drive to commodify everything around us will seem a logical and natural extension of the way our everyday lives are organized. It is unlikely, therefore, that society will be reconstituted around non-market values so long as the market permeates one of the most basic and fundamental aspects of our socio-economic existence.[14]

But what would it mean to decommodify labour? How might we envision a society that is not based upon a labour market? And how might we build mass movements to decommodify labour?

As our historical analysis suggests, at its most basic level, the decommodification of labour requires the recreation of common property and common rights that guarantee non-market access to the means of subsistence.[15] In modern capitalism, as we have seen, most people's access to housing, food, electricity, recreation, higher education, and so on depends upon finding a buyer for their labour in the market (or, in the case of children or "dependents" on parents, guardians, or partners finding such buyers). Fail to locate a buyer for our labour on the market and we (along with those who depend directly upon our earnings) run the risk of not procuring housing, adequate food, and so on. The first decisive step toward decommodifying labour, then, involves providing guaranteed (non-market) access to such fundamental goods as housing, food, electricity, recreational goods and facilities, education, health care, child care, and the like as basic rights. Individual subsistence and survival would, in such circumstances, no longer be determined by the vagaries of the labour market, by whether or not one manages to find a buyer for one's embodied abilities. Market dependence would thus be broken.

To be sure, the guarantee of universal rights and entitlements to the goods and services provided by a socialized consumption sector would require a commitment by healthy adults to performing social labour, to doing some of the work necessary for society to meet the needs of its members. In my view, which I have set out at some length elsewhere, such social labour ought to be organized in terms of worker-managed, communally owned workplaces that operate according to eco-logical and democratic principles. In addition, they should be based upon a radi-cal reduction in the length of the ordinary workday or workweek. By eliminating wasteful forms of production, unemployment, massive product duplication, enor-mous war industries, and the huge resources devoted to advertising, marketing, product promotion, and so on, society could provide work to all healthy adults and improve the conditions of life for the majority of humankind while also signif-icantly reducing the hours (and upgrading the conditions) of social labour.[16]

By organizing the allocation of fundamental goods and services on the basis of rights, not ability to pay, we would supplant the market as the mechanism by which people guarantee their survival—or fail to do so. This is not to say that all market transactions would necessarily disappear, and certainly not overnight. It is instead to propose that people's survival would be secured outside the market, in what I have called the socialized consumption sector, which would be governed by need, not ability to pay.[17] Freeing our socio-material reproduction from the market is the decisive step toward de-marketizing and decommodifying human labour.[18] If the first wage-labourers were driven into the labour market as the only available means of survival, then the construction of a socialized consumption sector that guarantees survival, comfort, and socio-material reproduction as social rights would eliminate this market dependence. In such a society, social labour would be performed as a social responsibility, not out of coercion enforced by the threat of poverty.

There is no doubt that a variety of transitional arrangements would be neces-sary before a society could be said to have accomplished the full decommodifica-tion of labour. Over time, more and more goods and services would have to be encompassed by the socialized consumption sector; correspondingly, the sphere of market transactions would tend systematically to contract. And this is what it means to decommodify human labour: to make the market increasingly marginal, rather than central, to the procurement of the necessities of life.[19] As our socio-material needs are increasingly satisfied outside the market, as we become less and less reliant on market exchanges (via money) to "make ends meet," then the notion of human life as based upon rights to goods and services can be expected to supplant the commodified view of the world in which everything ought to be for sale. In a society that treated people as inherently valuable ends in themselves and not as means to the expansion of capital, new social values—non-commercial and non-commodity ones—based upon fundamental principles of human dignity, integrity, freedom, and self-development could be expected to flourish. People in a decommodifying society would learn to value themselves, others, and the natural environment in qualitatively new ways, opening the way to a radically different form of society.

ANOTHER WORLD IS POSSIBLE

To talk about a radical transformation of world society is, of course, to invite the charge of utopianism. Yet this is to miss two crucial points. First, our adversary—neoliberalism—has succeeded in part because of the boldness of its (reactionary) utopianism, what we might call capitalist utopianism. At the core of neoliberalism is a dramatic vision in which the whole world really is for sale, a world without unions, environmental regulations, minimum wage laws, and so on. Neoliberalism imagines a world organized simply on the basis of private property rights (which would apply effectively to everything) and global market competition. And it is not just our planet that is supposed to be regulated by property law and corporate ownership: recently, a private corporation was granted legal rights to explore, photograph, and land on the moon—part of a long-term plan for the privatization and corporatization of lunar space. Not surprisingly, corporations have also been offered the opportunity to have their logos emblazoned on the side of lunar space shuttles—for a mere $25,000 US. Neoliberalism thus projects a radical corporate utopianism in which everything from the human genome to the moon is privately owned.

But the second crucial point about a radical perspective is that the emerging global justice movement, particularly in the South, is itself beginning to formulate a powerful counter-utopia. Occupying land in Brazil, fighting giant dams in India, resisting water privatization in Bolivia, striking against layoffs in Korea, throwing up barricades against structural adjustment in Argentina: in all these ways and more, mass movements of millions of people have challenged the fundamental premises of global commodification.[20] Rising to new levels of militancy and defiance, they have also begun to formulate their own social vision. Until recently, the opposition to neoliberalism generally lacked the audacity and boldness of outlook that sustained its capitalist adversaries. But the new grassroots popular movements of workers and peasants have increasingly proclaimed, as the banner of the World Social Forums of 2001 and 2002 in Porto Alegre, Brazil declare, that "Another World is Possible." In so doing, they have started the process of reclaiming utopia, of envisioning a world organized on the basis of popular democracy, global justice, full gender and racial equality, ecological sanity, respect for the rights of indigenous and oppressed peoples, and production for human needs, not profit.

The new movement is very much one in formation. More mainstream and "respectable" elements, particularly non-governmental organizations (NGOs) and moderate trade union leaders, often try to constrain the movement's propensity to militant struggle and direct action and to divert its energies into demanding a few seats among the elites at the negotiating table, rather than overturning the whole structure of elite power. But against these moderate and bureaucratic forces, there are powerful movements that seize land, occupy the streets, wage mass strikes, confront the riot police, throw up barricades—in short, do whatever is necessary to roll back the neoliberal juggernaut. And in demanding land for the landless, jobs for the jobless, and water, electricity, and homes for all, they are challenging the very logic of commodification.

Yet, as I have argued throughout this piece, commodification cannot truly be uprooted without undermining the market character of labour in modern society. And this social and political project—the overturning of the commodity structure of modern life—is not possible without a radically anti-capitalist movement, one which intends to break corporate-capitalist power and create new forms of communal property regulated by radical, grassroots democracy. The task is thus a revolutionary not an ameliorative one.

How could it be otherwise? To decommodify society, to make it effectively impossible for people to even imagine that someone could own the world's water or the human genome, means to strike at the deepest roots of our own commodification. It means, in short, to create a world in which the buying and selling of labour is as reprehensible as the buying and selling of body parts.

Notes

1. I would like to acknowledge funding by the Social Sciences and Humanities Research Council of Canada that has assisted my work on this article. I would also like to thank Sue Ferguson for her comments on an earlier draft.
2. This article clearly illustrates the way in which class and race issues figure in the buying and selling of body parts. These issues, along with gender, are also raised by a recent Canadian example (Priest, 2002).
3. This is the heading of the final chapter in Andrews and Nelkin. Radin's argument (2001) in defence of "incomplete commodification" works in a similar direction.
4. This emphasis on embodiment had earlier proponents in political philosophy, but Hegel was unique among German Idealist philosophers in accenting it in this way.
5. See, for instance, Rinehart (1996).
6. Taussig has often been criticized, with some justification, for idealizing pre-capitalist arrangements in these regions as "natural" and "organic." This criticism should not, however, detract from the great power of his reading of cultural understandings of capital as a diabolical power in these societies.
7. See for instance Meyer (1990, 1995) and Drohan (2000). These are not the only countries where such tales abound at this moment of late capitalist anxiety. One also finds them in other parts of Africa, East Asia, and Latin America. See, for example, Jean Comaroff and John L. Comaroff (1999, p. 291).
8. For a detailed account of the English common lands, see A.W.B. Simpson (1986); for an insightful interpretation of their meaning for common rights, see E.P. Thompson (1991).
9. For a more detailed discussion, see David McNally, *Against the Market* (1993), chapter 1.
10. By no means do I intend to idealize the feudal system: it was oppressive, exploitative, and patriarchal in the extreme. The key point in my account is the transformation to modern forms of capitalist property and the way in which this transformation required the destruction of communal lands in order to create a modern capitalist labour market.
11. For descriptions of the process by which this takes place, see McNally (2002, pp. 73–78).
12. I do not believe these processes are ever totally complete. See, for instance, McNally (2001), chapters 4 and 5.

13. I recognize that many people do in fact contest the commodification of such things. In doing so, however, they are acting counter to the logic of commodification that is inscribed in the experience of wage-labour.

14. I would also argue, much as I have in the final chapter of *Against the Market* (1993), that society cannot be reorganized according to non-commercial values so long as it rests on the buying and selling of human labour. An unwillingness to confront this is the great weakness of Radin's important book, *Contested Commodities* (1996). While occasionally acknowledging the alienating effects of at least some forms of wage-labour, she hopes to challenge "commodification as a worldview" without decommodifying labour—an impossible task in my view. Similarly, the absence of human labour on the impressive list of goods and services that Barlow and Clarke (2001) suggest ought not to be commodified (noted previously) represents, in my view, a major flaw in their critical analysis.

15. The idea of recreation here does not mean a return to the medieval or early-modern system of common lands. To begin with, these were ultimately subordinate to the social power and property of landowners. More than this, in modern society, we would have to think in terms of common forms of industrial and "post-industrial" property.

16. See McNally, *Against the Market* (1993), chapter 6.

17. See McNally, *Against the Market* (1993), p. 196. As I argue there (e.g., p. 197), such a sector need not rigidly lock in consumption patterns, but could provide for a range of individual "trade-offs." Nevertheless, some of its basic elements are certain to be more or less fixed, such as housing, food, clothing, and so on.

18. I refer to socio-material reproduction here in distinction from socio-biological reproduction (conception, pregnancy, childbirth, and child-rearing). Socio-material reproduction refers to the recreation of the basic means necessary to human life in its modern forms.

19. The notion of necessities is, as I argue in *Against the Market* (1993, pp. 188–90), an historically malleable one. This is not to say that there are no natural needs—without water, oxygen, etc. we perish, after all—but simply to point out that human needs are open-ended and culturally shaped. On the general point, see my *Bodies of Meaning* (2001, pp. 7–9) for a discussion of "historical bodies."

20. See McNally, *Another World is Possible* (2002), chapter 6.

CHAPTER THREE

On the Ownership of Nature

Birgit Müller

Two big international treaties at the end of the twentieth century—the Convention on Biological Diversity (UNEP Secretariat, 1992) and the Marrakech Agreement (1994) founding the World Trade Organization (WTO)—have helped to redefine legally humanity's relationship to nature.[1] While the Convention on Biological Diversity instituted private property rights over wild nature to prevent bio-piracy (the limitless exploitation of the rich genetic resources of poor countries), the Marrakech agreement made the recognition of patents for the discovery of micro-organisms and genetic components of naturally occurring plants and animals obligatory for all signatory countries. In the wake of these two agreements, the question of who can earn what out of nature has increasingly become a pressing concern for life science corporations, national governments, local communities, and international non-governmental organizations (NGOs).

This newly instituted property regime represents a new benchmark in the commodification of nature, but is in many ways an expression of broader historical forces that have, for centuries, fuelled the plundering and despoliation of the global environment. In this chapter, I discuss the commodification of nature as a political and theoretical problem that is inextricably bound up with prevailing Western assumptions about human ownership of and power over nature. After briefly considering how this reductive conception of nature has become an integral part of the dominant intellectual and political paradigm of contemporary capitalism, I critically discuss some projects of common ownership and stewardship that help point the way to a more just and sustainable alternative in the future.

REPLENISH THE EARTH AND SUBDUE IT

The verb "to have," along with the associated idea of having and possessing, is largely unique to Indo-European languages, and corresponds to a particular worldview and way of defining our relationships to persons, objects, time, space, and even our own individual selves. This worldview has become so deeply embedded in our consciousness that it has gradually acquired an intuitive, taken-for-granted, and inescapable quality. In their everyday mode of thinking and interacting with the world, English speakers can scarcely formulate alternatives to "having," "possessing," and other notions associated with the ownership of property.

As an idea, and as a project for society, the notion of "privatization" is premised upon the conviction that private ownership can greatly enhance the sense of value and importance that individuals attribute to the objects, ideas, and resources at their disposal. By exerting ownership over such things, this view holds, the individual simultaneously carves out an inviolable space of freedom and autonomy for him- or herself. The problem with this free market ideal, however, is that the powerful few in capitalist society can, through their private control over the majority of collective resources, deny the many precisely this space of freedom. A thoroughly "privatized" society is one composed of selfish, competing individuals that work against and not with one another. The "invisible hand of the market" has no divine principle behind it. While the free interplay of self-interested property holders exchanging on the market certainly makes social relationships quite dynamic, it also presupposes a very particular relationship between human society and the natural environment. Indeed, what happens when private property becomes the universally accepted paradigm determining our collective relationship to the environment?

Regarding society as apart from the natural world and as transcending it provides the intellectual basis for treating nature as a lifeless "resource" that can be owned and exploited at will (Ingold, 2000, p. 215). With the Christian dictum "replenish the earth and subdue it," nature became primarily a thing "out there" to be used by humans and to serve human needs. According to the Judeo-Christian tradition, humans are not only created separately from the plant and animal kingdom; more importantly, they are created in God's image in order to have dominion over the rest of creation. While science gradually came to replace religion as a source of cultural authority in the Western world, it merely enhanced and reinforced this established instrumental relationship to the natural environment. The modern scientist, as a dispassionate observer of the natural world, systematically devalued spiritual and subjective experience in favour of cold quantification. The seventeenth century embraced the transformative possibilities of science with unqualified optimism, giving rise to utopian visions of nature laid bare to human understanding and harnessed to the goal of human progress. Science, philosophers like Francis Bacon suggested, would enable humanity to build a new Atlantis, where, through a program of scientific study and rational reform, poverty, sickness, and the rest of the world's ills would be vanquished (Geisinger, 1999).

The capitalist system, with its inherent goal of unlimited wealth creation, reinforced the Baconian vision of ongoing social progress driven by constant scientific advancement. Together, these forces provided the basis for a worldview that conceived of civilization in the role of actively dominating nature, and of nature as existing solely for the benefit of people. Economic liberalism's hallowed ideal of constant economic growth was based on a particular view of human nature. Happiness, as Adam Smith and others believed, was based on an individual's unfettered ability to enjoy the necessities, conveniences, and amusements of life to the fullest. This basic assumption was, eventually, to dominate the worldviews of capitalist and socialist societies alike. Throughout much of the twentieth century, the two competing political systems measured their success in terms of their ability to continually spur economic growth and increase human consumption.

Marx, however, had criticized the nature-culture divide as a particular feature of capitalism that lead to the intensive exploitation of both workers and nature's riches. Marx maintained that human history was, at the same time, natural history, that nature was shaped historically through creative human activity (Marx & Engels, 1978, p. 43). Through work, humans regulate and control their metabolic relationship with the natural substances that they transform for their livelihood (Marx, 1977, p. 192). The ideal of preserving nature in a state untouched by human action was not part of Marx's thinking, because for him human labour was a force that necessarily transformed nature. Marx was thus not overly worried about the transformation of nature through human agency, as change in the state of nature was constant and unavoidable in the process of historical development. Nature changes through the actions of humans, while humans themselves transform their own nature and develop their capacities in the process. The specific way in which we use natural resources depends upon the manner in which production is organized socially. In capitalism, Marx asserts, the processes of production inevitably destroy their own sources of wealth: the land and the worker (Marx, 1977, p. 529).

This particular line of reasoning, of course, does not necessarily make Marx an environmentalist ahead of his time. Neither environmental concerns nor central planning were on his agenda when he sketched out the rough contours of the socialist society he envisioned for the future. There is nowhere in Marx, nor in later Marxists, an adequate analysis of the replacement of used-up means of production in an economy based on exhaustible resources (Martinez-Alier, 1987, p. 219). Marx (1973), writing in 1875, underlined the need to postpone communist redistribution until the development of the productive forces had proceeded much further. Some of his followers, writing later, maintained that environmental problems were entirely unique to capitalist society. As Richta, an influential Czech ideologue, stated in the 1970s:

> Socialism, in contrast to capitalism, creates the conditions for altering nature in a purposeful and controlled way, because central leadership and planned economic and social development make it possible to realise the interests of the whole society and to prevent the destruction of the natural environment. (quoted in Vanek, 1996, pp. 22–23)

In spite of such claims, actually existing socialism proved to be as exploitative of nature as any capitalist regime, if not more so. The gigantic development schemes that dominated socialist economies, providing their outward symbols of progress, went ahead with scant regard for the natural environment. It was the state that planned the systematic transformation of nature into productive resources and engaged in the wasteful and unaccountable central planning strategies that squandered collectivized natural resources. The destruction and pollution was such that environmental protests were the most visible expressions of discontent in actually existing socialist societies during the 1980s.

After 1989, private companies accelerated the private appropriation of industry, services, and natural resources formerly owned by the state, not only in the former socialist countries but in the First and Third Worlds as well. Neoliberal economists legitimized this strategy as the only rational and viable economic option in a "post-socialist" world. They justified the growing inequalities that immediately ensued by claiming that the disempowered would one day catch up to the levels of wealth and social development enjoyed by the global elite. Biotechnology was increasingly projected as one of the miracle solutions for achieving this goal. It was to increase agricultural output by creating high yielding species resistant to herbicides and pesticides and to remedy the exhaustion of fossil fuels by producing plastics through micro-organisms. The fantasies connected with these new technologies merged seamlessly with established ideas about unlimited economic growth. Speed and efficiency were at the heart of the genetic revolution (Rifkin, 1998, p. 46), and heralds of the emergent biotech utopia ignored the large amounts of energy that would be needed in the enormous agro-factories growing new foods, medicines, and industrial raw materials. Early experiments with genetically modified organisms (GMOs) in agriculture proved to be costly for farmers, demanding high levels of expensive inputs and holding farmers in direct personal dependence upon the big seed corporations.

Biotechnology, far from being neutral, threatens to cement the relationships of power and unequal exchange upon which the unjust flow of money and resources from poor developing countries to rich industrial countries has been based. The controversies surrounding its development in recent years point us directly to the broader moral and political issue we confront today: whether the dominance of market principles is compatible with and even conducive to environmental preservation, or whether market principles have to be strictly reigned in and regulated to allow a diverse environment to survive.

MAKING THE COMMODIFICATION OF NATURE THE DOMINANT PARADIGM

With the fall of actually existing socialism, the concept of private ownership became enshrined at the beginning of the 1990s as the dominant principle guiding economic and political life, and as the only remedy for the social and environmental problems we face. The Earth Summit of 1992, which brought us Agenda 21 and the Convention on Biological Diversity, was a turning point in the international legal framing of human society's relationship to nature. Faced with climate change, the decline of fresh water resources, the disappearance of forests, the rapid extinction of numerous animal species, and the extreme poverty of more than a billion of the world's population, the principle of market liberalization was advanced as an all-purpose solution. The principle of ecological efficiency, based on the goals of increasing production with fewer inputs, "dematerializing" the economy through technological progress, and privatizing natural resources and their management through the market, was presented as a means of guaranteeing the sustainability of economic growth (Nansen & Villareal, 2002, p. 12).

Sustainable Development became the guiding principle of the Rio Declaration, and has since become one of the most ubiquitous buzzwords in our contemporary political vocabulary. Although there is no single, agreed-upon definition of Sustainable Development (Geisinger, 1999), virtually all definitions conceived of it in terms of a basic tension between the goals of economic development and environmental protection, with a marked preference for the goal of growth. Virtually echoing the words of Adam Smith, the Brundtland Commission report (Brundtland, 1987) observes "[s]o-called free goods like air and water are also resources. The raw materials and energy of production processes are only partly converted to useful products. The rest comes out as waste" (p. 46). Accordingly, as subsequent advocates of "sustainable development" would forcefully argue, the means of increasing awareness of the value of our limited natural resources was the generalization of the principle of private property over nature—over water, forests, genetic resources, and so on.

As the most visible outcome of the Rio conference, the Convention on Biological Diversity was strongly reflective of this ideological trend. It stipulated that systems of private ownership rights would encourage the preservation of biodiversity, the protection of rare plants and animals, and sustainable patterns of resource use. Hardin's evocative picture of the "tragedy of the commons" (Hardin, 1968) served as an argument for introducing private property rights into this international convention to protect nature from human short-sightedness. It is rational for a herder on a common pasture, so Hardin's argument runs, to add extra animals to the pasture although this will collectively result in overgrazing. To say it in more general terms: where individual interests would push members of a collective to the boundless exploitation of collective resources, private property would work towards the preservation of privatized resources. The Convention accepts profit-maximization as the driving motive of economic action and choice, while also holding to the view that rules of access are needed to allow inhabitants of bio-diverse but poor countries to take a fair share of the profits that biotechnology corporations make from their genetic resources.

However, the Convention also acknowledges that "customary use of biological resources" (UNEP Secretariat, 1992, art. 10c)—that is to say, a use embedded in a large array of social practices, religious beliefs, and political convictions—should be protected and encouraged. It expresses the conviction that "indigenous and local communities embodying traditional lifestyles" have knowledge and practices relevant for the conservation of biological diversity (UNEP Secretariat, 1992, art. 8j). This holistic vision of humanity-nature symbiosis, however, expresses itself in an idealizing discourse that projects onto so-called "traditional" societies human-ity's hopes for preserving nature. In the system of protected areas that the Convention proposes to establish, indigenous and local communities are expected to practice a lifestyle that preserves biodiversity. The same is not expected from Western industrialized countries and their economic institutions, whose role it is to develop relevant technologies and to provide for "substantial investments to con-serve biological diversity" that will bring "a broad range of environmental, eco-nomic and social benefits" (UNEP Secretariat, 1992, Preamble).

The question, however, is this: benefits for whom? According to the Convention, developing countries would gain the possibility of sharing the benefits arising from the use of their genetic resources. Eighty per cent of genetic resources exist naturally in the poor developing countries of the South, but after 500 years of colonialism, specimens of about 80 per cent of these plants have already been transferred to the botanical gardens in the North, where they are conserved far from their natural habitat, *ex situ*. The Convention affirms that states have sover-eign rights over their own biological resources without specifying whether this applies to *in situ* or *ex situ* resources. This ambiguity serves the rich countries with low levels of biodiversity well, as it allows them to legitimize an appropriation that has, de facto, already taken place.

Knowledge about the healing and nutritional properties of many plants, how-ever, is still in the hands of so-called traditional communities, without being the exclusive property of any of them. This gives rise to a diversity of agendas sur-rounding the concept of indigenous environmental knowledge, creating fields of power within which alliances may be formed, struggles waged, claims made, and rights asserted and denied (Li, 2002). Often, similar plants are used by several communities, in one or more countries, that could thus equally lay claim to them. Biological traits recognized and used in one culture could be extracted from related or unrelated species in other parts of the world. Indigenous knowledge obtained from one community could allow companies to utilize that knowledge while obtaining biomaterials from *ex situ* botanical gardens, herbaria, zoos, cell libraries, tissue collections, and so on. In each case, benefit-sharing possibilities could be contractually avoided (RAFI, 2000, p. 3). Biotech companies negotiate their access to genetic resources through states that often have conflict-ridden rela-tionships with their own indigenous communities and want to extract a maximum of financial benefit from the deal. The result is that all parties—biotech companies, governments, and indigenous communities—start to regard plants and animals mainly as sources of income and profit.

The primary concept around which controversies about access to knowledge about plants and animals revolves is that of intellectual property. Over the last twenty years, all rules of the game have changed regarding intellectual property rights, both in terms of how they have been put into practice and how these changes have fundamentally affected the patenting of life forms. From protecting inventions for a certain period of time, patent law has moved towards allowing the private appropriation of "discoveries." Genes isolated in naturally occurring plants and animals, synthesized active ingredients of medicinal plants, and the processes by which genetic components have been isolated can all now be patented. With the signing in 1994 of the Agreement on Trade-Related Aspects of Intellectual Property Rights (TRIPS) by the member countries of the WTO, intellectual property rights regimes compatible with those that evolved in the countries of the North over the last 100 years have to be introduced by all signatories, including the non-industrialized countries of the South. In article 27.3(b),[2] the agreement asserts that intellectual property rights over living organisms and life forms are possible and that patent-protection for micro-organisms and genetically modified organisms needs to be made possible worldwide. The article obliges all signatories of the TRIPS agreement to provide for intellectual property rights protection for plant varieties, although it allows them to choose their own regime of protection.

By requiring WTO members to grant patent-protection for naturally-occurring micro-organisms and, as most industrialized countries would argue, also for genetic materials from plants and animals, the TRIPS agreement extends the realm of patent law far beyond the common practice of most countries. Analogous to the colonialist "discoveries" of the fifteenth to nineteenth centuries, when whole continents that had been settled for millennia by indigenous populations were "discovered" by white Europeans and appropriated by force and deceit, the regulations of the WTO opened the possibility of private companies getting legal access to natural organisms, traditional lineages of food-crops, and the knowledge about them that has accumulated for centuries among indigenous populations and traditional peasant communities.

In September of 1999, for example, the multinational company Monsanto filed a patent in 81 countries on soybeans with enhanced yield (WO 0018963). It covered any cultivated soybean containing segments of DNA from "wild" or "exotic" soybeans identified through marker-assisted selection (MAS). The group of genes, which was only vaguely defined in the patent description, was said to be responsible for enhanced yield. Not only did the patent claim an important trait in soybean breeding, but it also gave Monsanto monopoly rights on *Glycine soya* (wild soybean), particularly PI 407305 from Southern China and all its progeny. Furthermore, the patent extended to any soybean carrying the high yield genes (Kuyek, 2001, p. 14).

Five life-science corporations[3] currently hold more than 75 per cent of all biotechnology patents in the world (Ribeiro, 2003). Even if small laboratories in developing countries make discoveries of potentially lucrative natural ingredients, the patents often end up with one of the powerful companies following mergers and buy-outs. Attempting to palliate the appropriation of natural resources of poor yet bio-diverse countries by corporations from rich countries with declining biodiversity, some government officials and NGOs have placed their hopes upon *sui generis* procedures for protecting plant varieties. Others have started to denounce any legalization of the appropriation of genetic resources as *legal* biopiracy.

The African Model Law has been heralded by some environmental and development NGOs as an effective weapon against bio-piracy. Principles other than those of private appropriation are stated in the introduction to the commented version of the African Model Law:

> The OAU's Model Law is based on the principle that the biodiversity-related knowledge, innovations and practices of local communities are a result of the many tried and tested practices of past and present generations. In order to maintain and ensure their continuity and evolution, they must be passed on to future generations. This is a fundamental right and responsibility of each generation to the one following it. Therefore, no one has the right to appropriate, sell or monopolize any component of biological resources and the associated knowledge, innovations, and practices of local communities.... In this sense, community rights are said to be *inalienable*, and cannot be taken away from those who hold them. They are inter-generational rights and responsibilities, and the individual has no personal authority to take decisions that undermine or destroy them, but instead has the duty to develop them and pass them on to future generations. These rights are thus also *imprescriptible*. (Organization of African Unity, 2000, Introduction to the commented version of the African Model Legislation)

In spite of claiming in its introduction that community rights are inalienable and imprescriptible and cannot be individually appropriated, the model law of the OAU falls into the trap of the Convention on Biological Diversity by stipulating that the transfer and exploitation of biological resources can happen with *the prior informed consent* of the communities that traditionally dispose of these resources. This means that relations of (intellectual) property can be established over biological resources if the communities and especially the State authorities that are to defend their interests give their consent. Relationships of power between local communities and the state officials that are to represent their interests in the so-called "Competent National Authorities" are, however, unequal, often to the detriment of the former. Needless to say, powerful industrialized countries also exercise tremendous pressure on the governments of developing countries to open up access to genetic resources.

Confronted with such pressures and with the prospect of making money if they successfully claim certain biological resources as part of their traditional knowledge, more and more leaders of so-called traditional indigenous communities attending international fora—such as conferences of the signatory parties of the Convention on Biological Diversity—no longer contest the principle of sharing the access to and benefits from their biological resources with multinational corporations. Instead, they try to negotiate the most favourable conditions for themselves. In such fora, laying claim to an "indigenous point of view" becomes part of a strategic struggle for legitimacy upon a highly contested terrain. Different versions of the "indigenous point of view" are constructed here as coherent discourses that can be quite detached from the actual diversity of indigenous societies, their diverse economic and social conditions, and their varied relationships to the natural environment.

That said, some of these viewpoints are clearly opposed to the idea of access and benefit sharing. They lay claim to an indigenous way of life in which their communities are inextricably "part of a natural world" whose resources can neither be privatized nor negotiated away (Muelas Hurtado, 2000, p. 24). Increasingly, however, such viewpoints seem to be losing ground in international negotiations. At the same time, the "indigenous way of life" is now also increasingly heralded by radical ecologists and international environmental agencies as an alternative to the commodification of nature to which most parties seem to have resigned themselves. In reality, however, this romantic image of indigenous communities participates in the construction of an ideal Other, disinterested and non-materialistic, that is going to save islands of pristine nature for the rest of humanity—which is, predictably, going about business as usual.

THINKING UP ALTERNATIVES TO THE COMMODIFICATION OF NATURE

In attempting to confront the commodification of nature at a practical level, we run up against a number of unresolved questions. What alternative could lie beyond private appropriation? Collective ownership? No ownership at all? In all societies, control over and access to things, ideas, and resources is regulated—though not necessarily through legal systems or private property. Regulation may be through rituals, customary conventions, or forms of political power that can also be extremely constraining, non-egalitarian, and wasteful. If one takes property as a bundle of power, as Verdery (1998, p. 161) in her analysis of post-socialist systems suggests, then all other forms of control over things, ideas, and resources can be analysed in the same way, with respect to the exercise of power. This approach allows us to look also at the idea of a global commons in a critical way—not as a ready-made solution to the problem of commodification that we are encountering, but as the beginning of a new challenge that we are just getting ready to confront.

A radical alternative to attempts at drafting *sui generis* pieces of legislation that would comply with the regulations of the WTO is the initiative to draft a Treaty to Share the Genetic Commons, which opposes the extension of intellectual property rights to all living things and their components. The draft treaty is designed to make every government and indigenous population a "caretaker" or "steward" of its particular geographic part of the global genetic commons and to ensure that the gene pool remains a global commons that cannot be sold by any institution or individual as genetic information. To quote from the text of the Treaty Initiative:

> The nations of the world declare the Earth's gene pool, in all of its biological forms and manifestations, to be a global commons, to be protected and nurtured by all peoples and further declare that genes and the products they code for, in their natural, purified or synthesized form as well as chromosomes, cells, tissue, organs and organisms, including cloned, transgenic and chimeric organisms, will not be allowed to be claimed as commercially negotiable genetic information or intellectual property by governments, commercial enterprises, other institutions or individuals.

> The Parties to the treaty—to include signatory nation-states and Indigenous Peoples—further agree to administer the gene pool as a trust. The signatories acknowledge the sovereign right and responsibility of every nation and homeland to oversee the biological resources within their borders and determine how they are managed and shared. However, because the gene pool, in all of its biological forms and manifestations, is a global commons, it cannot be sold by any institution or individual as genetic information. Nor can any institution or individual, in turn, lay claim to the genetic information as intellectual property. (Draft Treaty to Share the Genetic Commons, 2002)

The Treaty Initiative is an attempt to challenge the generalization of the principle of privatization with a radically different way of thinking in terms of the common good. Natural resources—in this case genetic resources or, in the recent initiative advocated by the Council of Canadians, water—should remain common goods under collective stewardship. Humans should safeguard these resources for themselves and for future generations; accordingly, the protection of natural resources should be regulated democratically and not left to the vagaries of the market. One consequence of this treaty would be the abolition of all patents on life forms, genetically modified or not, and of plant breeders rights (according to UPOV 78 and 91).[4]

The Treaty Initiative was signed by 200 organizations and presented to the wider public at the World Social Forum in Porto Alegre in 2002. The support for the Treaty Initiative is far from unanimous, however, among those NGOs who have been struggling for the last ten years for a more equitable sharing of benefits from the use of genetic resources. They fear that a global genetic commons would once again profit the big corporations and deprive indigenous groups of much-needed means of income and self-determination. The Convention on Biological Diversity is regarded as a milestone among environmental treaties that activists don't want to put into doubt. Indigenous groups claim rights and protection for the "land varieties" they have developed over the centuries and which are now exploited by the big seed companies for developing genetically modified varieties—as in the case of the development of GM Texmati rice out of the traditional Basmati variety. In short, the Treaty Initiative encounters resistance among the ranks of indigenous and environmental movements that see the possibility of benefit sharing vanishing without adequate recompense.

The conflicts of interest that a Treaty to Share the Genetic Commons could provoke become apparent if we examine the controversies surrounding a slimming pill that hit the news in the spring of 2002, which involved the commercial exploitation of genetic components of the South African Hoodia cactus. The San Bushmen had relied on the cactus for generations on their hunting trips in the Kalahari desert. Eating its flesh provided them with vital moisture and suppressed hunger. This quality came to the knowledge of a South African laboratory of the Council of Scientific and Industrial Research (CSIR), which isolated the appetite-suppressing component (dubbed P57) and patented it. A small English pharmaceutical firm, Phytopharm, obtained the development rights from the South African laboratory and soon afterwards sold the licensing rights for the drug for 21 million dollars to Pfizer, the US company that made its name as the manufacturer of the impotence drug Viagra. With these rights, Pfizer intends to develop a slimming pill for the millions of overweight Americans—a potential market of several billion dollars. The case became known to the larger public when representatives of the San filed a claim for compensation for the use of their traditional knowledge of the Hoodia plant for commercial purposes. After months of haggling, the CSIR and the representatives of the San reached an agreement, which recognized the San as bearers of traditional knowledge and attributed to the CSIR the intellectual property rights over the appetite suppressing ingredient that the group had isolated. The CSIR and the San agreed further that they would co-operate in the future to identify plants that could contain commercially interesting components. The amount of money that the San would receive from the deal was not made public.

Had the Treaty to Share the Genetic Commons existed, neither the San nor Pfizer or any other pharmaceutical corporation could have profited financially from exclusive knowledge of the Hoodia cactus. The San, as "stewards" of the plants, could have refused the pharmaceutical laboratories access to it. If they had allowed the laboratory to isolate the appetite-suppressing substance, it would have become part of the public domain and could have been used by small pharmaceutical firms all over the world, including India for example, to produce slimming pills for the US American market. Indeed, supporters of the Treaty Initiative put their hope in the fact that big corporations would lose interest in genetic resources if they could not obtain exclusive property rights that would allow them to make substantial profits.

However, for the time being, the notions of common ownership and stewardship are confined to protected natural areas under the auspices of international environmental organizations and taken care of by indigenous communities. Here, however, the mystified notion of the indigenous as "part of nature" becomes a new means of exploitation, since a type of behaviour is expected from "indigenous" people that all others are not required or expected to follow. To anchor indigenous legal rights in specific identities or sets of practices, and to make these conform to territorial units, replicates old patterns of discrimination in new environmentalist garb (Li, 2002). The participation of indigenous groups in the administration and stewardship of nature reserves happens according to an essentialist image projected from outside. Life-science corporations or logging companies, in contrast, are not expected to abandon their profit-maximization priorities, but to make them coincide with the priorities of the park administration. The idea of "stewardship" over land and resources upon which indigenous land and resource rights are often made contingent only weakens their position in negotiations with government and international environmental agencies. Instead of guaranteeing them substantive control over the territories and resources they are to protect, such arrangements force them to play a token role that enforces their economic and political dependence rather than alleviating it.

Participation in environmental protection measures according to designs imposed from outside thus becomes a "new tyranny" that reinforces rather than overthrows existing inequalities (Cooke & Kothari, 2002). The creation of the protected area Montes Azules (Blue Mountains) in Mexico provides an excellent example here. The land rights over the vast area of Montes Azules (614 321 ha) was attributed in 1972 to 66 families of the Caraibes tribe, to the detriment of other Indian populations living in the area (Bellinghausen, 2002). With the creation of the protected area (331 200 ha) in 1978, the Caraibes became the "stewards" of the area, profiting from the financial aid of international environmental agencies while the other Indian populations were stigmatized as destructive peasants destroying pristine nature (Dumoulin, 2002). Opponents of the idea of environmental stewardship, therefore, affirm that members of indigenous societies have to catch up with the disadvantage of being excluded from the profit that is made from their resources and their knowledge about these resources. For the treaty initiative to become credible as a radical alternative, it has to oppose appropriation wherever it occurs and to ask for the same standard of behaviour— responsible stewardship over nature—from city dwellers and multinational corporations, as well as from so-called indigenous peoples.

Some environmental anthropologists, however, reject the idea of stewardship as establishing once again a hierarchy between humans and other living beings. Instead of attempting to protect nature from humans, human beings and especially those of industrialized societies have to rediscover that they are living and thinking with and through nature. They are "dwelling in the environment," as Ingold formulates it. "Human beings must simultaneously be constituted both as organisms within systems of ecological relations and as persons within systems of social relations" (Ingold, 2000, p. 3). Who and what, however, set the standards for these relations and determine whether they pertain primarily to the survival of the human species, the quest for a better life, or the attainment of the highest profit?

Various attempts have been made over the last hundred years to take into account the ecological conditions of human economy in order to conceptualize adequately the mechanisms that generate inequalities in distribution and lead to the squandering of resources (Hornborg, 2001, p. 36). Ecological economists like Martinez-Alier have attempted to combine the Marxist paradigm of exploitation with the theory of thermodynamics. They have stated that the basic principles of human ecology and economy could perhaps best be analysed in terms of the concept of energy return to human energy input. Large scale mechanized agriculture and increasing industrial production lead to a loss of energy accumulated on earth through the irremediable transformation of natural resources. The flows of energy between populations and ecosystems are asymmetrical. The industrial machine saves time and/or space for some social categories of people while taking it irremediably from others. The method of accounting in terms of energy loss allows us to demystify modern agro-technologies as being a waste of energy resources. Measuring the degree of exploitation of nature and humans in terms of energy not money allows us to throw light on its mechanisms from a different perspective. Once again, however, it also poses nature as a resource that is quantified in yet another unit of accounting. As the example of the carbon credits sanctioned by the Kyoto protocol shows, this same reasoning has already enabled less industrially developed countries to begin to market their unused "quota" of carbon dioxide emissions to the rich polluter countries.

There are no simple alternatives to the ongoing processes of the commodification and privatization of nature. They are linked not only to legal frames and practices of power and exploitation at the global level, but also to deeply ingrained worldviews, customs, and convictions. Resistance to the commodification of nature thus has to begin at the level of everyday life, with our perception of our place in nature, while at the same time challenging the rules of the global market economy enshrined in international treaties. It is not sufficient simply to create spaces of exception where, for certain categories of people, rules should prevail that are not respected in broader global struggles for power, money, and control. The parks, nature reserves, bio-corridors, and so on that the international community creates to preserve biodiversity may save particular plants from total extinction, but they cannot compensate for the continuing destruction of the natural environment outside of these enclaves in the name of progress and economic growth. The concept of stewardship over nature is highly ambiguous if it is used to coerce indigenous people living in areas declared as nature preserves into so-called sustainable practices that government administrators and international bio-technology corporations are not ready to respect.

In the short term, remaining conscientious about our embeddedness in our natural and social environments and striving to achieve a greater degree of local autonomy and democratic power provide important sites of struggle. This struggle may not entirely reverse the commodification of nature, but it may slow the processes of destruction and exploitation. On the level of ideas, instead of making nature into a metaphysical concept or a resource to be exploited, we need to reacquire the capacity to think of ourselves as inside and part of a natural world we cannot totally control. Acknowledging the complexity and non-instrumental value of natural systems is the first step towards acting responsibly within them. This is particularly true with respect to genetic resources that can naturally reproduce and mutate and are thus never entirely under human control. The second step towards developing the capacity to act against the commodification of nature is understanding that private ownership of genetic resources will increase not so much human control over nature as the domination and exploitation of humans by humans themselves.

Notes

1. The UNEP Secretariat refers to the United Nations Environmental Programme, Secretariat of the Convention on Biological Diversity.
2. Article 27.3(b) of TRIPS (1994) provides the following: "Members may also exclude from patentability.... Plants and animals other than micro-organisms, and essentially biological processes for the production of plants or animals other than non-biological and microbiological processes. However, Members shall provide for the protection of plant varieties either by patents or by an effective *sui generis* system or by any combination thereof. The provisions of this subparagraph shall be reviewed four years after the date of entry into force of the WTO Agreement."
3. DuPont, Aventis, Bayer, Dow, and Monsanto.
4. UPOV or Union for the Protection of New Varieties of Plants is an international agreement regarding the ownership of plant varieties. It was established initially in 1961, but it was revised in 1972, 1978, and 1991.

CHAPTER FOUR

Cosmopolitan Elites Versus Nationally-focused Citizens—Cycles of Decommodification Struggles

GORDON LAXER

Globalization is not an inevitable process; this first wave [of globalization] was reversed by a retreat into nationalism. (World Bank Report, 2002)

To globalize the economy by erasure of national economic boundaries through free trade, free capital mobility, and free, or at least uncontrolled migration, is to wound fatally the major unit of community capable of carrying out any policies for the common good. (Herman Daly, 1994)

We all need to be as free as possible of interference from economic changes elsewhere in order to make our own favourite experiments towards the ideal social republic of the future. (John Maynard Keynes, 1932)

Corporate elites in Canada, many of whom work for foreign transnational corporations, no longer want a separate country in North America. They continually pressure Canada to join the US in foreign aggression, so Canada can retain US market access. They also pressure Canada to adopt US-style, for-profit health care, US immigration and refugee policies, and guaranteed oil and gas exports to the US even if Canadians face shortages. These policies are called "deep integration" or a "North American security perimeter."[1] But, Canadians continually show they very much want an independent, pro-peace, more "caring and sharing" country than they perceive the US to be (Adams, 2003). Citizens punish politicians who threaten to privatize health care or who advocate that Canada be America's "deputy sheriff" abroad. The question is this: if Canada lacks sovereignty, can its citizens deepen democracy and reclaim their "commons"?

This issue is not unique to Canada. Corporate elites, the rich and their political allies are not really part of Latin American nations. They are anti-nationalists, who seek to remove sovereignty for citizens (McCaughan, 1997, pp. 166–67). As Jorge Castañeda (1993) put it,

> Even in Argentina, Chile, and Uruguay, which ... constitute the continent's most socially [and ethnically] homogeneous societies, the sense of belonging to a national community that has been confiscated or sequestered by the 'foreigners' and the elite amalgamated into one is undeniable. The real nation in these lands is perceived by the poor as theirs, while the rich—the landowning aristocracy in Argentina and Uruguay, with their continental or upper-class vocation ... belong elsewhere. (p. 276)

In a similar vein, Castells (1997, p. 30) argues that nationalisms these days are, more often than not, reactions against cosmopolitan elites.

Almost everywhere, corporate elites have, even more than in the past, disengaged from their fellow citizens, living in "segregated communities secured by armed guards and electronic surveillance," expressing a distinct transnational class consciousness, sharing similar lifestyles, and attending the same educational institutions (Sklair, 2001, pp. 20–21). Not all come from Western countries, but their shared culture is Western, largely American (Cox, 1987, pp. 358–60; Huntington, 2004).

Corporate elites move in the rarefied air of frequent travellers, with allegiance to a global elite and the universality of capitalist greed. They seek political influence as much as ever, particularly to protect their property interests through state guarantees and international investment agreements. But, in many periphery and semi-periphery countries, elites rely as much on US power as on their own state for protection from popular rule.

Core states are rich countries that dominate and exploit weaker and poorer periphery countries. Semi-periphery countries are in between regarding power and exploitation, but are not necessarily poor. Unlike the core, they may have the consciousness of subordination, but better means to escape subordination than the periphery (Chase-Dunn, 1990).

Disengaged elites battle rooted citizens over leadership of the nation, regarding who best represents the political community. Under the surface, these are struggles over class power, colonialism, and popular sovereignty. Adversaries clash about the terrain over which the principles of popular democracy and the commons should expand, versus the spheres over which the logic of capitalism and commodified markets should expand. This is a zero-sum struggle. The expansion of one contracts the other.

This chapter looks at cycles of global economic integration and renationalization (or deglobalization). I contend that hyper commodification has been strongest in phases of global integration and that, in contrast, the renationalization of economies has produced the most conducive conditions for decommodification. I outline a radical strategy for decommodification, which emphasizes its egalitarian and communitarian character, and contrast this with reactionary variations that support patriarchal and hierarchical versions of decommodification.

My arguments find parallels in the concrete programmatic strategy for radical decommodification in the work of Patrick Bond (2002a, 2005) and others in the South African Left. Bond (2005) argues that a progressive program of decommodification necessitates the "deglobalisation and delinking" of South Africa's economy from "the most destructive circuits of global capital" (p. 5). "The South African decommodification agenda is based on interlocking, overlapping campaigns to turn basic needs into genuine human rights including: free anti-retroviral medicines to fight AIDS, at least 50 liters of free water and 1 kilowatt of electricity for each individual each day" (Bond, 2005, p. 5).

By commodification I mean the production of goods and services for the portion of the economy organized on a for-profit basis. Decommodification on the other hand is a process that transforms activities away from production for profit for the purpose of meeting a social need, meeting a use value, or restoring nature. As was outlined in the introductory chapter, it is possible to measure the extent to which activities have been commodified or decommodified, although, to date, such measurements have been made only in the contemporary period and only for some spheres of activity.

The outcomes of contestations over what is, and what is not, for sale as commodities are not simply determined structurally. Agency and contingency shape political outcomes. It is further, more speculatively, contended that a renationalization phase began in 1997–2001 and that framing campaigns as popular national sovereignty versus the American Empire is likely in many countries to enhance decommodifying efforts over public life and nature. The *social imaginary*[2] or popular expectations underlying such contestations are to support inter-national, people-to-people solidarity and "defend the local nationally" (Canadian Dimension, 1995). My argument runs directly counter to the claims of "inevitability" that have been used to bolster the neoliberal goals of the elites in their project of scaling back the public sector; deregulating corporations and speculative capital; and commodifying, as much as possible, people, services, and the planet in order to expand the opportunities for profit making.

ELITES OPPOSE NATIONAL SOVEREIGNTY IN THE SEMI-PERIPHERY AND PERIPHERY

In the 1980s and 1990s, the new Right repeatedly portrayed a stark choice between the forces of good—liberalism = capitalism = freedom = democracy—versus the forces of bad—socialism = nationalism = statism = authoritarianism (McCaughan, 1997, p. 43). These campaigns helped alter popular consciousness and were bolstered by the fall of communism in the Soviet Union and Eastern European.

However, the Right's campaigns obscured basic realities. Profits can be made only on commodified goods and services. Capitalism brings strong pressures to break people away from collectives of various kinds and remake them into individual consumers. Capitalism cannot exist without a great deal of inequality, for reasons outlined following. Conversely, deep democracy is about equality and the collective good. When a service or good is moved into the democratic sphere, for example, guaranteeing equal access to health care, then citizenship principles apply. Such public, not-for-profit services are provided on the socialist basis of "to each according to her need" and "from each according to her ability" to pay taxes. But, if health or other services are transferred to the private-for-profit sphere, then capitalist principles apply. The rich can buy the fastest and best quality health care services, just as for any other commodity, and the health of the poor suffers.

Thus, the battle to contract or extend the public sphere is about expanding or shrinking the areas over which citizens have a democratic, communitarian say and right of access. The battle is over expanding capitalist commodification principles or non-capitalist decommodification principles.[3]

Upholding corporate property rights means entrenching inequalities. Property rights are about class power relations, not mainly about things. Why acquire money if it does not mean commanding the labour of others, who have little choice but to sell you their labour power, so you can pursue your goals, not theirs?[4] James Mill, who with Jeremy Bentham conceived the utilitarian basis for neoclassical economics in the 1820s, understood this:

> That one human being will desire to render the person and property of another subservient to his pleasures, notwithstanding the pain or loss of pleasure which it may occasion to that other individual, is the foundation of government. (Macpherson, 1977, p. 26)

Today, corporate elites continue to entrench inequalities by, amongst other things, meeting regularly at the Bilderberg Conference, at Davos in Switzerland, and at other fora, where they network about extending profit-making and corporate property rights. They also imbibe "neoliberal globalism" (the reigning ideology popularly called the "Washington Consensus"), free trade, and Structural Adjustment Programs. Neoliberal globalism has two components—neoliberalism and globalization. *New York Times* columnist and popularizer of neoliberalism Thomas Friedman (1999) summarizes its "golden straitjacket":

> A country must either adopt, or be seen as moving toward, the following golden rules: making the private sector the primary engine of its economic growth, maintaining a low rate of inflation and price stability, shrinking the size of its state bureaucracy, maintaining as close to a balanced budget as possible, if not a surplus, eliminating and lowering tariffs on imported goods, removing restrictions on foreign investment, getting rid of quotas and domestic monopolies, increasing exports, privatizing state-owned industries and utilities, deregulating capital markets, making its currency convertible, opening its industries, stock and bond markets to direct foreign ownership and investment, deregulating its economy to promote as much domestic competition as possible, eliminating government corruption, subsidies and kickbacks as much as possible, opening its banking and telecommunications systems to private ownership and competition.... (pp. 86–87)

The second component is globalization. In the 1990s, the dominant but con-tested assumption was that global integration was quickly and inevitably happen-ing across most, if not all, economic, cultural, and political spheres. National economies, nations, and states were becoming submerged and rearticulated into an increasingly borderless world. These assumptions were widely shared across the political spectrum. The Right's version, the dominant one, combines neoliberal-ism with faith in the inevitability of global integration and envisions a capitalist world, governed globally from above. It is "neoliberal globalism" or "globalism" for short. The model was *procedural democracy* in which voters periodically get to choose whether they want team A or team B, both representing elite interests, to rule them. The Left's vision was a mirror opposite: economic and environmental sustainability, communitarianism, and "rule by the people" in participatory democracies, at global and local levels. Differences aside, both assumed the inevitability of global integration and the "weakening of state sovereignty and state structures" (Beck, 2000, p. 86).

Although globalization and globalism talk appear to have passed their peak, they disarmed much of the Left, stunting imaginations and shutting out thoughts of alternatives that did not follow cosmopolitan premises. Some on the Left have rejected national sovereignty, assuming it cannot coincide with the "multitude," diversity, popular sovereignty, or working class power (Hardt & Negri, 2000, pp. 93–113).[5]

Most corporate executives embrace the globalism agenda. But corporate sup-port for the sovereignty of the country of these executives tends to vary directly with the power of that state.[6] The more "core" a country, the more its elites tend to support its sovereignty, attempting to wield this sovereignty to pursue imperial and capitalist policies and to mobilize popular support for military and prestige projects, which supposedly represent the whole nation. A major exception is the European Union, where corporate elites widely sought to diminish the sovereignty of their countries in order to weaken their domestic working class and left-wing opponents, who exercised power more effectively at national than at European levels (Bratt, 1993-4; Laxer, 1995).

Conversely, as George Grant (1965) noted long ago, the more peripheral a country, the less its elites are prone to support its sovereignty,

> No small country can depend for its existence on the loyalty of its capitalists. International interests may require the sacrifice of the lesser loyalty of patri-otism. Only in dominant nations is the loyalty of capitalists ensured. In such situations, their interests are tied to the strength and vigour of their empire. (pp. 69–70)

In the majority of non-core countries, economic and political elites have acqui-esced to US power, or acted as its junior partners. After decades of incursions by US capital into their class formations, 25 years of globalism talk, and the over-whelming power of the US military, bourgeois nationalism is all but dead in most countries (Panitch & Gindin, 2004, p. 18).[7] In such countries, economic elites often count on the US, as well as their own state, to protect their property and guard against reform and revolution. They still try to control their state, but usually want to throttle its sovereignty through various means, including neoliberal agreements like NAFTA, backed by the implied might, or sometimes the explicit might, of the US.

Economic elites in most, but not all non-core countries have largely abandoned nationalist leadership.[8] Instead, they often condemn nationalisms as outdated and invoke the globalization theology and liberal cosmopolitanism to defeat popular sovereignty and social ownership projects. This strategy worked better before Latin Americans, Africans, and others experienced economic stagnation and growing inequalities associated with globalism policies and before the US so blatantly asserted its unilateral right to breach other countries' sovereignty rights. Abandoning leadership of the nation opens political space for the Left to lead the "true nation," the one normatively identified with "the people" (Castañeda, 1993, p. 273). The great fear of elites everywhere is *popular sovereignty* at national or local levels.

Political elites in most non-core countries also support US hegemony and diminished sovereignty for their own country, for several reasons: it is difficult to buck the coercive power of the US, the World Bank, and the International Monetary Fund; political fallout from lost jobs should TNCs depart; and close ties with economic elites. In the semi-periphery and periphery, on the other hand, more national sovereignty creates openings for more popular sovereignty, the redistribution of wealth, and the protection of citizens from the ravages of free market capitalism. Such courses of action are by no means assured, but if implemented, they tend to decommodify services, labour, and resources.

THE US EMPIRE SPARKS COUNTER-NATIONALISMS

Fear of popular sovereignty is the reason neoliberals oppose "too much" democracy. One strategy they employ to achieve the consent, or at least the acquiescence of the governed, is to use "globalization" and "globalism" talk to undermine popular national revolts. Richard N. Haass (2000), President of the US Council on Foreign Relations, asserts that immature democracies "are all too prone to being captured by nationalist forces," meaning independence from US policies. Haass argues that promoting democracy, while laudable, should not be a fundamental US foreign-policy goal, "given that other vital interests often must take precedence."[9] By immature democracies, Haass can only mean those in the global South and Eastern Europe, regions where democracy is recent almost everywhere and anti-imperial nationalisms tend to be popular. The US has shown little compunction about violating national sovereignty in these regions.

The US dominates the global economy and politics largely through an informal empire, whose great appeal has been that it has not appeared to be an empire.

Instead of invading and planting the flag for the long-term, the US almost always rules by influencing other states and their ruling classes. Since 9/11, however, the US has acted more overtly like an empire. Occupations in Iraq or Vietnam are exceptions, which hurt the image. To gain domestic support for occupation, US leaders use fear and American nationalism. The latter tends to spark counter-nationalisms elsewhere. Ideas associated with America fall into disrepute, and US officials interpret opposing perspectives as anti-American (Castañeda, 2004).

Nationalisms occur in waves. From 1945 to 1975, during a phase of renational-ized economies, "national and social liberation" were widely seen as essential to escape from colonial and neocolonial rule and as the first steps towards socialism, equality, and democracy. But in the late twentieth century, Ahmad (1998) argued, the newsworthy nationalisms were mostly narrowly ethnic, and often racist and vicious, displacing the predominance of anti-imperial, progressive nationalisms. Consequently, left intellectuals tended to dismiss all nationalisms as irrational, mas-culinist, Western, and reactionary. Such nationalisms still exist, but now have vigor-ous competitors in progressive, internationalist nationalisms. An exemplar of the latter is the Bolivarian Revolution, led by Venezuelan President Hugo Chávez, a self-described "patriot nationalist." He simultaneously advocates Venezuelan sov-ereignty vis-à-vis the US, and also an independent Latin American region, integrated along non-neoliberal lines, to which Venezuela would cede some sovereignty. It is what Gilberto Gil, Brazil's Minister of Culture, calls a "sovereign nations commu-nity" (2005). Such an integrated Latin America could gain more effective auton-omy from the United States than could any of the countries on its own.

The character of recent nationalisms has changed. Bourgeois nationalisms, which were historically the chief competitor to Left nationalisms, have died or greatly atrophied in most countries, especially peripheral ones, in the face of glob-alist ideology and the penetration of US corporate interests into their midst. Racist or expansionist versions of pre-1945 nationalisms, which explicitly advocated overthrowing democracy, have been widely discredited. Nevertheless, their pop-ulist successors have made inroads into, and even alliances with, the established party system in Europe and in some other areas. Current Right populist discourses claim to represent "the people," meaning the dominant ethnic group, against the elites. By couching their appeals in anti-elitist rhetoric, they compete directly with anti-racist class appeals from the Left to workers and citizens of all origins, and against elite power (Goodman, 2003). Although right populist parties are danger-ous and influence the centre-right to enact anti-immigrant and anti-minority laws, their appeal in most countries remains limited (Betz & Johnson, 2004).

Positive, inter-nationalist nationalisms are inclusive, embrace deep diversity including recognizing rights for minority nations within the country, are substan-tively democratic, avoid expansionism, and support people-to-people inter-nation-alism (Laxer, 2001, p. 15). The main struggles in each country involve turning corporate-oriented, pro-US Empire states into citizen-oriented states that support popular national sovereignty abroad. Current examples include struggles in Bolivia, Uruguay, and Venezuela.

Not all current nationalisms are positive and anti-imperialist. Some are traditionalist or fundamentalist and may or may not be anti-imperialist. Some fundamentalist movements are not nationalist, but seek a religious rather than a political community. It is the latter that makes a nation.[10]

DEGLOBALIZING TRANSNATIONAL CORPORATIONS

During the 1930s depression, John Maynard Keynes (1932–33) urged countries to make their own national experiments at social change:

> We do not wish, therefore, to be at the mercy of world forces working out or trying to work out some uniform equilibrium according to the ideal principles ... of laissez-faire capitalism.... We wish ... to be our own masters.... We all need to be as free as possible of interference from economic changes elsewhere in order to make our own favourite experiments towards the ideal social republic of the future. (p. 761–63)

Keynes, a future architect of the post-war, Bretton Woods international financial system, which helped reglobalizing trends in the post-1945 economy under US hegemony, wrote this when deglobalization winds blew strongly. Keynes was optimistic, then, that countries could forge independent, democratic alternatives to liberal global capitalism.

Some would argue that Keynes's plea shows how much the world has changed. My perspective is different. Taking the long view, I argue that global integration has ebbed and flowed and that national and regional experiments are likely to return. If I am right, it would improve the chances to decommodify many aspects of public life and nature. My case rests on two broad arguments. First, the previous wave of global economic integration, from 1872–73 to 1913, was substantially reversed, and economies were considerably "renationalized,"[11] turning toward more inwardly articulated development. There was also decommodification, likely on a substantial scale, in positive and negative ways, of what had been hyper commodified economies. Many transnational corporations (TNCs) were deglobalized. If economic globalization was reversed in the past, it makes it more plausible to argue that such reversals are likely in the future.

Second, the US is promoting the interests of US-based corporations such as Halliburton at the same time as it claims to champion international agreements guaranteeing generic rights for all corporations. The reassertion of US imperial might is fostering popular national revolts against it. Proponents of movements or parties for peace, opposition to corporate globalization, and popular national sovereignty have taken power in several states or will likely take power soon and boost opposition to US domination at the level of states (Bello, 2004). The invasion of Iraq fractured America's military alliances. NATO partners France and Germany broke ranks. Amongst other things, this encouraged Canada, Mexico, and Chile, key allies on NAFTA and the Free Trade Area of the Americas, to join them. Public opinion turned decisively away from US leadership in all these countries (GlobeScan, 2004). American unilateralism also undermined support for its neoliberal agenda at the World Trade Organization (WTO) and other international fora. The emergence of the Group of 20 countries, led by Brazil, India, South Africa and China, at the 2003 WTO meetings in Cancun marked the resurrection of an independent voice from the global South, ready to challenge the US and other great powers. Between 2002 and 2004, two US-backed attempts by local elites to oust Hugo Chávez, the popular nationalist President of Venezuela, a leading oil exporting country, were defeated. These were major blows to US power.

Citizens' movements and some governments are groping toward alternatives to neoliberalism, and reverting to practices from the era of more nationally articulated economies (Bello, 2002, pp. 95–104). Despite such breaks against the US model, there are not yet widely accepted, new visions of regaining control nationally.[12] Agreement on new social imaginaries to replace the globalism agenda has not yet fully emerged. However, there is a wide, if often tacit, consensus on the following components: re-embedding economies and the environment in sustainable communities; participatory democracy at all levels—local, national, and international; citizen-oriented states to replace corporate-oriented states; pluralism and diversity of thought; and redistribution of wealth to the global South (Patomäki & Teivainen, 2004, p. 151; Conway, 2004, p. 367). Implementing this program would require relatively sovereign, socially transformative states working with citizens' movements and counterparts in other countries.

I put forward one such vision: deglobalizing the TNCs, something that happened massively in the 1960s and 1970s, despite fierce opposition from corporate elites and US and allied powers. This vision holds that for political communities to gain deep democratic control over their collective social, environmental, and economic lives, they must deglobalize TNCs and place TNCs' constituent parts under domestic, democratic control. Governments and citizens need to be able to rely on capital with "location commitment," which will not be lured to more profitable venues. Putting renationalized corporations in the hands of co-operatives or government-owned industries subject to "workers control" at local and national levels would build in structured location-commitment. It is only when communities of wage earners and peasant farmers are assured of continuing jobs, income, or land that they are likely to feel secure and sufficiently non-competitive with each other to support a program that returns resources to nature and provides universal public services for the common good and high social wages for all. This is a program of radical, democratic decommodification.

Before developing my argument further, I need to show that reversing global integration and deglobalizing TNCs are plausible alternatives. The globalism theology holds that the direction of history can go only towards ever-greater world integration, eclipsing states, nations, national identities, and commodifying almost everything. This ahistorical view is being increasingly challenged. The World Bank (2002) acknowledges, albeit disapprovingly, that the earlier wave of globalization, which they date at between 1870 and 1914, was substantially thrown back. "Globalization is not an inevitable process, this first wave was reversed by a retreat into nationalism" (pp. 24–30). If true, politics superseded economics then. What about now? The current US aphorism that, after 9/11, "security trumps trade" implies that the state is again taking precedence over global economic integration.

The re-emergence of the state, and concomitantly of nationalisms, after unparalleled global capitalist integration, occurred before. Confident predictions of world integration and the eclipse of nations and states just prior to World War I vanished after radical or catastrophic ruptures led to substantial renationalizations of economies and widespread deglobalizing of corporations and capital. Wars, revolutions, depression, social reform in the North, and decolonization in the South were the ruptures that significantly reversed global integration for 60 years after 1913. We turn to those events and their consequences for expanding or contracting what is, and is not, for sale.

CYCLES OF GLOBALIZATION AND RENATIONALIZATION

Nicolai Kondratiev outlined long cycles of economic boom and bust, which repeat every half century (45 to 60 years).[13] Longer than short-term business cycles, they are apparent only to historians. Their causes are debated, but there is widespread agreement on their existence, measurability, and dates. There are different versions of long economic cycles. I find Kondratiev cycles the most useful (Suter, 1992, pp. 19–29).

I leave others to ponder the whys of long economic cycles, but assume that long economic cycles have occurred and will likely recur (Kondratiev, 1998; Kuznets, 1930/1967; Schumpeter, 1939; Mandel, 1980; Hopkins & Wallerstein, 1977; Suter, 1992; Boswell & Chase-Dunn, 2000). Alternating economic cycles profoundly affect cultural and political moods and changes. Less has been written on how these cycles have affected long political cycles, why certain movements and ideas fare better or worse in different periods, although Boswell and Chase-Dunn (2000) provide a comprehensive account.

The existence of long cycles, implying the reversibility of history, does not mean that history simply oscillates back and forth. There is forward movement, trends or historical irreversibles, which make each century different from the last. History may repeat itself, but, as Marx wrote, never in exactly the same way. Nor is it all predetermined. People shape what structural conditions establish as possibilities, in one direction or another. It is helpful to learn about past patterns because they can inform historical actors about likely future possibilities.

According to world systems theorists Hopkins and Wallerstein (1977) and Chase-Dunn (1989, pp. 51–53), the historical trends in the capitalist world economy have been an expanding economy and international state-system, mechanization and automatization of production, and deepening of the global disparities between core and periphery. They add two more: the internationalization of production and the deepening of commodification.[14] I concur on the first set of trends, but not the last two. I see commodification and the internationalization of production as cycles, not trends. Both have been reversed in the past.

Kondratiev cycles coincided with the two most recent cycles of global economic integration. It is generally agreed that a cycle of hyper global integration began around 1872–73 and then, a century later, around 1973 (Suter, 1992, p. 66).[15] It is no accident that these years also mark the start of long "bust" phases, when profits were squeezed.

When a downturn starts, profitable outlets are scarce, so businesses shift strategies and invest in new technologies, which do not promise high profits immediately (Suter, 1992, p. 36). They also aggressively attempt to commodify new areas of labour, services, and nature, and pierce the borders of relatively uncommodified countries and regions. Aggressive capitalist strategies and high unemployment often weaken workers' and citizens' demands on corporations and governments, and these reshape policies towards greater commodification. Also, recessions usually lead to sea changes in dominant ideas and the politics of support received by their political and cultural protagonists. Politics and culture affect economies as much as the reverse. Writers as divergent as Samuel Bowles (1982) and those at the World Bank (2002, pp. 24–30) contend that politics have affected long waves of growth and profit rates.

After the 1872–73 to 1913 period of hyper integration, World War I, the Russian Revolution and the politics of the Great Depression reversed global capitalist integration. In the 30 years after 1945, the forces of further nationalization of economies and of global reintegration counteracted each other, leading to a rough stalemate. I examine the long cycle of renationalization, but first I discuss Karl Polanyi's (1944) concept of a "double movement" and then democratic struggles more broadly.

The first of Polanyi's historical movements involved free market policies in the 1800s turning everything into commodities, including "fictitious commodities"— land, labour and money—that were never created for the purpose. The result, Polanyi contends, spontaneously led to defensive counter-movements. Communities protected themselves and re-regulated markets. In the 1873–1913 cycle of global integration, aggressive capitalism turned people into factors of production (labour), encroached on nature (resources), and threatened community life. The most powerful counter-movements in the global North, which pushed back, were 1) communist, 2) fascist, and 3) democratic and socialist.

Not all counter-movements were democratic. At first, the Russian Revolution showed promise for ending exploitation and even for freeing intellectual and cultural expression in the wake of Czarist dictatorship. However, military siege against the revolution by old ruling elites and foreign armies created conditions conducive to the victory of Stalinism over more pluralist voices. The Czarist economy had comprised a great deal of foreign ownership and loan capital, and was rapidly moving towards capitalism. The Soviets reversed these trends by renouncing Czarist debts and cutting ties with capitalist economies.[16] "Socialism in one country" was a radical experiment in renationalizing and decommodifying an economy, but not mainly in positive ways.

Fascists, Nazis, and right-wing authoritarians dominated much of Europe and Asia in the 1920s to mid-1940s. Under fascism, the state rather than capitalists took the lead role. Foreign conquest, the stamping out of dissent, and the Holocaust took precedence over profit making, but these were thriving capitalist economies, in which most businesses either collaborated with or acquiesced to fascist governments (Hobsbawm, 1994, p. 129). Directing economic resources for the state and war had deglobalizing consequences, but not in positive ways. Fascism had an international component, which explains why Hitler found collaborators in conquered countries. As Hobsbawm (1991) argues, "a part of numerous ruling classes appeared to opt for an international political alignment of the right in support of fascism" (pp. 146–48).

In a third pattern, workers, farmers, and citizens campaigned for the vote for workers and women and organized powerful socialist parties and unions. When war, revolution, and the *Great Slump* came, these movements pushed governments to create universal public services, which reversed commodification but also had the unintended effect of renationalizing economies. After fascism's defeat, the model these democratic struggles created spread to most of the global North and some of the South. In the next section, I look more generally at the struggle for democracy and contrast it with the expansion of capitalism.

CAPITALISM VERSUS DEMOCRACY

The past two centuries have witnessed clashes between two expansionary and conflicting tendencies: capitalism versus democracy. Battles to extend or contain capitalism have engaged pro-business forces versus their adversaries over the extent to which people, nature, and essential services are bought and sold for profit. From the start, capitalism has had globalizing tendencies, while democracy has had strong nationalizing effects. At the risk of oversimplifying, capitalism is global, democracy national and local.

Capitalism is globalizing because, while needing a state to protect private and corporate property rights, it is not rooted in communities. Rather, capitalism continually breaks up traditional farming and indigenous communities and those created and then abandoned by capitalism, such as mining communities, which last a generation before the resource runs out. It also creates and then destroys communities of blue-collar workers, which begin and evolve after corporations start up and then dissolve when they relocate. In theory, capitalists oppose institutions larger than the firm and smaller than the world market that hinder profit making (Hobsbawm, 1991, p. 26).

Capitalist industrialization did not evolve from local to national to global levels. It was born global. Take cotton textiles, the first commodities produced by the revolutionary new techniques that swept England in the late eighteenth century, now known as the Industrial Revolution. From raw materials to final market, cotton was global. England imported raw cotton from the US South, picked by slaves who had been forcefully removed from Africa. Manufactured in Lancashire England, much of the product was sold in India.

In contrast, struggles to gain bottom-up democracy and citizenship rights have pitted supporters against opponents around issues of the power of people to determine collectively their social, political, and economic lives. To the extent that deep democracy has existed, it has taken root only at national and local levels. While not necessarily national in theory, democracy needs stable political communities of place to thrive in practice. It takes time, frequent interactions, and shared histories to create strong identifications with one's political community, and caring about distant citizens, to prepare the soil in which democracy grows (Barber, 1995, p. 278). It is not that nations and nationalisms always support democracy, nor that transnationalizing power must thwart it. But, so far, we have no examples of transnationalism coinciding with deep democracy. Europe's largely impotent Parliament confirms this. As we saw in the introductory chapter, capitalism and democracy have diametrically opposed principles. Capitalism is about individual gain and inequality, while democracy is about equality and the common good.

As Weisskopf, Bowles, and Gordon (1985) contend, profits can fall when capitalism is too strong, but also when it is too weak. The latter can occur when citizens' movements and progressive governments restrict the capitalist sphere by expanding public, not-for-profit sectors. A stalemate ensues between contending forces. The system either tilts back toward ruthless capitalism (e.g., neoliberalism) or moves on to a non-capitalist society. Thus the outcome of battles over deep democracy affect and are affected by Kondratiev cycles and globalization-renationalization cycles.

GLOBAL INTEGRATION 1872–73 TO 1913

The dominant view is that global integration is much greater than ever before. Compare Jules Verne's 1873 dream of travelling around the world in 80 days with today's reality of instant, virtual access to anyone on the globe who can afford to be wired, and to rapid air travel to anywhere for a price. Instant communications enable corporations to coordinate production transnationally and investors to move massive amounts of speculative capital around the world daily.

In the late 1800s, protectionist tariffs were the rule in most of the global North (Clough, 1952, p. 611). This contrasts with today, when most tariffs are negligible, except for farm products. Add to this the empires of a century ago that restricted trade. British colonies traded largely with Britain, French colonies with France, and so forth.

Given the barriers to world integration, could anyone contend that the 1872–3 to 1913 period was as globally integrated as now? I will argue it was both less integrated and more integrated then. Which dimensions should be compared? The

World Bank (2002) states that economic integration occurs through "trade, migration and capital flows" (p. 23). To this, I suggest, should be added currency and monetary policy dimensions.

Historical comparisons are complicated because there are now more than three times as many independent countries. Estimates for 1910–13 are 56–60 countries, compared to 192 to about 200 today (Boli-Bennett, 2000, p. 97; Statesman, 1913, pp. ix–xxx). Each time a border was added, what had been counted as "internal" trade and "internal" migration moved to the "international" categories. Thus, even with no rise in long distance trade and migration, the multiplication of borders produces statistical increases in these numbers and misleads today's observers into believing there is much greater global integration now.

Most tariffs may now be gone, but in their place governments added quotas and regulations intended to block imports. Domestic policies, which had no such intentions, can also reduce imports. Of course, tariffs did not always make countries' markets impenetrable. Confronted with tariffs, corporations jumped over them and set up subsidiaries within their walls.

With new technologies to transfer capital and coordinate production around the world instantly, and with recent neoliberal agreements to protect privileges of foreign corporations, we would expect the relative level of foreign ownership capital to be much greater now. But it is not so, at least in the global South. The World Bank (2002) states that net private capital flows to developing countries "remained more modest than during the first wave [of globalization]. By 1998 the foreign capital stock was 22 percent of developing countries' GDP, roughly double that in the mid-1970s, but well below the 32 percent reached in 1914" (pp. 42–43).

Neither did the transportation revolution lead to higher relative levels of people moving permanently to other countries. Despite the multiplication of borders, the total percentage of permanent migrants is now only 2.3 per cent compared to 10 per cent a century ago (World Bank, 2002, pp. 10–11). Thus, technological revolutions are not sufficient to produce greater global integration. States now erect political boundaries much more effectively. A century ago, one did not need a passport to move within Europe (Zakaria, 1995, p. 1). People freely crossed the Canada-US border to work or live as they pleased. Then, the US beckoned the "poor and huddled" masses; now it is a gated country, where security trumps unrestricted immigration.

At the height of the gold standard era, 1890 to 1914, all the major economies used the gold standard to determine prices and interest rates, with less variation and less government intervention than today. In many ways, it was a more truly transnational system than in the late twentieth century (de Cecco, 1974). In contrast, today the interest rates of central banks vary greatly by country. Nor have economic shocks usually spread from one region to the next, as they would if the economy were truly global. The devastating Asian financial crisis of 1997–98 did not spread to North America and Europe (Glick & Rose, 1999). Stagnation and deflation in the 1990s in Japan, the world's second largest economy, did not drag down other core economies.

High levels of foreign investment, much greater international migration, and less sovereignty over currency and monetary policies made the pre-1914 period more globalized, in crucial respects, than today. Glowing predictions by contemporaries about global integration, an end to wars, nations, and nationalisms were shattered by historical ruptures, to which we turn (Angell, 1913).

RENATIONALIZATION AND DECOMMODIFICATION: 1914 TO THE MID-1970S

Globalization before 1914 was followed by a long cycle of renationalization in the era of the world wars, 1914 to 1945. Then a stalemate period ensued from 1945 to the mid-1970s, when trends towards global reintegration and further renationalization likely roughly nullified each other.[17] After this stalemate, the world shifted decisively toward greater global integration. Although it is too early to be sure, I speculate that events between 1997 and 2001 have sparked a return towards a renationalization phase, which, the past tells us, is conducive to decommodification struggles.

The literature on decommodification has been applied to welfare states in Northern countries in the past 30 years in the works of Esping-Andersen and others and, regarding unpaid and non-marketized work, in the literature of Colin C. Williams and Jan Windebank (2003) and others. In both these spheres, the extent of commodification and decommodification has been measured fairly extensively. However, equivalent work has not been done for earlier periods or for other spheres, including the five ruptures I am discussing here. Thus, at this point, I am able to make broad links between deglobalization and decommodification but not to measure the exact extent of decommodification. I welcome the aid of researchers who will help take up the task.

The world wars had strong deglobalizing effects, and probably decommodifying effects too. These wars ended most commerce between combatants, led to seizures of corporations owned in enemy countries, increased the state's economic role, and originated state planning in capitalist countries. The Soviets expropriated foreign and domestic property and repudiated foreign debts. In the capitalist world, the 1930s depression led to protectionism and a drop in world trade. The US stock market crashed to 9 per cent of its 1929 value and did not recover for 24 years.

The 1945 to mid-1970s "golden years" saw rapid growth in the global North and much higher living standards, leading to mass consumerist lifestyles and much greater commodification. The value of international trade and foreign ownership investment outpaced growth (World Bank, 2002, p. 28). The size and concentration of TNCs recovered. Unity against communism in the global North under US hegemony undermined economic nationalisms in allied countries. However, contrary trends towards renationalization also counteracted global integration. Communism spread. Keynesian welfare states expanded, and colonies gained sovereignty. What were the decommodification implications of the five ruptures?

On balance, the world wars likely decommodified, but not mostly in positive ways.[18] Wars certainly renationalized economies. There was some reversion to production for use value to meet subsistence needs, but it is not likely that much decommodification resulted from renationalized trade and increased domestic corporate ownership. Nor is it likely that much decommodification occurred as a result of increases in all the government-owned and government-run industries that were crucial to conduct the wars (Sciabarra, 1980; Bothwell & Kilbourn, 1979). The employment of millions of soldiers was, in Marxist terms, non-commodified labour. But ordinary soldiers were not treated better than exploited workers as a result. Certainly, there was a lot of popular anger about "war profiteering." During World War I, labour and farm organizations in western Canada for instance, called for conscripting wealth before conscripting men (Conway, 1994, p. 87). Working class demands were ignored then, but some came to fruition during the next world war.

At the beginning of the 1930s depression, all governments in capitalist countries were in the grip of orthodox liberal economics, which, like today, said "markets know best, don't touch them." When catastrophic unemployment rates did not soon reverse, citizens polarized and were attracted to the political Right and Left, as do-nothing political centrist parties lost credibility. Centre-left governments took office a few years into the depression in the Nordic countries and the US, and they began government spending to create jobs. But many governments did not create or expand activist, welfare states much until World War II. Universal public services and legal recognition for the rights of unions made major gains in Britain, Canada, and the US during World War II.

The depression had strong renationalizing effects. As unemployment skyrocketed, most countries erected trade barriers to shut out imports, in desperate efforts to retain some jobs at home. Exports fell back to 5 per cent of world income, a low level not seen since 1870 (World Bank, 2002, p. 27).[19] Some people moved back to the land; others reverted to production for use value; families shared living spaces; and some used barter and local currencies (Berton, 1990, pp. 12, 184; Mitchell & Shafer, 1994). Such experiments were ways of coping, out of want. Unemployed workers became uncommodified. Their labour power was no longer bought and sold at "capitalist auctions," which conventional economists call "labour markets." But it was worse to be unemployed and without access to public unemployment payments.

In the stalemate period after 1945, there were three tendencies towards renationalized economies, which I briefly examine. In the first, the expansion of communism to China, Southeast Asia, Eastern Europe, and Cuba removed huge areas from capitalist profitability. This was massive deglobalization. We discussed the Soviet economy's renationalizing effects, which also reflect similar tendencies in other communist countries. Especially in the early days of communist regimes, there was massive decommodification, in collectivizing farms and in producing more for use value. Commodity production for profit virtually disappeared. However, except for early forms of heavy industrialization, which developed impressively in the Soviet Union and other communist countries, these were stagnant economies where workers pretended to work, employers pretended to pay them, and governments pretended to be democratic.

Second, the decolonization of the global South from 1946 to the mid-1960s was accompanied by radical, anti-colonial nationalisms, which asserted that the people of a country, not foreign capitalists, should control their resources, economies, cultures, and polities. People wanted to end colonial economic and political control, which had forced colonies to buy finished goods from the "mother country" and export to them only raw materials. A creative United Nations model called *inwardly directed development* (Prebisch, 1971) and *import substitution industrialization* (ISI) aimed to build independent national economies in newly decolonized countries and in Latin America, which although formally independent, was dominated "neocolonially" by the US (Frank, 1967, p. 86). The strategy was to use imported machinery from industrial countries to make, for domestic markets, goods that had been imported. Tariffs would keep out cheap imports, thus creating an opening for domestic manufacturing jobs and production. Diverse governments in the global South adopted the model.

In the early 1970s, governments took ownership control over TNCs on a massive scale in 10 countries in the global South, combining revolution with decolonizing nationalisms (Kobrin, 1982, p. 36). The scale of state nationalizations was large in some industries, such as oil. However, the 559 major acts[20] of nationalization in the world from 1960 to 1979 comprised less than 5 per cent of foreign affiliates in the global South (p. 13).

Success generally eluded "inwardly directed" development strategies because of the very restrictive context. Corporations and northern countries pushed their own products and technologies on the global South and influenced the *terms of trade*, so resource and farm exports from the global South were devalued relative to finished goods from the global North (Amin, 1974, pp. 53–59). The US and Europe subsidized their own farmers so highly that peasants in the global South could not compete in these lucrative markets. It was protection for the privileged North and "free trade" for the South.

Before most *inwardly directed development* strategies achieved much decommodification, they were killed off in the early 1980s, by Reagan-Thatcher style *globalism*, which openly promoted corporate control over former colonial and neocolonial economies. US monetary policy between 1979 and 1982 raised interest rates excessively around the world, and sparked a debt crisis in many countries of the global South.[21] Unmanageable debts provided an opportunity for the IMF and the World Bank, which work on behalf of large private [northern] banks with states acting as guarantors, to require that indebted countries dismantle nationally oriented development policies (George, 1989, p. 47). Governments asking for debt relief were forced to allow mainly northern TNCs and banks to dominate their economies. This economic domination also greatly influenced their political life too. Such requirements, called "Structural Adjustment Programs," followed *globalism's* "golden straitjacket" rules.

However, there are signs that economic sovereignty policies are returning to the global South. In 2003, Chávez's Venezuelan government wrested control of the national oil company from the local elite who ran it like an autonomous, private preserve. Chávez imposed much higher royalty rates on foreign oil corporations. Venezuela's increased oil revenues were redistributed, taking money from well-to-do Venezuelans, who had spent most of it on highly commodified products and services, many imported, and put it into the following largely decommodified programs: public health care, literacy programs, education for the poor, subsidized food, and land redistribution (Wilpert, 2004, p. 1; Kozloff, 2005, p. 2). In Cochabamba, Bolivia, citizens' movements successfully fought to regain public control over a foreign-owned water corporation. Water now flows again to all as an uncommodified good (Olivera & Lewis, 2004).

Third, in the global North, governments followed Keynesian models of mildly redistributing income to the poor to stimulate consumer demand, in the political context of historic compromises between corporations and growing union movements. The IMF and the World Bank were originally set up to promote Keynesian national development (Chase-Dunn, 2004, pp. 14–15). Although there were early welfare states, most developed in the democratic half of the long renationalization cycle, 1945 to 1970s. These were national, not international, class compromises. The assumption for most northern countries was that capital would be invested largely domestically to ensure full employment. The transformation of states post-1945, from minimalist institutions that did little more than support the military, distribute the mail, and indoctrinate primary-aged school children to deluxe, cradle-to-grave welfare states, expanded public sectors from about 10 per cent to roughly 50 per cent of economies in the global North (Desai, 2000). In the US, where the welfare state remained less developed than elsewhere in the North, military Keynesianism rivalled welfare Keynesianism in expanding the state. Public, not-for-profit sectors are necessarily national and almost entirely excluded from international trade and investment. Keynesianism in core countries can be characterized, without too much distortion, as having been *capitalism in one country* (Desai, 2000).

Not all northern countries renationalized their economies. Canada, small West European countries, Australia, and New Zealand did not have nationally oriented economies from 1914 to the mid-1970s. Canada continued a colonial pattern of exporting raw materials to the US and doing limited manufacturing, substantially in US-dominated branch plants.

Despite the Keynesian emphasis on boosting consumption as a way to stimulate economic growth, the so-called Keynesian welfare state had strong decommodification effects. The ways it led to a "social wage," freeing workers from total dependence on capitalist labour-market earnings, and greatly expanded public, not-for-profit health care, education, fire services, and public transit are outlined in the introductory chapter. They need no elaboration here. In the current era, in contrast, TNCs are demanding access to public health care, education, and municipal services around the world, "investment opportunities," as they see it, from which they have been largely excluded for decades. These services cannot be profitable unless sold on the capitalist principle that those with the most money get better access. (See Gould's chapter.)

To sum up, history shows that capitalists have relentlessly tried to commodify most areas, certainly those in which they thought they could turn a profit: people's work, nature, and essential services. However, faced with insecurity or ruin, communities everywhere also resisted much of this drive to commodify. I have made a connection between a deglobalization phase and success at reversing commodification. In the twentieth century, it was during or through wars, communist revolutions, depression, decolonization, and revolution in the global South and through the Keynesian welfare state in the global North that decommodification took place the most. But not all reversals were positive or progressive. Wars, depression, and communist revolutions often led to autocratic rule and forms of traditional or reactionary decommodification. The Keynesian welfare state and anti-colonial revolutions in the global South produced more positive kinds of decommodifying, often giving rights and security to workers and citizens and reclaiming commodified tracts of land and returning them to nature. Even so, however, the tendency was to do progressive things in top-down, bureaucratic ways.

Renationalization of economies and moves away from capitalism do not necessarily lead to decommodification. It depends on how state-owned corporations, war production, public services, and other institutions are organized. Radical decommodifying requires trusting the people and putting real power into their hands. In the following section, I discuss prospects for a new phase of renationalization and democratic reversals of the sell-out of nature, public services, and workers.

NEW CYCLE OF RENATIONALIZATION AND DEGLOBALIZING THE TNCs?

It is too early to be sure that the world is entering a new cycle of renationalization, but I make such a case. The US shift towards explicit empire partly resulted from the rupture initiated by the 11/9 attacks, which provided an opening for right-wing Republicans to implement a long-standing agenda of asserting unilateralism and "pre-emptive war" (PNAC, 2000). These policies initiated trends toward a re-bordered world, the reinvigoration of the state, and anti-imperial nationalisms.

However, the US shift also resulted from structural crises in the globalism project, which Walden Bello (2003) argues peaked in 1995 with the founding of the World Trade Organization (WTO). The first blow to globalism was the 1997–98 Asian financial crisis, which showed that allowing capital to flow freely across borders can be profoundly destabilizing. Consequently, several key intellectual advocates, including Jeffrey Sachs, Joseph Stiglitz, and George Soros, deserted the neoliberal ship. Second was the collapse of WTO talks in Seattle in 1999 and in Cancun in 2003. Third was the stock market collapse and end to the *Clinton boom* in 2001. Economic weakness led to US protectionism and policies that weakened its dollar. Both hurt the economies of US allies and undermined their support for US leadership on multilateral agreements. These structural crises led to stalemates on the neoliberal agenda at the WTO. They weakened globalism's ideological dominance and set conditions for economic renationalization and progressive decommodification (Broad, 2004).

Believers in the strong globalization thesis assume that recent global integration created a qualitatively new era, which will not repeat the past. If so, there would be no reason to think that the five catastrophic ruptures leading to the renationalizing cycle in the twentieth century are likely to recur. That would rule out wars, depressions, renewed social reform in the North, and the reinvigoration of decolonizing and revolutionary movements in the South. What are the prospects for their recurrence?

The post-1945 age of nuclear weapons deterred war among major northern countries. Such wars are unlikely to reappear soon, although Chase-Dunn (2004) sees such a danger, ironically if US hegemony weakens (p. 25). Chances of revolution are very remote in the North and would be likely only after a severe and prolonged deflationary depression. The latter is not impossible, given the speculative capital sloshing around the globe, the massive monthly additions to the debt the US owes other countries, and the "irrational exuberance" of corporate and real estate values. But we cannot rule out the re-emergence of strong pressures to extend universal, not-for-profit, public services in the global North, nor the resultant decommodifications.

The 1930s depression resulted from capitalists being so strong they were able to suppress wages. This led to speculative growth in the 1920s, but, longer term, low wages created insufficient demand, as workers did not have enough income to buy back the things they made. The Depression had political consequences, provoking workers and citizens to campaign for a social wage to counteract the Great Slump. It also led to a limited confluence of interests between workers and many business owners to support a "social wage" [government income supports] and recognize union rights, thereby increasing effective demand. A similar political cycle could recur in a future global depression. Recently, capitalists have become too strong again and have suppressed purchasing power by widely lowering wages. The interests of workers' and citizens' movements for reinvigorated, activist states may coincide with the interests of enlightened capitalists to refloat economies by boosting labour market wages and social wages.[22] But, if such alliances recur, they would not solve the major contradictions of capitalism, nor radically decommodify public life and nature.

When it comes, the radical break is likely to emerge in the global South. Several of the types of ruptures in the last century have already appeared: severe economic dislocations, former revolutionary movements coming to power, and the revitalization of anti-colonial, sovereignty movements. Currently, Latin America seems the most likely place for a major shift. We are already seeing victories for Left parties and anti-capitalist globalization movements, which both reject globalism and US domination. For instance, access to water was endorsed as a decommodified, human right in a referendum in Uruguay in 2004. Left-wing governments in Venezuela, Uruguay, and Brazil reject the neoliberal *Free Trade Area of the Americas* initiative, and they are trying to create instead an integrated South America with much autonomy from the US. If a new cycle of renationalization is starting, then conditions should become more favourable for deglobalizing TNCs. What forms would the latter likely take? Current grassroots and anti-statist inclinations of citizens' movements mean that efforts to tame global capital are likely to be defensive and avoid more radical measures like state nationalizations. For example, *Attac*, perhaps the most powerful anti-globalist citizens' movement in Europe adopted the following platform in 1998: (1) hinder international speculation; (2) tax financial capital transactions; (3) sanction tax havens; (4) inhibit privatizing pension funds; (5) oppose abandoning state sovereignty to investors and markets (Birchfield & Freybert-Inan, 2004, p. 293). Such measures would help to halt the advance of global corporate capitalism and hinder further commodifications. But they would just be a start. If citizens' movements and radical governments are intent on creating, rather than just imagining, "another world," they will have to develop positive and more radical alternatives.

CONCLUSION

If unilateral US nationalism continues, we will likely see a return to struggles for popular national sovereignty elsewhere, of kinds which are similar to the decolonization struggles from 1945 to the mid-1970s. In the last decade of that period, the decolonization movement deepened national self-determination and social transformation, by deglobalizing the greatest number of TNCs outside of wartime. In 1973, the United Nations set up a Commission on Transnational Corporations and the General Assembly agreed in principle on a Code of Conduct for TNCs. Two of the clauses were particularly pertinent. One stated that "Transnational corporations shall respect ... the right of each state to exercise its permanent sovereignty over its natural wealth and resources" and another that "States have the right to nationalize or expropriate the assets of a transnational corporation operating in their territories, and that adequate compensation is to be paid by the state concerned." When people look to positive alternative international agreements to replace neoliberal ones, the 71-clause UN Code of Conduct on TNCs would be a good model. The premise was to take powers from unelected corporations and give them to governments.

Today's sovereignty struggles are infused with a greater international and transnational spirit than those 30 years ago. Gilberto Gil (2005) stated it best when he said "we need sovereignty so we can interact with other people to maintain cultural diversity and share our distinct cultures with the world. In constructing the new society we want, we must maintain, in tension two contradictions, sovereignty and mutual dependency on all humanity. Both must be held up at the same time. The new sovereignty is a beautiful thing."

Citizens continue to support domestic ownership and national cultural expressions even when political parties and citizens' movements of all stripes have abandoned such positions. In the past, for instance, Canadians expressed a willingness to promote "Canadian ownership, even if it meant a lower standard of living" (Canadian Gallup Polls, 1980, p. 135). Concern over foreign ownership continues at 60 to 80 per cent levels despite the issue not being championed by significant political voices over the past 20 years (Hurtig, 2002, pp. 48–49). Canadian ownership has a strong tendency to mean public or social ownership because Canadian elites are so tied to their US counterparts that they have no interest in Canadian economic sovereignty. It is within struggles around economic sovereignty, economic security, and economic democracy that non-commodified public and social ownership can reach fruition.

Whatever alternatives political communities devise, they must find ways to raise sufficient capital so that all who want paid employment will have the means to do technologically dynamic, productive, and meaningful work. Corporate capitalism is a very unequal way to raise such capital. There are better ways. As we have seen, it is in the nature of corporate capitalism to escape responsibilities to communities of place and go anywhere to get the best deal. In contrast, to ensure responsibility to communities and nature, a new ethic of ownership must be built into the structure of control. A family of democratic alternatives, explored in the introductory chapter, is democratic social ownership. It can take many forms, including worker co-operatives and worker-owned enterprises, community-controlled development funds, worker-controlled pension funds, investment capital controlled by unions and citizens movements, and government-owned industries run by workers' control.

Efforts to deglobalize the TNCs must begin at home, spearheaded by local political mobilizations and national states. To be successful, grounded movements in many countries would have to coordinate internationally and campaign for international agreements to regulate and control TNCs and encourage domestic ownership. However, if popular democratic control is to grow, countries would have to regain sufficient sovereignty so that immobile labour and citizens in national and local political communities could "defend the local, nationally."

Notes

1. Since 9/11, elites based in Canada have carried on well-organized campaigns for "deep integration." See the CD Howe Institute's "border papers" (www.cdhowe.org), the North American and Security Prosperity Initiative of the Canadian Council of Chief Executives (CCCE) (http://www.ceocouncil.ca/en/), and the trilateral task force of the US Council on Foreign Relations and the CCCE (CCCE website).

2. I use the term *social imaginary* in Charles Taylor's (2002) sense, meaning not a set of ideas, but popular self understandings, practices, and common expectations, not always explicitly articulated, which give people a sense of shared group life.

3. There are traditionalist or conservative bases for decommodification, as well as socialist ones. See introductory chapter.

4. "Commanding the labour of others" could happen directly through hiring a servant or worker or indirectly by purchasing something that another person made last week or a hundred years ago.

5. Rosa Luxemburg (1908–09/1976, pp. 101–10) was critical of the right of national self-determination, arguing that it did not support working class power or socialism and that "rights" were undialectic.

6. Whether the government is perceived to be pro-business or not also influences elite support for its own state's sovereignty.

7. By bourgeois nationalism, I mean states promoting domestically owned businesses rather than foreign-owned ones.

8. An exception is Australia. Howard's government has adopted a mild version of the anti-immigrant, anti-refugee ideology of Pauline Hanson's One Nation Party.

9. Haass argued this before the US occupied Iraq and before the US switched its justification for being there from finding weapons of mass destruction to promoting democracy.

10. An al Qaeda broadcast referred to the "Muslim nation." See "Qaeda Deputy Says Attacks Won't Stop," *New York Times*, February 22, 2005, A9.

11. I use the term to mean economies that are largely nationally articulated. I do not mean state ownership.

12. A promising new vision, "Socialism of the XXI century" has been articulated by Heinz Dieterich Steffan and endorsed by Hugo Chávez (Pozarnik, 2005)

13. Kondratiev used the term "cycles," but the first English translations of his work came from a German translation of the original Russian, substituting "waves" for "cycles" (Louçã, 1999, p. 172).

14. Chase-Dunn and his associates are more nuanced than this. They see limits to commodification, especially those involving emotional relations (Boswell & Chase-Dunn, 2000, p. 31), uneven progress and reversals (Chase-Dunn & Hall, 1997, p. 47), and even efforts to decommodify labour and communities (Chase-Dunn, 2004). Still, they present commodification as a trend more than a cycle.

15. This skips over the intervening Kondratiev downturn—the Great Depression, followed by World War II. This was not a period of global integration. Wars, revolution, and depression may explain differences between the preceding and following cycles.

16. In 1921, the Soviets made a brief opening to the capitalist West in *The New Economic Policy*.

17. The World Bank (2002, p. 28) characterized this period as a second wave of globalization, which was followed by a third wave of sharply greater integration after 1980.

18. The boost in female employment during the wars commodified women's work (in largely positive ways) and counteracted to some extent general trends towards more production for use value.

19. This was a 1950 figure, so it also included the effects of World War II and the expansion of communism to China and Eastern Europe.

20. This number was for the world, not just for the global South.

21. The collapse of high world oil prices at the same time contributed greatly to southern countries' indebtedness. Many countries had relied on oil exports to pay their way in the world.

22. It is more difficult to pull off such alliances at the national level if economies remain globalized because reflated economies may stimulate imports and balance of payments problems as much as increases in domestic jobs.

part two

DYNAMICS OF COMMODIFICATION

CHAPTER FIVE

The General Agreement on Trade in Services—Politics by Another Means

ELLEN GOULD

The General Agreement on Trade in Services (GATS) of World Trade Organization (WTO) is one of many international trade agreements that threaten to place large areas of public policy out of reach of democratic decision making. A top WTO official even promoted the GATS as a way to make liberalization irreversible (Hartridge, 1997). The goal appears to be to achieve an end of history, an anti-democratic one where the Washington Consensus favouring privatization and deregulation will set the course for public policy forever.

In pursuing new profit-making opportunities through commodification, unfet-tered access to natural resources, and business-friendly regulatory reforms, cor-porate strategies can founder on unpredictable political responses. For example, the public uproar sparked by large death tolls in train accidents prompted the United Kingdom (UK) government to undo some of the privatization of the coun-try's railway system. Faced with consumer outrage at high prices following elec-tricity deregulation, California imposed price caps. The privatization of the city's water utility in Cochabamba, Bolivia ignited so much resistance that authorities had to cancel their contract with a company partially owned by one of the world's most powerful transnationals—Bechtel Corporation. The GATS has the potential to make such democratic responses to crises violations of international law and subject to WTO sanctions.

In the GATS' peculiar wording, the agreement imposes bindings and disciplines on government. This terminology reflects more than just the tendency of trade lawyers to use obscure language. Under the GATS, governments volunteer to be tied down and restrained. Feminist scholar Zillah Eisenstein (1996) describes a current trend towards the privatization of public life that results in the depiction of the public as the enemy—as the arena of special/divisive interests that Balkanize the country (p. 61). The GATS embodies this view. Rather than increasing govern-ment responsiveness to citizens, the GATS serves the opposite purpose: the development of enforceable restrictions on governments to prevent them from responding to political demands.

In order to become a WTO member, and almost all countries of the world now are members, a government is obligated to sign the GATS. The GATS requires WTO members to engage in repeated rounds of negotiations to expand what the agreement covers with the result that their public policy is bound ever tighter by GATS rules, and their policy space is increasingly restricted.

The GATS is about far more than privatization, deregulation, and the commodification of services. The analysis that follows explains the specific mechanisms used in the agreement to tie governments' hands and to take policy decisions permanently out of the political domain.

THE CURRENT ROUND OF GATS NEGOTIATIONS

The creation of the GATS in 1995 had little immediate effect. Coming at a time when countries were privatizing and deregulating many areas covered by the agreement, the GATS was overshadowed by the neoliberal changes countries were making on their own. As WTO Director General-designate Supachai Panitchpakdi (2002) stated,

> Although the Uruguay Round succeeded in creating the GATS, at the end of the Round a number of issues ... [were] left untouched and the initial commitments made by the members were at best modest: mostly only guaranteeing the existing levels of access. GATS commitments reflect mostly existing levels of unilaterally determined policy ... (p. 3)

Negotiations to expand the agreement began in January 2000 and were originally scheduled to conclude in 2005.[1] The negotiations were intended to go far beyond locking in the liberalizing decisions governments had already taken. Not only would whole new service sectors be opened up to foreign competition, but also new restrictions would be placed on domestic regulation. This dual privatization and deregulation agenda was reflected in the 1999 Congressional testimony on the GATS by Dean O'Hare, Chair of the US Coalition of Service Industries. O'Hare argued that one of the GATS objectives should be to encourage privatization of health care systems, allowing for complete foreign ownership of health facilities. But he also wanted the negotiations to address regulatory problems such as excessive privacy rules over medical records.

The bargaining positions adopted by governments in the negotiations indicated the radical transformation being pursued. On October 10, 2002, the UK Department of Trade and Industry released a summary of the requests it had received from other countries in the early stage of negotiations (UK, 2002). The sweep of the requested changes was breathtaking. Among other things, the UK was asked to open up all hospital and social services, rest, convalescent and old people's homes to unlimited foreign ownership; to allow foreign majority ownership of all suppliers of medical, dental, and related services; to make government subsidies specifically directed to UK cultural producers available to foreign competitors; to allow foreign ownership as well as cross-border delivery of all adult and higher education services; to allow foreign ownership and cross-border delivery of all services related to libraries, archives, museums and other cultural services; to relax restrictions on store hours; and to entrench deregulation of energy services.

One of the negotiating requests, originating with the US according to leaked documents, indicates how far the negotiations are intruding into areas that have nothing to do with trade. To enhance the transparency of local regulations, the US asked that UK local governments be required to set up meetings for developers who want a forum to respond to residents' concerns about planned projects. This would effectively create an obligation, enforceable under international law, for local governments to assist retail interests in getting community acceptance of their development proposals.

The UK gave its citizens fewer than three months to respond to the major changes to public policy that would result from acceding to the GATS requests, changes that would normally be debated for years in the domestic context. The UK also provided only a summary of the requests without attributing them to a specific government. This secrecy enabled governments to take extremely aggressive positions without having to defend them in the court of domestic or international opinion.

Citizens outside the UK, though, were even worse off, as other governments refused to reveal any of the requests they had received. This approach is an example of how trade negotiations tend to remove deliberations about public policy from the public arena and treat them as confidential contractual matters between private parties.

THE EFFECT OF GATS BINDINGS ON GOVERNMENTS

The GATS is sometimes promoted as the inevitable product of technological advance. The argument is made as follows. With the Internet, services that were once thought impossible to trade across borders now can be. Just as international rules were needed to govern trade in goods, similar rules for services must be developed as they become more tradable. The coverage of services by multilateral trade agreements is presented as merely a natural evolution of the post-war reduction of trade barriers.

An emphasis on historical continuity is a device used to promote both the GATS and the WTO. The underlying message is that citizens need not be concerned because they are dealing with the same multilateral trade system that has been around for decades. However, the WTO's establishment in 1995 represented a significant break with the past. The WTO's dispute settlement system inverts the conditions under which trade dispute panel decisions are adopted and enforced, resulting in a substantial reduction in national governments' authority over public policy. Under the previous rules of the General Agreement on Tariffs and Trade (the GATT), dispute panel decisions were adopted only if all members agreed, including the country that lost the case.[2] Now, under the WTO, all members have to oppose a panel decision for it to be rejected, including the country that won the case. Sanctions for refusing to comply with WTO panel decisions are so strict that countries almost always make the changes required. There is no avenue for appeal other than to the WTO itself. No relief from a judgement can be sought from domestic courts and constitutions, or from international bodies such as the United Nations.

Furthermore, the inclusion of an agreement entrenching intellectual property rights (the TRIPS agreement) and one covering services (the GATS) vastly extended the WTO's mandate into areas that are illegitimately defined as trade. Cross-border trade in services actually makes up only a relatively small aspect of what the GATS covers. As part of the effort to categorize services, which usually involve face-to-face contact between consumers and suppliers, as tradable the GATS defines trade so broadly that it includes activities that occur completely within a country's borders. Because the agreement covers foreign investment, corporations are effectively granted a range of new rights, such as the right to establish for-profit health clinics in foreign countries. The WTO Secretariat has described the GATS as the world's first multilateral agreement on investment, and advocates of the agreement have said it is a way many of the goals of the failed Multilateral Agreement on Investment can be achieved but with less risk of non-governmental organization (NGO) activism (Sauve & Wilkie, 2000, p. 338).

The GATS definition of trade also includes consumption of services abroad (e.g., students attending foreign universities) and individuals supplying services abroad on temporary work visas (e.g., Indian software developers working for Silicon Valley firms). The WTO Secretariat has described increased employment of foreign workers on temporary visas as a strategy to lower health costs (WTO, 1998a). Lowered wages for health care workers, who are primarily women, is therefore one anticipated result of subjecting services to GATS rules.

The fact that the GATS applies to all levels of government—national, state, provincial, municipal, and even non-governmental organizations with delegated governmental authority—means it can be used as a way to force neoliberal restructuring onto subnational governments. As Rudolf Adlung (2000), the WTO's chief health economist, has explained, "the commitments negotiated by senior governments can be used as an instrument of central policy surveillance and enforcement over member states or regions" (p. 118).

THE GATS AND PRIVATIZATION

In March 2001, WTO members agreed to formal negotiating guidelines that meant no service would be left off the table, with no exception made for sectors like health, education, public utilities, or cultural services. This decision, as well as the secrecy of the bargaining process, paved the way for requests to be made in the most politically sensitive areas, particularly services that are often delivered in the public sector. A German government report (2002a) observed that the GATS requests the European Commission (EC) had received included demands for "abolishment" of "common EC restrictions for services that are considered part of the civil service" (p. 2). As the substance of the requests leaked out, the threat to public services became clear and refuted official denials that public services were not threatened by the negotiations.

It is true that under the GATS, WTO members can decide which services they commit to the agreement's most powerful provisions ("market access" and "national treatment") and the extent to which these provisions will apply. In this narrow sense, governments are under no compulsion to privatize public services under the GATS. But in the current round of negotiations, the WTO's most powerful members have requested that countries make the kinds of commitments that would entail privatization, and are exerting substantial pressure to achieve this end. The flexibility governments have, in theory, under the GATS is consequently qualified in practice by the political realities of the negotiating process.

It is also true that the GATS exempts services supplied in the exercise of "governmental authority" from commitments. Officials often cite this exemption as a protection for public services. Reading the actual wording of this exemption, though, exposes how limited it is. GATS Article I, "Scope and Definition," states:

For the purposes of this Agreement:

...

(b) "services" includes any service in any sector except services supplied in the exercise of governmental authority;

(c) "a service supplied in the exercise of governmental authority" means any service which is supplied neither on a commercial basis, nor in competition with one or more service suppliers.

Since there are few examples of public services that operate without any private sector competitors or without any commercial aspects, this exemption appears to provide very little real protection for public services. Despite the problems with the exemption, EC and US trade representatives at a 30 October 2002 meeting with consumer groups in Washington, D.C. stated that they would not seek to clarify the exemption through an amendment to the GATS. Instead, they said they were content to allow a WTO panel to interpret the issue in the event of a challenge to a public service. In other words, the EC and the US have decided to delegate authority over the fate of key public services to unelected WTO dispute panels. This decision is just one example of how democratic control over policy is being surrendered through the GATS. If a WTO panel ruled that the governmental authority provision did not exempt a public service from a government's GATS commitments, the service could have to be opened up to foreign, private competition regardless of what the affected populations wanted.

The political pressures involved in the negotiations combined with the weak protection in the agreement for services "supplied in the exercise of governmental authority" mean that the GATS negotiations are a threat to key public services. For example, leaks of the European Commission's bargaining demands indicate the EC is seeking *unlimited* commitments of drinking water services. The GATS rules on "market access" mean it is a violation for a country that makes unlimited commitments of a service to maintain monopolies or exclusive suppliers of this service "either on the basis of a regional subdivision or on the basis of its entire territory" (GATS Article XVI.2).[3] If governments succumb to pressure and fully commit drinking water services to GATS rules, public utilities providing this service could be challenged as a violation of the GATS. The decision of whether the supply of drinking water should be provided by private, for-profit companies or by public utilities might never again be one that could be made democratically at the local level.

Another example of the threat to public services is the impact on public subsidies. The official WTO guidelines to the GATS, agreed to by all WTO members, states unequivocally that government subsidies are part of what is covered under the rules of "national treatment" (WTO, 2001a). Making unlimited national treatment commitments of a service means governments have to treat foreign suppliers of this service no less favourably than they treat domestic suppliers (GATS Article XVII.1). For example, the US is requesting unlimited commitments in the higher education sector. If Canada agreed to this American request, provincial governments would be expected to make all the assistance they provide to Canadian public universities equally available to foreign, for-profit institutions like the US-based University of Phoenix. Since it is unlikely that taxpayers would accept government subsidies going to foreign, for-profit corporations on the same basis as they are granted to domestic, non-profit institutions, GATS commitments are a powerful tool to get rid of government subsidies altogether.

In the current negotiations, some requested commitments would result in complete privatization of public services, while others would open up to commercial development as many aspects of the particular sector as possible. For example, in reviewing the health and social services sectors, negotiators acknowledged there was significant government involvement but concluded that this did not mean that the whole sector was outside the remit of the GATS. Members also noted increasing possibilities for private participation, whether domestic or foreign, in various health and social-related activities (WTO, 1998b).

GATS commitments also tend to preclude permanently the creation of new public services, because the agreement makes it so difficult to withdraw commitments once they are made. If a government commits to have a sector fully covered by the GATS, then to subsequently create a new monopoly public service, it would have to withdraw these commitments. The GATS provisions spelling out what governments have to do create a public monopoly in a committed sector (Article VIII, Article XXI) are extremely onerous. They indicate why liberalization under the GATS is considered irreversible. To withdraw a commitment, governments have to wait three years and provide compensation in the form of substitute commitments sufficient to satisfy all other WTO members.

GATS commitments made by one government are intended to be very hard for subsequent governments to undo, no matter how strong the popular demand for change. As the WTO's online course on the GATS states, "By guaranteeing that investment and trading conditions will not be changed against their interests, a commitment in the GATS provides the security which investors need" (WTO, 1998c). A WTO paper on the benefits of the GATS also states, "… [B]indings undertaken in the GATS have the effect of protecting liberalization policies, regardless of their underlying rationale, from slippages and reversals … (WTO, 1999a). Locking in liberalization permanently is presented as a positive development rather than an erosion of democracy.

DEREGULATION UNDER THE GATS

While trade officials often protest that the GATS is not about deregulation, the opposite is stated in WTO documents. For example, in one paper, the WTO Secretariat itself states that genuine deregulation and liberalization measures have been negotiated under the GATS (WTO, 1999a). The US has said that "many WTO Members, from the least-developed to developed, are proceeding to deregulate their services sectors…. The GATS negotiations should recognize and encourage these initiatives" (WTO, 1999b).

Many of the problems experienced by ordinary citizens in the first years of the twenty-first century can be attributed to the failure of governments to regulate adequately. Just a few examples of these failures are the discovery that arthritis medications, approved for sale by pharmaceutical regulatory agencies, actually might have contributed to many tens of thousands of heart attack deaths; the loss of hundreds of billions of dollars, sometimes destroying the lifesavings or pensions of families, due to inadequate regulation of corporate accounting; and epidemic levels of obesity among children, the target of massive junk food advertising campaigns. Yet governments' ability to introduce stronger regulations in all of these areas—scientific research, accounting, and advertising—could be severely curtailed by the GATS.

Because the GATS primarily governs activities that occur entirely within the borders of countries, it is argued that the agreement should address domestic regulations as barriers to trade. When countries make unlimited commitments of particular services under the GATS, they explicitly agree to deregulate. Under full *market access* commitments, governments are forbidden from imposing certain kinds of regulatory limitations on the supply of a service, regardless of whether the suppliers are domestic or foreign.

The deregulatory potential of GATS market access rules became clear in November 2004 when a WTO dispute panel published its ruling in the "US-Gambling" case (WTO, 2004). This case involved a challenge by the island nation of Antigua to US prohibitions on Internet gambling. Antigua claimed that its Internet gambling companies had suffered when the US increased its enforcement of federal and state regulations prohibiting online gambling. Antigua argued, and the WTO dispute panel agreed, that US regulations violated GATS commitments the US had made to allow foreign companies cross-border access to the American gambling market.

When the US appealed, the WTO Appellate Body overturned much of the panel's decision but upheld one critical part of it—that countries violate the GATS when they ban any service covered by full market access commitments spelled out in Article XVI of the agreement (WTO, 2005b). The US government in its submission to the Appellate Body criticized the panel's interpretation of market access, stating this interpretation "unreasonably and absurdly deprives Members of a significant component of their right to regulate services by depriving them of the power to prohibit selected activities in sectors where commitments are made"(WTO, 2005a, p. 62).

The US gave the example of regulatory efforts to eliminate "spam," defined as an unsolicited form of advertising through email or fax. In the US view, such regulations should not be considered violations of GATS market access because they are neutral in the sense that they restrict domestic spammers as much as they do foreign ones. But the US warned that if the panel's interpretations of market access were upheld, spam restrictions would be in trouble as violations of Article XVI Market Access. The US defined the dire consequences of the panel's ruling this way:

> ... [T]he very concept of regulation of a service typically rests on the power of the state to prohibit services not supplied in accordance with state-imposed norms. In that sense, most regulation involves prohibiting that fraction of the service which, although abstractly possible, does not conform to the relevant norms. Under the Panel's interpretation of Article XVI, however, it would appear that very little domestic regulation could "escape" Article XVI if it can be described as prohibiting part of a sector or part of a mode of supply.... (WTO, 2005a, p. 61)

Despite these warnings about the impact on government's right to regulate, the Appellate Body agreed with the panel's interpretation of market access. This ruling opens the door to many new GATS challenges to domestic regulation.

While there has not yet been a panel decision about government regulations and GATS "national treatment" rules, national treatment commitments also appear to make regulations vulnerable to a variety of GATS challenges. Any regulation would be a violation if it affects the conditions of competition so as to favour, however unintentionally, domestic firms. For example, in discussing barriers to trade in the construction industry, the European Commission describes how building regulations could violate national treatment: "Even if the same measures are applied to all suppliers, domestic or foreign, they may be found to be more onerous to foreign suppliers" (WTO, 2000). The concern would be that special construction standards intended to address local problems, such as extreme weather conditions, would be a violation of GATS commitments because foreign firms would tend not to have the same expertise in working with these standards as local firms.

But despite these existing provisions, the GATS Working Party on Domestic Regulation (a special committee set up as part of the overall GATS negotiations) is drafting yet another mechanism by which WTO members can challenge each others' services regulations through the WTO dispute system. This Working Party is negotiating constraints on licensing, qualifications, and standards over services to eliminate regulations that constitute "unnecessary" barriers to trade in services.

Under the necessity test being proposed, governments would be required to revise all existing and proposed regulations to ensure they had an objective that a WTO dispute panel would consider legitimate. Even if governments correctly anticipated what a panel of trade lawyers would accept as legitimate, they would have to ensure that the regulation they chose to fulfil this objective was the least trade restrictive or no more trade restrictive than necessary.

If approved, this new GATS regulatory obligation would obviously lead to deregulation, but it could be used to force privatization as well. In the event of a challenge, a dispute panel could rule that providing universal access to basic health care was a legitimate goal, but requiring hospitals to be non-profit was not the "least trade restrictive" way of meeting this goal. Panels might decide that, instead, governments should provide assistance to needy individuals so that they can buy hospital services from private, for-profit suppliers. The "least trade restrictive" obligation would tend to make governments transform all services into commodities, governed by market rules.

To make concrete the kinds of regulations that could be challenged under this new GATS provision, negotiators compiled a list of regulations "to be disciplined." This leaked list (which the WTO refuses to make public) proves the extent to which WTO negotiators are intent on curtailing governmental regulatory authority. Some examples of the regulations targeted are regulations relating to zoning and operating hours, restrictions on advertising and marketing, and "restrictions on fee-setting"—which means that government limits on electricity, telephone, or water fees could potentially be challenged. The list was drawn up by consulting exclusively with businesses on what regulations they wanted disciplined by the GATS. No consumer, environmental, or other public interest group was invited to comment (WTO, 2002).

If implemented, this new GATS restriction on domestic regulation could mean governments will not be able to regulate privatized services to guarantee public policy objectives are met. Negotiators have not even agreed to include a list to illustrate what objectives would be considered legitimate. So even the most fundamental goals, such as that there should be universal access to basic services like safe drinking water, could be challenged. The privatization of public services through GATS commitments and the disciplining of domestic regulation, therefore, can be seen as a two-pronged attack on the public interest.

THE GATS AS THE POLITICAL PROJECT OF US AND BRITISH FINANCIAL CORPORATIONS

The GATS originated with the US financial sector's interest in expanding into foreign countries in the early 1980s. David Hartridge (1997), former director of the WTO Services Division, once commented, "Without the enormous pressure generated by the American financial services sector, particularly companies like American Express and Citicorp, there would have been no services agreement and therefore perhaps no Uruguay Round and no WTO."

The US Coalition of Service Industries (CSI) was founded in 1982 and has been dominated since then by the largest American banking, accounting, and insurance interests. Arthur Andersen, The Chubb Corporation, Citigroup, Goldman Sachs, J.P. Morgan Chase and Co., MasterCard, and New York Life are among its members. A paper written at the US National Defense University analyzed the identity of interests between the executive branch of the US government and the financial sector, and why this led to the close collaboration that established the GATS. According to the paper's author, James Zumwalt (1996), while the executive of the US government can usually be counted on to favour trade negotiations, Congress is considered a perennial obstacle because it is less cohesive than the executive branch and more subject to political pressure. The lobbying of Congress by domestic manufacturers and unions threatened US support of the Uruguay Round, because Congress has to pass implementing legislation for any trade and investment agreement that the executive branch negotiates. The executive branch, specifically the Department of Commerce and the office of the US Trade Representative (USTR), worked closely with the services sector to overcome the political problem posed by Congress.

The very idea of a services sector, though, is a political construction. Prior to the fight over so-called "free trade" agreements, the businesses that ultimately joined the Coalition of Service Industries (CSI) did not even identify themselves as having cohesive interests distinct from those of other US corporations. A group of New York bankers persuaded executives in telecommunications, entertainment, tourism, and transportation companies to join the financial services lobby. According to American Express vice-president Joan Spero, these bankers persuaded companies in other sectors that a large coalition could more effectively change public policy if they redefined themselves as comprising a service industry.

Spero revealed the key public relations messages CSI used to promote the notion of the services economy and the need for free trade in services:

1)   services are important to the economy,

2)   services companies employ many workers in quality jobs (CSI stressed the high-tech nature of many services jobs to counter a "hamburger flipper" image),[4]

3)   services boost the economy by facilitating technological improvements and productivity, and

4)   services are a tradable good that can and should be covered by international rules. (quoted in Zumwalt, 1996, p. 5)

Twenty years after the CSI developed the original public relations arguments for the GATS, politicians, trade officials, and academics make GATS promotional speeches structured around these exact same talking points. Just because services are important to the economy and can boost productivity, it does not follow that they should be opened up to foreign, private competition. Sectors like education were kept out of the market precisely because they are too critical to be subjected to the vagaries of the market. Experiments with privatized education have had disastrous outcomes. In October 2002, students in Philadelphia schools managed by the Edison Corporation were left short of textbooks and computer equipment after these had been sold to pay corporate debts (Saunders, 2002). Public electrical utilities were originally established in Canada to provide reliable power at low cost. However, in Ontario's newly privatized electrical market, companies like Dofasco Steel have complained that the wildly fluctuating prices charged by private utilities make it very difficult to operate.

As the groundwork was laid in the free trade agreements of the early 1980s, the public relations strategy to convince Americans that services jobs were good jobs was key to counteracting concerns about the loss of US manufacturing jobs to low-wage, overseas competition. American labour had been haunted by the image of displaced manufacturing workers forced to take minimum wage jobs in hamburger restaurants. CSI lobbied successfully to have the Commerce Department required, by law, to collect data under services as a separate category of economic activity. Economists were hired to study the significance of the US services sector, and opinion pieces touting its value appeared in the US media.

Besides shaping public opinion, CSI established strategic alliances within the domestic and international civil service. Zumwalt documents how CSI worked from its very beginning with the US Trade Representative to get international negotiations on services started. USTR, "with intellectual support from CSI," then moved the plan for multilateral negotiations on a services agreement through the trade committee of the Organization for Economic Cooperation and Development. This committee published a study in 1985 laying the groundwork for services to be incorporated into the Uruguay Round, which was launched the same year.

Once the GATS was established as part of the WTO in 1995, negotiators' priorities to expand the agreement reflected CSI's priorities. Trade representatives in
Geneva concentrated their initial work on developing a separate financial services
agreement and draft rules to govern the accounting profession. The WTO repeatedly looked for advice from CSI member Arthur Andersen, the now disgraced and
defunct US-based auditing firm. An Andersen representative revealed to the *New
York Times* that his firm helped draft the GATS disciplines on accounting
(DePalma, 2002).

One of the CSI's main successes has been to cast the financial sector's narrow
interest in overseas expansion as being in the general interest of Americans, a view
echoed in the mainstream media. In contrast, editorialists denounce the US administration when it departs from its "free trade" policies and bends to the vested
interests of domestic manufacturers. But the evidence suggests that NAFTA, the
WTO, and dozens of bilateral investment agreements signed in the 1990s have not
resulted in higher incomes for the average American. The US Center on Budget
and Policy Priorities reports that during the 1990s, the wages of lower- or middle-
income Americans either declined or stayed the same, whereas the real income of
high-income families grew by 15 per cent. The trend towards increasing inequality in American society that began in the late 1970s established new records during the "free trade" era.

The British business lobby "LOTIS," developed at the same time as CSI, outdis-
tances even the latter in the degree to which it directly formulates public policy.
With its meetings attended by senior government officials and top British financial executives, LOTIS has been described as a veritable corporate state alliance
in which the distinction between public and private has become completely blurred
(Wesselius, 2002b, p. 1). Leaked minutes of the group's 1999 to 2001 meetings
reveal that the dynamics go far beyond business executives giving input into government policy.[5] Civil servants and chief executive officers speak interchangeably
about goals for upcoming negotiations, problems they face with NGOs opposed
to the GATS, the need to develop anti-GATS countermeasures, and how to research
and publicize a response to critics. At the same time they were strategizing with
business on how to undermine NGOs, British officials were promising on their
department's Internet site to engage with NGOs and take the interests of all sectors
of society into account in the GATS negotiations.

GAINING SUPPORT FOR THE GATS OUTSIDE OF THE US AND THE UK

While key individuals in the US and UK financial sectors created lobbies for the
GATS in their countries, elsewhere trade officials organized domestic business lobbies when they did not get the pressure they wanted to justify aggressive positions
at the GATS negotiations. Through its international conferences attended by foreign civil servants and academics, the American services lobby has extended its
influence beyond the US border. The CSI has helped generate a kind of ideological

boosterism for the GATS that is embraced in countries even where there is no organized business pressure backing the agreement.

In his study "Behind GATS 2000: Corporate Power at Work," Erik Wesselius recounts how the European GATS business lobby—the European Services Forum (ESF)—was founded on the initiative of a civil servant, Sir Leon Brittan, the European Trade Commissioner at the time. Rather than ensuring business interests did not gain disproportionate influence in the development of public policy, Brittan created an organized lobby that was subsequently granted access to negotiators and key negotiating documents.

Andrew Buxton, Chair of Barclay's Bank, explained Brittan's pivotal role:

> Significantly, the European Commission also saw the benefits of strong business participation in the process, and in 1998 Sir Leon Brittan, Vice-President of the Commission, asked me to create and chair a select group of European business leaders in the service industries, to act as a link between the Commission and a wide range of service industries as the World Trade Organization Talks widen their horizons into other service industries. (Wesselius, 2002a, p. 8)

Brittan told the ESF founding meeting that he was "in their hands" with respect to setting priorities for the GATS negotiations. Another top European Commission official told a business audience he considered the ESF as ranking on par with countries of the European Union in setting negotiating objectives (Wesselius, 2002a, p. 9).

The marginalization of elected representatives contrasts sharply with this active pursuit of business interests. A report by members of the German Bundestag on globalization observed that parliamentarians have little influence in contexts like the WTO, and "are all too frequently treated as if they were merely annoying bystanders, when they are not excluded altogether" (Germany, 2002, p. 11).

EC officials circulated the initial draft European position to business in May 2000, the second draft in September 2000 and pleaded for business input in October 2001 and January 2002 as documents were being finalized. In contrast, the Commission refused to make the European position publicly available and it became known only through leaks.

In Canada, the Canadian Manufacturers and Exporters, a business lobby with extensive involvement of American subsidiaries and headed by a former Cabinet minister, took the lead in promoting the GATS negotiations. Aside from this group, however, officials from the Department of Foreign Affairs and International Trade had a very difficult time engaging business support for the agreement's expansion. In 2001, they organized meetings across the country, inviting primarily business groups. Turnout from business was poor in contrast to the interest shown by NGOs and unions concerned about potential negative impacts.[6]

To organize business support and get positive media coverage, the Canadian government hired public relations firms to find spokespersons who could provide first-hand accounts of restrictive trade practices in other markets and/or offer informed opinion on this subject to media (FWJ Advertizing, 2001). In 2001, the PR firms mailed out stock responses to counter criticisms of the GATS. These talking points labelled critical views as *Misperceptions* and responded to these with "THE FACTS," such as that the GATS was not established in the sole interest of multinationals.[7]

The mailing to informed business leaders gave examples of what the federal government characterized as barriers to trade that Canada would seek to eliminate through the GATS negotiations. Virtually all of the listed "Examples of Restrictions Canada Will Target" were developing countries' regulations designed to ensure that their citizens benefit from foreign investment.

THE GATS AND DEVELOPING COUNTRIES

Given the lack of domestic businesses in most developing countries that could benefit from the GATS, it is not surprising that their governments generally resisted the establishment of the agreement and have opposed its expansion through new rounds of negotiations.[8] Specific articles were made part of the GATS in order to overcome this resistance. The articles provide for differential treatment of developing countries, such as allowing them to make GATS commitments of fewer services.

But once developing countries allowed the establishment of the GATS, the US and other countries set out to erase the differential treatment the agreement is supposed to provide. The US, the European Commission, Canada, and Japan opposed the broad-based assessment of the experience with services liberalization that some developing countries said was a pre-condition for further GATS negotiations.

Developing nations stand on solid ground when they demand that their actual experience with liberalization of services has to be assessed before they are pressed to make further commitments, because such an assessment is called for in Article XIX.3 of the Agreement. Pakistan's delegate stated at a GATS meeting that assessments had to go beyond a mere tallying of export data to consider liberalization's actual impacts on access to basic services (WTO, 2001b).

For US audiences, GATS promoters argue that expansion of services trade through the GATS will help counteract the domestic trade deficit in goods. But the same argument cannot be used in developing countries, which tend to import far more services than they export. So these countries are told that being a net importer of services can be positive. Even though their balance of payments will suffer, developing countries are encouraged to import services on the basis that the superiority of imported services will benefit other areas of their economies.

Charles Heeter, an executive with Andersen International, gave presentations to both the WTO and to the US Trade Commission on the need for liberalization of the accounting profession under GATS rules. In his April 1998 testimony to the Trade Commission, Heeter said developing countries particularly needed Andersen's services:

> Accounting and audit, two central areas of our practice, are especially crucial in the processes of development and transition.... By providing the type of market-oriented, state-of-the-art accounting and bookkeeping services that are in short supply in developing and transition economies, professional services firms such as Arthur Andersen contribute directly to the market economy's development. (Heeter, 1998, p. 5)

The inherent superiority of American services may be a tougher sell, though, after the collapse of Enron Corporation and its accounting firm Arthur Andersen in an enormous accounting scandal.

CONCLUSION

Despite efforts to cast it as a politically neutral agreement that leaves key policy decisions to governments, the GATS has, from its beginning, been a profoundly political project. The agreement does not have specific clauses called privatization, deregulation, and commodification, but, nonetheless, it has powerful provisions that will lead to these outcomes if governments make full commitments of public services in the current negotiations. And this is exactly what they are being pressured to do in the current round of GATS negotiations.

The audacity of these proposals may prove to be their undoing. The notion that a trade agreement could reverse locally made decisions over zoning offends the most basic understanding of democracy and raises questions about whose interests are driving the negotiations. The concept that decisions to privatize can be locked in and made irreversible under the GATS, no matter what crises emerge, appears to be an extremely high-risk gamble even for those willing to consider privatization. The transfer of authority to WTO panels to decide which domestic regulations are too "burdensome" sounds highly autocratic. Those who learn about the substance of the GATS negotiations come to realize that this trade agreement encroaches on extensive areas of domestic policy. A broad consensus can be built around the modest idea that trade agreements should be about trade and not about undermining legitimate public policy and democratic governance.

Notes

1. At the beginning of 2005, the end of the year target for the conclusion of negotiations looked doubtful as many countries had missed the deadlines for submission of negotiating offers.
2. The WTO's glossary of trade terms gives the following explanation for the GATT: "GATT—General Agreement on Tariffs and Trade, which has been superseded as an international organization by the WTO. An updated General Agreement is now one of the WTO's agreements." The WTO administers both the GATT, which covers trade in goods, and the GATS, which covers trade in services. The WTO glossary is available on the WTO Internet site at http://www.wto.org/english/thewto_e/glossary_e/glossary_e.htm, accessed May 3, 2005.
3. For the articles of GATS, see the World Trade Organization (1994).
4. Bracketed text in this quotation inserted by Zumwalt (1996).

5. The minutes of the LOTIS meetings are available at http://www.gatswatch.org/LOTIS/ LOTISapp1.html

6. The lack of interest in these meetings by Canadian business may have been because the major obstacles to Canadian firms in exporting services are often experienced at the Canada-US border, and these obstacles are theoretically supposed to be already resolved under NAFTA.

7. Ironically, at a time of a severe nursing shortage in Canada, the mailing was sent to nurses asking them what kind of obstacles they faced in working overseas.

8. A notable exception is India. The Indian delegation to the WTO has promoted the GATS as a way to ensure that large corporations based in developed countries continue to send more and more services work overseas.

CHAPTER SIX

Frontiers of the Market
Commodifying Human Body Parts[1]

TREVOR W. HARRISON

If anything is sacred the human being is sacred. (Walt Whitman, "I Sing the Body Electric.")

We are now eyeing each other's bodies greedily, as a potential source of detachable spare parts with which to extend our lives. (Sociologist, T. Awaya.)

2.50 for an eyeball, and a buck and a half for an ear. (The Tragically Hip, "Little Bones.")

Beginning in the 1980s, the world was suddenly gripped by a new wave of capitalist expansion. Underpinned by a series of political victories in the Anglo-American democracies and the later collapse of communism in Eastern Europe, and operating under the rubric of "globalization," capitalism spread like a pandemic. For neoliberal zealots, the market itself became sacred. All relationships were to be subjected to exchange. Everything—mind, body, and soul—was to be made a saleable commodity.

Indeed, in the case of the body, quite literally. For, little analysed on the margins of globalization (at least at first) there emerged a global trade in human body parts (HBPs)[2] for transplantation,[3] tacitly condoned and sometimes aided and abetted by a few governments and involving a range of actors.

Many have greeted the emergence of a commercial market for human organs with concern. These concerns are heightened by reports of human body parts being obtained coercively from the young, the poor, the homeless, the illiterate, the captive, and the infirm. (See *National Film Board of Canada* [NFBC], 1993; McCullough, 1993; "An Abominable Trade," 1995; Scheper-Hughes, 2000.) In the words of Scheper-Hughes (1998), "the movement and flow of living donor organs ... is from South to North, from poor to rich, black and brown to white, and from female to male bodies" (p. 15).

These concerns are an integral backdrop to this chapter. I argue, however, that the emergence of the HBP trade, along with the application of new technologies, must be understood in the broader context of globalization, specifically the extension and intensification of a capitalist mode of exchange. I argue further that the HBP trade mirrors the "normal" system of unequal exchanges that mark other forms of trade between developed and developing regions of the world, and between classes, ethnicities, genders, and ages within and across these same regions.

THE MARKET FOR HUMAN BODY PARTS

The first successful human organ transplant—of a kidney—occurred in France in 1906. More transplants were attempted in other parts of Europe during this period and later in the Soviet Union. But the modern era of transplants began only in the 1950s, and even then remained largely experimental until the mid-1970s (Patrick, Phillips, & Diethelm, 1991).

Thereafter, the number and variety of human organ transplants performed steadily increased, especially in the wealthier and technologically more advanced Western countries. In 1975, for example, Europe recorded a total of 2,273 transplants. Even in 1990, the total number of European transplants was 11,836 (European Renal Association-European Dialysis and Transplant Association [ERA-EDTA], 1996); in Canada that same year, 1,255 (Canadian Organ Replacement Registry [CORR], 2002); and in the United States, 14,978 (Organization Procurement and Transplantation Network [OPTN], 2002). Yet, worldwide, by 1994, there were nearly 300,000 transplants of all types conducted (CORR, 1996, pp. 3–7; Childress, 1992, pp. 1240–42; United Network for Organ Sharing [UNOS], 1996a; ERA-EDTA, 1996). The new millennium saw over a million transplants conducted in one year alone (Business Communications Company [BCC], 2003).

While the number of transplants performed has increased, reflective of an increase in supply and trained medical personnel to do the procedures, demand—spurred by technological improvements that ensure "safe" (or relatively safe) outcomes—has vastly outstripped supply, resulting in longer waiting lists. Figures for the United States provide stark evidence of this fact (Figure 6.1).

Between 1993 and 2002, the number of donors in the United States went from 7,866 in 1993 to 12,800 in 2002 (an increase of 65 per cent), while the number of transplants went from 17,640 to 24,901 (an increase of 41 per cent). At the same time, however, the number of persons awaiting transplants went from 31,694 to 79,387 (150 per cent) (calculated from OPTN, 2003).

Data for six central European countries (Netherlands, Austria, Germany, Belgium, Luxemburg, and Slovenia) in the latter part of this same period (1999 to 2003) exhibit a similar trend, though not nearly the same steep and continued increase of demand over supply (Figure 6.2).

In 1999, for the six European countries in question, the number of transplants performed was 5,523, while waiting lists stood at 14,174. In 2003, 5,903 trans-

FIGURE 6.1	Total US Organ Donors by Donor Type, Total Transplant Recipients, and Total Waiting List Patients, 1993–2002

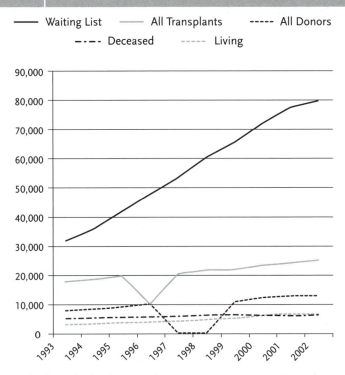

Source: Data for the graph taken from United States Organ Procurement and Transplantation Network (2003), *Annual Report*, Table 1.1, Table 1.11, and Table 1.4. US Transplant Website: <http://www.ustransplant.org/>.

plant operations were performed (a 7 per cent increase) compared with a waiting list of 15,548 (up 10 per cent) (calculated from Eurotransplant Statistics, 2003).

In short, demand easily outstripped supply in many countries during this period. The result was an increasingly bullish market for HBPs as the twenty-first century began. The emergence, however, of an international market for HBPs cannot be separated from broader trends. Indeed, the HBP trade is notable precisely because of its generality to recent processes of globalization.

THE GLOBAL CONTEXT

The internationalization of market capitalism has been going on for hundreds of years (Panitch & Leys, 2003). But capitalism is also dynamic, and, by the mid-1970s, signs were apparent the "world system" was once again undergoing fundamental changes (Wallerstein, 1979). In the developed capitalist countries, these

NOT FOR SALE

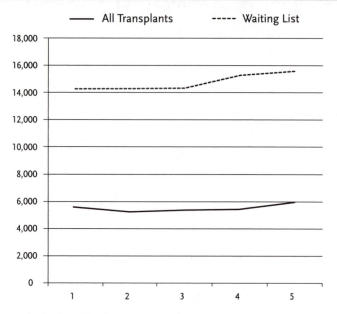

| FIGURE 6.2 | Total Transplant Recipients and Total Waiting List Patients for the Netherlands, Austria, Germany, Belgium, Luxemburg, and Slovenia, 1993–2002 |

——— All Transplants   - - - - - Waiting List

Source: Data for the graph taken from Eurotransplant Statistics by country, 1999 to 2003. Eurotransplant Website: <http://www.transplant.org/>.

signs included a growing crisis of capital accumulation and of state legitimacy, as the Fordist compromises that had underpinned the post-war welfare state gave way to renewed conflict between labour and capital. Likewise, the formerly peripheral or semi-peripheral regions of the world also experienced a series of changes, including rapid urbanization; intensified industrialization, proletarianization, and feminization; mounting external debt; and growing social and political unrest (Mittelman, 1996; Panitch & Leys, 2003).

The summary term frequently used to describe the changes is "globalization." What is globalization? The term is open to considerable debate. For one thing, it is not of one piece; rather, it is more accurate to speak of a series of "globalizations," interrelated and overlapping, but also sometimes contradictory and often opposed. Moreover, it manifests itself in several spheres, economic, political, cultural, and ideological.

Economically, globalization involves the establishment of a complex series of world-wide market exchanges in labour, trade, technology, and capital between countries possessing different economic, military, and political powers. More than past eras of capitalist expansion, it also involves a substantial reorganization of production over space (Mittelman, 1996; Lairson & Skidmore, 2003; Panitch & Leys, 2003).

Politically, globalization manifests itself in increased interconnectedness and interdependence, though not necessarily unification (Boyer & Drache, 1996), as attested to since the end of the Cold War by a series of regional wars, not to mention the so-called "War on Terrorism." While states remain powerful actors, the politics of globalization can also be seen in changing state roles, powers, and functions, underpinned by new regimes of moral regulation and accumulation (Aglietta, 1987).

Globalization, however, is not merely political or economic; neither is it simply geographic or social. It is also cultural and ideological, marked by the entry of primarily neoliberal (capitalist) values into previously unpenetrated cultural corners and ideological spaces (Mittelman, 1996; Boyer & Drache, 1996; Robbins, 2005). As such, globalization's neoliberal bias supports the transformation and extension throughout the world of *specifically capitalist exchange relationships*. It replicates a series of traditional unequal relationships between developed and developing countries, and between classes, genders, etc. across and within the same countries, while also creating new avenues for exploitation and control.

Moreover, globalization also fosters a form of particularly capitalist alienation. Labour itself becomes an object; likewise, the objects produced no longer appear in their human, relational form. Rather, in Marxist terms, they are "fetishized"; that is, they become viewed as capital or products of capital, thus obscuring and mystifying the actual human process of their creation, procurement, or exploitation (McNally, 1981; Robbins, 2005, p. 44).

In capitalism, all objects lose distinction. They stand apart merely on the basis of their relative equivalence, each with a price, or rather an exchange value. Thus, wombs are rented; sperm is sold; and, finally, human organs, "harvested."

TECHNIQUE AND TECHNOLOGY IN THE HBP BUSINESS

Clearly, human organs have a use value. It was only recently, however, in the context of globalization, that HBPs acquired an exchange value. A series of technological advancements contributed to this development.

Although experiments in human organ transplants date to early in the last century, as recently as the 1950s few physicians believed in their practicality. Experiments at Harvard University, followed by the first successful human kidney transplant at Boston in 1954, between identical twins, furthered the possibility, but three prime technical problems remained: removal, preservation (in conjunction with transportation), and anti-rejection following transplantation. Slowly, however, each of these technical problems was resolved.

Surgical techniques for removal were among the first problems overcome. Today, HBPs are procured from fully "living" donors, "brain dead" individuals (i.e., bodies only technically "alive"), and those recently deceased. Whereas organ extractions from living donors are legally restricted to kidneys, cadaveric (deceased) and near-cadaveric procurements are frequently more extensive, with little wastage. Today, corneas, hearts, lungs, kidneys, livers, pancreases, and (in rare cases) stomachs and intestines are often extracted from the dead.

The removal of body organs for future transplant requires a formalized and specialized technique, depending upon the organ being procured (Counce, Patrick, & Phillips, 1991, p. 210; Weber & Heinrichs, 1991, pp. 152–53). The need for precision is amplified by the fact that the specific organ must remain functional in order to retain its use (and hence) its exchange value.

Moreover, the technical phase of procurement does not end with extraction. The organ also must be preserved. For years, simple hypothermia was used to preserve human tissues. In the 1950s, this technique was expanded to whole organ storage, combined with flushing of the blood from the vascular system. More recently, flushing solutions have been developed, varying according to the organ in question. With extended preservation times, and with "the possible exception of the heart, cadaveric organs can now be stored long enough to permit relatively unhurried transportation" (Collins, 1991, p. 102). (See also McCullough, 1993, pp. 98–99.)

The latter is an important related issue. No market can exist unless a system is created to bring together supply with demand. In the case of transporting HBPs, two basic considerations are paramount: 1) time between organ extraction and transplantation and 2) temperature at which the organ is maintained during this time. Transportation and preservation procedures in the United States, and elsewhere in the developed world, have improved and today stipulate the size and material of containers, temperature ranges for shipping, and identification labels (Hoffmann & Belzer, 1991). Whereas chartered aircraft were used to ship kidneys, today regular flights on commercial airplanes are increasingly used. Finally, the melding of supply and demand is today facilitated by the use of information systems matching recipients to organs (Creger, Guindon, & Ferree, 1991).

Despite these technological developments, the problem of rejection remained especially problematic until recently. A partial solution was found in 1963 with the introduction of azathioprine and, later, prednisone. This new anti-rejection drug made it possible for the first time to conduct successfully both living-related and cadaveric renal (kidney) transplants. In the later 1960s, even more potent attempts at anti-rejection were made possible by the use of cyclophosphamide, antilymphocyte globulins, and radiation. Depending on the form of anti-rejection employed, and the condition of patients, survival rates ranged from 60 to 85 per cent.

Organ transplants entered popular consciousness in 1967 when the late Dr. Christian Bernard performed the world's first heart transplant. But for all the glamour thereafter attached to transplant procedures, human organ transplants continued to have a marginal and uncertain existence due to the threat of rejection. Indeed, after 1970, high failure rates resulted in a kind of moratorium over heart transplants in particular (Fox & Swazey, 1992, p. 7).[4] Then cyclosporine arrived on the scene.

CYCLOSPORINE AND THE CREATION OF DEMAND

As early as 1970, the Committee on Morals and Ethics of the Transplantation Society issued a statement affirming that "the sale of organs by donors living or dead [sic] is indefensible under any circumstances" (Daar, 1992, p. 2207). The concern expressed may have seemed unnecessary at the time; after all, organ transplants were still rare. Organ supply regularly outstripped demand, with supply being met almost entirely through "gifted" donations from relatives, where the risk of bodily rejection was reduced. In short, objective conditions were not "right" for a commercial market for organs.

All this began to change in the mid-1970s. Between 1975 and 1980, the number of transplants performed in the United States increased markedly. Demand rose even more sharply in the early 1980s with the introduction of cyclosporine (CyA), an anti-rejection medication.

Cyclosporine was first discovered in 1972 by a researcher with a large multinational, the Sandoz Pharmaceutical Corporation (Kahan, 1988). By 1978, it had moved from laboratory studies on animals to clinical trials on a small number of patients. Finally, the American Federal Drug Administration (FDA) in 1983 approved cyclosporine for general use. Despite some negative side-effects, it was quickly hailed as a "wonder drug," not only for its use in transplant surgery, but also for treating diabetes, as well as a host of dermatological, ophthalmological, rheumatological, nephrological, haematological, and neuromuscular syndromes. By 1989, cyclosporine had become the primary immunosuppressive drug used in organ transplant operations worldwide (Fox & Swazey, 1992, pp. 3–4).

Deliberate blood transfusions and improved surgical technique combined to enable the survival rate for not-related organ transplants to soar to over 80 per cent in heart, liver, and kidney transplants (Wolf, 1991). This improved survival rate had several important impacts upon supply and demand.

First, the decline in risk resulted in an increased demand for organs, especially kidneys. Kidneys are uniquely appropriate among body parts for sale as commodities because they can be removed from a living donor without the donor dying.[5] This possibility is important because kidneys from live donors are more valuable than those from cadavers. The "warranty" on live donor kidneys is 20 years versus 11 years for those taken from deceased donors (Finkel, 2001b). The gradual aging of the population after 1980 in many countries, including the United States and Canada, combined with rising incomes and a culturally induced desire to remain forever young, further stimulated demand for HBPs in the developed world.

Second, however, the increased demand in developed countries for HBPs (in general) was not off-set by similar increases in supply, either from living donors or through cadaverous organ donations (COD). While the supply of organs from living non-related donors increased in North America throughout the late 1980s and early 1990s, the number of COD actually declined, the result, in part, of increased safety measures that reduced the number of deaths through accidents of suitable (young, healthy) donors (Evans, 1992, p. 2152).

Third, the almost immediate increase in transplant survival rates resulted in the opening of several renal transplant centres, many in developing countries, notably India. These centres fulfilled the administrative function of acting as brokerage houses for facilitating the transaction between suppliers and buyers and the development of a process of unequal—and largely unregulated—exchanges in HBPs between developed and developing countries.

In short, the excess of demand over supply, particularly the failure of non-market solutions to meet this demand, provided the material basis for the emergence of a trade in HBPs (Evans, 1992; Turcotte, 1992; McCullough, 1993). As supplies from live donors and post mortem donors failed to meet demand, a market "niche" was created for purchased organs.

According to Finkel (2001b), the going price for a kidney transplant is between US$10,000 and US$30,000, though some buyers in Israel have been reported as willing to pay as much as US$145,000.[6] While little of this "transaction fee" goes to the donor—in India, perhaps US$500 to US$2,000, for Moldovans, perhaps US$2,700—such an amount may constitute an entire year's earnings for many people.

These journalistic accounts suggest that organ exchanges are occurring between wealthy recipients and poor donors. Table 6.1 provides statistical data broadly supportive of this belief. The table shows, for the year 2003, the top twenty cadaveric-donor countries and the top twenty living-donor countries (total and by donors per million population), and it includes GDP (in $US per capita).

Note that of the twenty top cadaveric-donor countries, only ten are repeated in the list of the top twenty living donor countries: the United States, Italy, Mexico, Brazil, Germany, France, the United Kingdom, Canada, the Netherlands, and Sweden. Of the ten countries that "drop out" on the donor list, six are European (Spain, Poland, Portugal, the Czech Republic, Austria, and Hungary), three are Latin and South American (Brazil, Cuba, and Chile), while the tenth is Australia. With the exception of Brazil and Cuba, all of the countries absent on the donor list have a per capita GDP of more than $US10,000. Moreover, the case of Cuba is made problematic by the fact that many necessities (e.g., health and education) are socialized. Thus, the actual standard of living for many Cubans is higher than per capita GDP figures suggest.

By comparison, the ten "new" countries on the living donor list include Pakistan, Iran, Japan, Egypt, Saudi Arabia, the Philippines, Jordan, Romania, and Switzerland. Excluding Switzerland and Japan, which changed its laws in 1997 allowing for living donor transplants to deal with a growing black market problem in organs (WuDunn, 1997), the remaining nine countries (five of them in the Middle East) have quite low per capita GDP. Only Saudi Arabia passes $US10,000 per capita GDP. The case of Iran is particularly striking. In 2003, Iran had 87 cadaveric donors (placing it twenty-fourth on an extended list), but, as Table 6.1 shows, it had 1413 living donors, fourth overall in that category.[7] At the very least, the data show a strong correlation between national income levels and the greater willingness of individuals within poor countries to make

TABLE 6.1	Top Twenty Cadaveric-donor and Living-donor Countries, 2003

(Total and Per Million Population) and Gross Domestic Product (Per Capita), 2003

Country	Cadaveric GDP/cap.	Donors	CD/mp	Country	Living GDP/cap.	Donors	LD/mp
USA	36,200	5921	20.4	USA	36,200	6188	21.3
Spain	18,000	1443	33.8	Brazil	6,500	1830	10.3
Italy	22,100	1402	18.5	Pakistan	2,000	1675	11.6
Mexico	9,100	1229	11.7	Iran	6,300	1413	20.8
Brazil	6,500	1179	6.7	Mexico	9,100	1132	10.8
Germany	23,400	1140	13.8	Japan	24,900	1075	8.5
France	24,400	1119	18.3	Germany	23,400	476	5.8
UK	22,800	644	10.9	Egypt	3,600	450	6.9
Poland	8,500	525	13.7	UK	22,800	442	7.5
Canada	24,800	428	13.5	Canada	24,800	438	13.8
Argentina	12,900	301	8.1	Italy	22,100	337	4.5
Netherlands	24,400	223	13.7	Saudi Arabia	10,500	228	10.9
Cuba	1,700	194	17.3	Netherlands	24,400	194	11.9
Portugal	15,800	190	19	Philippines	3,800	189	2.4
Czech Rep.	12,900	189	18.4	Jordan	3,500	183	36
Australia	23,200	179	9	France	24,400	178	3
Austria	25,000	176	22	South Africa	8,500	167	3.5
Hungary	11,200	161	16.1	Romania	5,900	156	7.4
Chile	10,100	136	9	Sweden	22,200	135	15.1
Sweden	22,200	114	12.7	Switzerland	28,600	106	14.7

Source: European Transplant Coordinators Organization (2004) and Time Inc. (2002).

living donations. Unfortunately, we do not know the individual donor's income, nor do we know the income or nationality of the recipients. Nonetheless, the data is suggestive.

The living donations are kidneys. The cost of other (cadaveric) HBPs varies, however. Cornea transplants cost roughly US$5,000, liver transplants about US$50,000—most of this being "pure" profit for the doctors and other middlemen insofar as the organs are often "sourced" from people, either dead or living, without recompense (NFBC, 1993; "Desperate Man," 1995b). With so much money at stake, it was not long before private European and American entrepreneurs emerged who viewed organ transplantations as a "potentially lucrative area to exploit" (Daar, 1992, p. 2207). (See also Sells, 1992.)

FROM SMALL ENTREPRENEURS TO BIG BUSINESS

Stories circulated by the late 1980s that human organs were being stolen from living subjects. At first dismissed in some quarters as merely "urban legends" (Brunvald, 1993), reports that children, the poor, the illiterate, and the mentally ill in some countries were being kidnapped and murdered for their organs gradually gained credibility. Central in confirming these reports was the National Film Board of Canada's "The Body Parts Business" (NFBC, 1993). The film provided exhaustive and convincing evidence of widespread corruption and human rights abuses related to a flourishing, illegal trade in human body parts, particularly in South and Central America and Russia. Since then, additional stories have arisen elsewhere. In 1999, for example, Egypt's prosecutor-general launched an investigation into the mysterious deaths over a three-month period of 25 children at a homeless shelter amidst allegations that their body parts had been sold to wealthy transplant patients in private hospitals ("Egypt Holds," 1999). As often is the case, the results of the investigation proved inconclusive.

But outright theft of body organs is not always necessary. The coercive effects of poverty and starvation have often led to people "choosing" to sell their kidneys. Such was the case in Iraq after the first Gulf War in 1990 and the UN sanctions that followed ("Desperate Iraqis," 1993; "Reporter Killed," 1996a) and in Eastern Europe following the collapse of communism (Finkel, 2001b).

People such as physician H. Barry Jacobs, founder and medical director of International Kidney Exchange, led the early commercialization of the HBP business. Jacobs proposed setting up a brokerage firm to purchase organs, particularly in the developing world, for sale and transplant in the United States (Fox & Swazey, 1992, p. 65; Childress, 1992). Another early entrepreneur was Rainer Rene Adelmann zu Addlemannsfelden, a German count and self-styled "specialist in legal loopholes," who similarly announced that he was setting up an "Organ Bureau" to broker in kidneys (Daar, 1992, p. 2207). This trade became almost immediately international in scope, directed by male entrepreneurs in developed countries with connections to similar "compradors" in developing countries whose role was to procure willing "sellers."

McCullough (1993, p. 90) tells the story, first published in the *Lancet* in 1989, of four healthy but poor Turks flown to Britain and paid to have their kidneys used in transplantation to wealthy patients at the Humana Hospital Wellington. He likewise tells of entrepreneurs in Bombay paying young peasants to allow surgeons to remove kidneys for transplants to wealthy Arab patients.[8]

The nascent HBP business had a seedy reputation. Sells (1992) contends that by 1985 there were regular reports of

> ... rampant commercialism, where profit, not patient care, was the primary motive, with surgeons and middle men taking huge cuts. Risks of disease transmission were ignored. Proper postoperative care was not provided.

Extortion and blackmail were reported, and the survival figures were terrible. (p. 2198)

Due to the logistics and costs of matching supply to demand, and the potential profits to be made, however, the trade in body parts quickly became more organized, and individual entrepreneurs gave way to corporations. By the early 1990s, extraction companies had been formed in Turkey, the former Yugoslavia, Russia, and several parts of the developing world for the export of organs to such places as Germany, Italy, France, and Cuba. In 1990 alone, for example, a Moscow "company" (Bio) exported to two German partners 18,718 thymus glands, 1,172 eyeballs, 3,187 testicles, and over 700 hearts, kidneys, and lungs (NFBC, 1993).

Few laws regulated the extraction and sale of organs. The unregulated market thrived especially in those areas—South and Central America, Russia, and much of the rest of Eastern Europe—where the state had either collapsed, often due to war, or was simply corrupt.[9] State corruption and laxity also meant few customs controls, allowing for easy transport of organs.

Gradually, however, the HBP business attracted a growing number of entrepreneurs, doctors, and various "middle men" (NFBC, 1993; "Abominable Trade," 1995). Under their management, the HBP business became sanitized and objectified, as did the language used to describe the business, as can be seen in a recent business promotion (Business Communications Company, 2003):

> The rapidly growing tissue and organ transplantation market, which recently topped 1 million procedures in a year, worldwide, is on the cusp of even more dramatic changes. While some sectors, such as bone and tissue grafts, are on a trajectory of rapid growth, others, such as heart transplants, are poised for sharp decline.[10]

Nonetheless, the international trade in body parts retains much of its former seediness. In some cases, HBPs are only one commodity in an entrepreneur's "general store" that might include also small weapons, stolen property, drugs, or prostitutes. Body parts are merely a specialty item (Jimenez, 2002). There remain also significant problems with the market's functioning. In particular, sellers/donors and buyers/patients alike—desperate and easily victimized—often risk their health, while unscrupulous doctors and notorious middlemen make substantial profits.[11] The result has been calls from doctors and various professional associations for the state to play a greater role in regulating the HBP trade. Amidst these calls, a debate has ensued centring on ownership of the parts themselves.

HUMAN BODY PARTS AS PRIVATE PROPERTY

In the late 1980s, some medical ethicists and practitioners began arguing for regulated commercial markets as a means of dealing with the problems of under-supply and abuse. As stated by Eisendrath (1992), "When we need something scarce but don't know how to get it, we resort to a combination of markets and regulations. Markets get the goods moving; regulation guides them toward fairness and social priorities" (p. 2214).

Proponents for the use of commercial markets invoke two arguments familiar to nineteenth-century capitalism: first, libertarian arguments "in support of the use of incentives and markets"; and, second, utilitarian arguments (Blumstein, 1992, p. 2193; Eisendrath, 1992). The former argument is buttressed by claims that individuals have proprietary rights over their own bodies that enable them to decide whether to alienate, not merely their labour, but also their body, including its individual parts.[12] The latter argument is supported by claims that payments actually lead to increased donations, thereby eliminating both an imbalance between supply and demand and the negative consequences of an unregulated market. While both arguments relate to the case of living persons owning their own bodies, and provide no guidance in the case of cadavers who might be "owned" (for example) by next of kin, they nonetheless betray a specifically capitalist conception of the human body as "just" another commodity.[13]

To date, such arguments have not garnered widespread public or political support in most countries. In every country but Iran, the sale of human organs, whether from living donors or the dead, is *officially* outlawed. Moreover, the controversy has resulted in mobilizations within civil society against commodifying HBPs. Human Rights Watch has intensified its efforts to fight the HBP trade. In California, meanwhile, a group called Organ Watch has been created. Its co-founder, Nancy Scheper-Hughes, a professor of medical anthropology at the University of California at Berkeley is blunt:

> Doctors should not be involved in transactions that pit one social class against another—organ getters versus organ givers. Doctors should be protectors of the body, and perhaps we should look for better ways of helping the destitute than dismantling them. (quoted in Finkel, 2001b)

Nonetheless, neoliberal arguments have provided a rationale and a kind of moral justification for the wealthy to purchase human organs from people less well off. More broadly, the arguments are reflective of the neoliberal thrust of globalization with which states, in the past twenty years, beginning in the late 1980s, increasingly contended and—too often—collaborated.

STATES AND THE HBP BUSINESS

That the state should become involved in the HBP trade is not surprising. Controlling and regulating human bodies is a central and perhaps defining role of the modern state (Corrigan & Sayer, 1985). The precise *form* of state involvement, however, varies according to historical, political, and cultural circumstances. While often indirect and normative, control may also be direct, especially by authoritarian regimes.

Today, however, the excesses of authoritarian governments regarding the trade in human organs do not contribute to ideology or racial experimentation but rather to the pursuit of hard currency (McCullough, 1993, p. 91). The People's Republic of China provides a well-documented example of an authoritarian state that today markets body parts for cash.

Although the issue of HBP trade is international, in practice, the markets function regionally. For example, the majority of "purchased" transplants in the Middle East and Europe are conducted in Turkey, drawing upon the populations of Eastern Europe and the Middle East for supply while avoiding European laws preventing such practices.[14] China, meanwhile, conducts the majority of transplants for Asia and Pacific Rim countries, including "tourists" from Canada and the United States, using prisoners as its chief source of supply.

An FBI "sting operation" in February 1998 provided a rare glimpse into the HBP business in the People's Republic of China. Two Chinese nationals, one of them a state prosecutor from Hainan Island in China, were caught by an undercover agent in the United States offering to sell "made to order" body parts. The Chinese prosecutor's "sales brochure" was chilling. Lungs from non-smokers went for US$20,000; livers, US$25,000; kidneys, US$20,000; and corneas, US$5,000 a pair ("Shot to Order," 1998). As prosecutor, he was in a perfect situation to ensure delivery, even just-in-time delivery.

Though American officials later dropped charges in this case, it substantiated previous reports from Human Rights Watch-Asia concerning the People's Republic of China ("Organs Removed," 1994; "Half-dead," 2001; McCullough, 1993; Scheper-Hughes, 1998, 2000). According to these reports, hospitals and prospective recipients are notified prior to executions that a particular organ, usually a kidney, will be available. Prisoners' consent is rarely sought, or it is coerced in the last few hours before death. In some cases, kidneys are removed from prisoners the night before execution. In other cases, executions are deliberately botched in order to keep the host body alive longer. The manner in which the execution is conducted also depends upon the organ required. It is reported, for example, that if corneas are required, the prisoner will be shot in the heart; if kidneys are required, the rifle shot is to the base of the skull.

The government of the People's Republic takes about 2,000 organs from prisoners every year (Scheper-Hughes, 1998, 2000). Recipients are usually from the Chinese mainland, often apparently members of the government bureaucracy, but surgeries are also available to foreign citizens ("Organs Removed," 1994).

China's involvement in the HBP trade is singular. Most states, particularly in the developed world, have attempted to shape the market for HBPs through regulation. These regulations are not uniform, however. For example, states invoke different ways of defining death, pursuant to organ removal.

Nonetheless, many states have moved to control, if not to ban outright, the sale of organs. United States' law makes it illegal to purchase organs, the National Organ Transplant Act (NOTA) of 1984 specifically making it illegal "for any person to knowingly acquire, receive, or otherwise transfer any human organ for valuable consideration for use in human transplantation if the transfer affects interstate commerce" (quoted in Childress, 1992, p. 2143). Most Western European countries have adopted similar laws regulating the definition of consent and the sale and purchase of organs (Sells, 1992; Land & Cohen, 1992). Even India, long "the world's largest reservoir of live kidney donors," has been pressured to put into effect a national statute outlawing the sale of human organs ("Abominable Trade," 1995; Sells, 1992), though one may ask to what degree this law is enforced.[15]

Finally, however, there is the question of whether regulations alone will address the real issues of exploitation and criminality underlying much of the HBP trade. The case of Japan is instructive. For a long time, Japan had laws prohibiting live donations. But the chief result of these laws was the stimulation of organ markets in countries that are on Japan's periphery (McCullough, 1993, pp. 88–90; WuDunn, 1997). As mentioned earlier, in 1997 Japan passed laws allowing for, but also regulating, surgical transplants.

This is perhaps the central lesson to be learned from the HBP trade: the resiliency of capitalism in making a profit under regimes of either regulation or deregulation. In this regard, the HBP business also can be viewed as reflecting broader realities of globalization today.

CONCLUSION

Neoliberal globalization has unleashed new forces of exploitation and liberation, of division and interconnectedness, of ethical absence and moral assertion. Its negative aspects are readily apparent, from brothels, to the drug trade, to sweatshops. This paper has examined a particularly unexamined aspect of globalization: the emergence of the global trade in HBPs for transplantation.

Until the early 1980s, organ transplantation remained a minor and uncertain medical procedure. A series of technological innovations changed this, however. Quickly, the supply of organs provided by donations alone began falling short of demand. A few individuals seized this opportunity to create a commercial market for organs, with organs obtained from "donors" in the developing world.

In the early stages, these entrepreneurs were small operators, frequently with connections to state facilities (morgues, mental hospitals) that allowed easily for organ procurement, either through physical coercion of the living or cannibalization of the dead. While these market characteristics still hold in many regions, many small operators have since been replaced by larger corporate or even state enterprises. Additionally, the unsavouriness of physical coercion has been "laundered" through liberal notions of property rights that defend economic coercion as legitimate. The result is that the wealthy today need not steal the body parts of the poor and desperate: They can simply buy them—all within contract law.

In a broader sense, the HBP trade holds a mirror to other more or less "acceptable" forms of unequal exchange between developed and developing regions, and between classes, ethnicities, genders, and other groupings within and across these same regions. Indeed, discussions of the global trade in HBPs cannot be separated from wider discussions of inequalities of power and wealth and the ideological constructs that support them. Marx thought the poor and the working classes had nothing to sell but their labour. It seems he was wrong.

What is the likely future of the HBP business? Despite the well-intentioned efforts of many to roll back the market for HBPs, in the short term, this seems unlikely. The demand for transplant organs continues to outstrip supply, and will likely widen with further technological advances. Governments facing rising medical expenses are also pushing demands for organ transplants. Far from being replaced by a sudden onslaught of altruistic donations, a more realistic challenge to the HBP industry comes from further medical and technological changes that might allow for either synthetic or animal-based transplant substitutes. But these alternatives remain some years off and fraught with uncertainty and risks. In the short term, the global trade in HBPs will likely continue to grow, pushing ever further the frontiers of commodification.

In this context, there is the need for a concerted effort by governments and non-governmental agencies to prohibit the sale of transplant organs. Similar campaigns were launched during the nineteenth century to end slavery and in the twentieth century to prohibit the use of land mines. Why not also the sale of human body parts?

Notes

1. This chapter updates and expands my article "Globalization and the trade in human body parts," published in the *Canadian Review of Sociology and Anthropology*, 1999, Vol. 26, No. 1, pp. 21–36. I want to thank Gordon Laxer for his useful comments on an earlier draft of this revised article.

2. An HBP is defined as "an organ, tissue, eye, artery, blood, fluid, or other portion of human body" (Childress, 1992, p. 2145), including foetal matter, zygotes, embryos and foetuses (Canada Royal Commission on Reproductive Technologies, 1993, p. 19).

3. There is also a market for body parts for purposes other than transplantation, for example, scientific research. In the interests of brevity, however, this discussion is restricted to surgical transplants.

4. Twenty-three heart transplants were conducted in the United States in 1968. Not until 1977, however, was this number surpassed (UNOS, 1996b).

5. Technically, eyes also can be removed, leaving the "donor" alive (if dismembered). The NFBC (1993) documentary told the chilling story of a young, mentally handicapped Argentine male whose corneas were removed with a kitchen spoon, and his body discarded in a sewer. Remarkably, the young man lived to tell his tale.

6. In 1994, a British Columbian realtor flew to India to buy a kidney. He declared his total expenses as $60,000 (CD), of which about $30,000 went for the kidney and transplant. Of the latter, perhaps $2,000 went to the donor, a seventeen year-old construction worker. According to the BC transplant society, Kinnee was not alone in his search. At least three other BC residents had travelled to India or China during the previous six months ("Organ Thugs," 1995a).

7. Altogether, the data set from which the table is taken covers 61 countries.

8. Dr. Colabawalla (1995), a noted Indian doctor, has told me similar tales of "donors" being flown from India to Europe.

9. In October 1996, Xavier Gautier, a reporter with *Le Figaro*, was found hanging on the Spanish island of Minorca. While local officials termed it a suicide, his family believed otherwise and claimed Gautier was investigating alleged trafficking in human body parts during the war in Bosnia. Allegedly, prisoners were specially selected and executed, their body parts being sold on the world market in order to purchase weapons. Gautier's family later handed over an eight-page list of names of people alleged to be connected with the illegal activity (Blockade Creates, 1996b). I do not know if the authorities followed up on this information.

10. A *Time* magazine article in 1996 listed 18 potentially transplantable human parts under a heading redolent with the language of modern industrial production: "A host of transplant possibilities, *if the parts are in stock*" ("Organ Transplants," 1996, p. 58). (The italics are mine.) Mocking this use of language, Kimbrell's (1993) scathing denunciation of the HBP trade is titled "The Human Body Shop."

11. The chief organ broker in Istanbul is referred to locally as "Dr. Vulture."

12. "Rationally, the analyst may note that the sellers deem themselves better off, do not consider the risk to be excessive, and deem organ donation to be an avenue of opportunity" (Blumstein, 1992, p. 2195).

13. In 1999, the family members of a deceased in England garnered public attention when they demanded that his organs be transplanted only to a white person.

14. Until the 2003 invasion, Iraq was another major Middle Eastern site for organ transplants.

15. India's Bill 1) regularizes genetically related live-donor transplantations, 2) makes trade and commerce in human organs illegal and punishable by law, 3) allows unrelated live-donor transplants only under very stringent circumstances as judged by an Authorization Committee set up by the government, and 4) recognizes brain-stem death as the sole means of establishing death (Colabawalla, 1995).

CHAPTER SEVEN

A New Gender (Dis)order?— Neoliberal Restructuring in Australia

RAY BROOMHILL & RHONDA SHARP

The concepts of commodification and decommodification have been widely used within political economy and social analysis to understand historical change and the different policy patterns that have emerged within countries. However, this conceptual framework has often lacked a gender perspective that enables an understanding of the different experiences of women and men as well as of different classes of men and women. In this chapter, we analyse how neoliberal restructuring, by producing changes to the complex processes of commodification and decommodification that emerged in post-war capitalist societies, has also produced significant changes in pre-existing gender arrangements within these societies. We analyse these processes through the development of a feminist regulation framework that is applied to an analysis of recent changes to the Australian gender order resulting from neoliberal restructuring. Our rationale for this approach is that analyses of neoliberal restructuring need to incorporate understandings of its social as well as its economic and political dimensions. Specifically, we need to better understand how restructuring has affected the various patterns, formal and informal, of social and cultural arrangements that contribute to social coherence and change in different societies. As Karl Polanyi observed in his classic 1944 study, capitalism is continually engaged in an internal struggle between the demands of capital accumulation and the need for social sustainability and reproduction (Polanyi, 1957). This struggle is played out in changes to the historical balance between commodification and decommodification.

One of the many significant transformations that capitalism is undergoing with the restructuring of the post-war era is the breakdown of the post-World War II male breadwinner gender order and the emergence of a new gender (dis)order. The term "gender order" is used to describe the combined set of institutional and informal arrangements that, together, define gender roles and relations in a society (Connell, 1987). In part, a "male breadwinner" gender order, which took different forms nationally, was embedded in the major institutions of many post-war capitalist societies, especially the institutions of the welfare state, education systems, and the processes of labour market and employment regulation. The post-war gender order also comprised more informal forms of social regulation, including specific gender norms, values, social patterns, and cultural behaviours. Together, these formal and informal processes of social regulation were crucial in defining and securing patterns of both social reproduction and capital accumulation across many countries that seemed unusually stable during the post-war era. However, the multi-faceted arrangements that comprised the various forms of the gender order in different capitalist societies during the long boom are now under challenge. In the current processes of neoliberal restructuring, patterns of both capital accumulation and social reproduction are undergoing profound changes.

GENDER AND COMMODIFICATION/DECOMMODIFICATION

Debates about the notions of commodification and decommodification have significant implications for our understanding of the changes currently affecting gender relations. Some of these implications have been developed in feminist critiques. However, mainstream debates generally have not adequately incorporated a gender perspective, and much of this literature has failed to recognize fully the different experiences of women and men in the context of neoliberal global restructuring. In his classic formulation of the theory of decommodification, Esping-Andersen (1990) portrayed the achievement of social rights that decommodify labour, such as unemployment benefits and pensions, as providing potential for liberating the working class from the discipline of the capitalist market. When viewed through this lens, the struggle by workers for decommodification measures that guarantee a standard of living relatively independent of market participation is of unambiguous benefit to all in the working class.

Feminist researchers have rejected Esping-Andersen's argument that the primary struggle of workers has been to achieve "decommodification" as being somewhat "myopic" and gender blind (Knijn & Ostner, 2002, p. 147). Struggles that provided male workers with greater bargaining power in the workplace often reinforced women's relegation to a secondary labour market role or even their exclusion from the labour market. Because his analysis effectively ignores the differences in the position of women and men in the labour market, it is not sensitive to the different gender impacts of state welfare policies that decommodify labour. In fact, such "decommodification" policies primarily benefit those whose labour has already been commodified. Similarly, because of its gender blindness in relation to women's and men's respective roles in unpaid labour within the household, the analysis fails to observe that social welfare policies had reinforced women's subordination in the household and maintained the male breadwinner model. While Esping-Andersen's more recent work (Esping-Andersen & Gaillie, 2002) has acknowledged that decommodification processes will not benefit women whose labour has not first been fully commodified, his analysis has changed little to incorporate the implications of this conclusion (Knijin & Ostner, 2002, p. 146). As a result, Esping-Andersen's analysis remains inadequate in dealing either with the role of gender or the role of the state in relation to the processes of commodification and decommodification.

In spite of these reservations, feminist critics of Esping-Andersen have nevertheless sought to engender his conceptual apparatus. This attempt has led to the development of an extensive literature on commodification/decommodification processes that seeks to identify and classify, along gender lines, the different forms of welfare state regime that have emerged within Western capitalism (Knijn & Ostner, 2002; Shaver, 2002; Orloff, 1993; Ungerson, 1997). This literature has added a much needed dimension to the mainstream accounts of welfare regimes by showing that the form the welfare state took in each country was profoundly influenced by the broader patterns of gender relations that existed in each society (Crompton, 1999; O'Reilly & Spee, 1998; Pfau-Effinger, 1998). Rather than focusing narrowly on the nature of welfare states, these researchers have examined broader structures and patterns of gender relations within the whole society.

However, the existing feminist political economy literature on national welfare regimes is underdeveloped in two important areas. One is the relative absence of any theorization of historical change and transformation within different national patterns of commodification/decommodification, especially those currently occurring as a result of neoliberal restructuring. While, historically, capitalism has been engaged in the transformation of labour into a marketable commodity, Polanyi (1953) emphasized that the drive towards the total commodification of society is fundamentally incompatible with capital's longer-term need to maintain a social structure that can ensure social reproduction. Typically, in times of strong economic growth and full employment, the bargaining power of labour increases, and the raw impact of the market is somewhat modified through the regulatory role of the state in decommodifying aspects of the market's activities. In times of crisis and restructuring, capital and the state invariably become more directly focused on the need to maintain or restore capital accumulation and hence far less willing to support social reproduction through policies and activities that increase decommodification. A second aspect of feminist political economy research that requires further development is the identification and analysis of the role of class and other socio-economic differences within societies. What are the implications for national gender arrangements of the increasingly uneven impact of restructuring on men and women according to their location, race, class, age, and other socio-economic variables? There has not been sufficient recognition of the complexity and diversity existing within national gender orders.

A regulation approach provides a framework that is capable of explaining the historical changes that occur in the gender order as well as analysing class and other complexities that exist in the patterns of gender relations within each society. It can therefore assist in the development of a more sophisticated strategy to promote progressive change.

130

A FEMINIST REGULATION APPROACH

The "regulation approach" is a research agenda and a methodology rather than a unified theory. It developed among left-leaning French social science academics in the mid-1970s, providing an influential new analytical methodology for mapping patterns of capitalist development (Aglietta, 1987; Leborgne & Lipietz, 1988). The regulation approach emphasizes the complex nature of the relationship between capital accumulation and capitalism's social, political, and cultural context, recognizing that, in order to achieve growth and stable capital accumulation, capitalism needs to provide for social reproduction (Jessop, 1994; Peck & Tickell, 1995). As such, this methodological approach provides a framework for analysing the role of gender within the broader context of capitalist restructuring. Regulationists have focused on identifying the key role of changes to the mode of social regulation in capitalist crises and restructuring. The form of any regulatory regime is not predetermined or predictable but is arrived at through political struggles, negotiations, and compromises. Ultimately, as capital accumulation falters and signs of economic crisis re-emerge, the institutional and informal regulatory framework also begins to fracture and come unstuck. In fact, crises in the existing regulatory arrangements may themselves contribute to, and accelerate, the next crisis of capital accumulation and period of restructuring. Therefore, it is not inevitable that there will be a stable and sustainable economic, political, and social framework at any particular stage in the cycles of capitalist accumulation.

However, more informal forms of regulation, including cultural and social processes, are also important in influencing the different patterns of social regulation and in providing social coherence. These can be described as constituting a "mode of social regulation." For example, the post-war period saw the emergence of patterns of nationally specific cultural norms and values that included a culture of mass consumerism, of state welfarism, and of variations on a "male breadwinner/female homemaker model" of the nuclear family. These cultural values played an important role in structuring social reproduction. Of course, even in periods of social stability, dominant value systems are usually far from hegemonic and are frequently contested by competing sets of values. They are also place-specific, reflecting the existing culture of different countries and regions as well as the social processes at work in each.

The regulation framework therefore provides a useful base for extending existing feminist political economy analyses of national welfare regimes because it adds both an historical and a class dimension to that analysis. A further reason that the regulation approach is a particularly useful starting point is that its emphasis on seeing the economy as deeply embedded in society creates a space for a feminist analysis of gender to be integrated into its broader analysis of the neoliberal global restructuring process. However, the framework clearly needs to be extended to bring into view more comprehensively the role of gender relations as a key element of social regulation. While some regulationists have recognized the need to give more attention to the role of gender in the regulatory framework (Low, 1995,

p. 213; Peck & Tickell, 1994), and a few have actually sought to incorporate gender in their studies (McDowell, 1991; Bakshi & Goodwin, 1995), in practice, most have ignored the significance of gender relations in the restructuring process. We argue, however, that, with the incorporation of a more gender-aware perspective, a feminist regulation approach can enable a better understanding of the relationship between global restructuring and gender in several key ways. First, it opens up a space for seeing gender as playing a central, rather than a peripheral, role in global restructuring. Second, it permits the inclusion of both the productive and reproductive (paid and unpaid) spheres of the economy and society in the analysis. Finally, with its emphasis on the dialectical nature of the relationship between capital accumulation and capitalism's cultural, social, and political context, it draws out linkages between the different levels of restructuring—in the market, the state, and the household spheres.

AUSTRALIA'S POST-WORLD WAR II GENDER ORDER

During the post-war era in Australia from the late 1940s to the mid-1970s, growth and stability were underpinned by gender structures and arrangements that were based upon a strong version of the "male breadwinner" model. While neither universal nor static, the norms, behaviours, privileges, and pressures of male breadwinning gained ascendency in Australia because, amongst other factors, it became feasible in the post-war period of full employment for almost all men to fulfil the role of breadwinner (Murphy, 2003, p. 103; Broomhill & Sharp, 2004). The dominant pattern within the gender order comprised strictly gendered divisions of labour in the labour market and in the household.

Australian governments played an important role in supporting the male breadwinner model in the Keynesian post-war period. While a Labor government held office during World War II and in the immediate post-war period, Australia was governed from 1949–72 by a Liberal/Country Party coalition that, though conservative in social policy areas, implemented liberal Keynesian economic policies. In both economic and social policy realms, post-war governments significantly influenced the position of men and women and the gender relationships that existed between them. A range of social provisions existed that cushioned white male workers to some extent from the disciplines of the market through the decommodification of their labour. Esping-Andersen himself saw the Australian welfare state as weak in its level of decommodification provisioning, but others have strongly challenged that view on the basis of the key role of the centralized industrial relations system in decommodifying market processes through guaranteeing minimum conditions of work and pay for workers (Castles, 1985).

Nevertheless, these decommodification provisions overwhelmingly protected male workers. In fact, the Australian welfare system has been characterized as the "wage-earners' welfare state" (Castles, 1989; Smyth, 1998, p. 82). The male breadwinner model itself was entrenched in "all aspects of public policy, social

and political culture" (Cass, 1998, p. 42). Policies including taxation, employment, wage fixation, and social security reflected assumptions about the predominance of the male breadwinner. Of particular importance in the Australian social
regulatory framework was the evolution of a centralized industrial relations system built around the gendered concept of a minimum family wage for male workers and reduced wages for women. While, at one level, the family wage might be
seen as a decommodifying influence for women by protecting married women
from having to seek paid work in the open market, in practice, it played a critical
role in blocking women's options in paid employment. The non-commodification
of women's labour was also reinforced by the constraint on the level of state intervention in maternity, parental leave, and childcare policies (Cass, 1998, p. 42).
However, while the male wage earners' welfare state acted primarily to decommodify and protect men's labour market position, the framework of wage earner
welfare state rights did also provide some degree of protection for those women
who entered the labour market. For example, in 1942, decommodified rights were
established for women who had lost their male breadwinner through the introduction of widowed, divorced, and deserted wives' pensions.

Australia's gender culture until the 1960s has been described as "remarkably
homogenous" (Probert, 2002, p. 10). In a study based upon interviews with about
85 men and women who had been young parents in the 1950s, Probert (2002)
found a coherent pattern of beliefs about the role of men as "breadwinners" and
women as "mothers and homemakers." As we have seen, these cultural norms
were reinforced during the post-war period in Australia by state policies and institutions that were imbued with similar values. Nevertheless, the shape of the
Australian post-war gender order was far from static. Although remaining fundamentally based upon a nuclear family structure and a male breadwinner norm, it
experienced significant changes during the 1950s and 1960s.

Throughout this period, women were increasingly drawn into the labour market. This was mainly due to the increasing demand for labour resulting from the
extended economic growth that accompanied post-war capitalist development in
Australia. However, changing child-bearing trends and changing attitudes to
women's role in society were also important. Women's increasing labour market
participation was also due, in part, to the increasing role of the state in providing
services that were previously women's family responsibilities. The steady growth
of the community services area of the economy, largely driven by the public sector,
provided an enormous area of growth in women's employment. As a result, the
state as the largest single employer in a tight labour market served to undermine its
role in upholding the traditional male breadwinner model, reflecting the conflicts
and a lack of coherency within the state in relation to women (Nolan, 2003).
Governments also provided a growing welfare state structure that underpinned
individual and family welfare and social reproduction where the family failed or
couldn't cope. This was especially so during the decade of the 1970s when Labor
governments, at the federal and state levels, became increasingly active in support
of welfare and social equity through involvement in a wide range of social policy

areas—including the expansion of housing, health, and education. During the 1970s, the Australian women's movement also played a crucial role in changing attitudes and government policies towards women's role in the labour market.

However, women's increased participation in the labour market was not on equal terms with men's. By and large, women entered into a peripheral labour market, one that was highly segmented by gender. The range and types of employment created ensured the maintenance of a fairly rigid sexual division of the labour market. Furthermore, the dominant gender culture ensured that women also remained primarily responsible for social reproduction within the home and the society. In spite of women's increasing participation in paid work, the values of the male breadwinner model were deeply embedded in dominant Australian social and cultural norms throughout the post-war period, and women remained primarily responsible for domestic labour and caring work (Cass, 1998, p. 42). Thus post-war capital accumulation and social reproduction were both constructed upon a quite unequal division of labour—in the labour market and in the household.

Nevertheless, the changes that occurred to women's role and to gender relations during the first three post-war decades had a profound effect on the gender order and, ultimately, on the mode of social regulation itself. The male breadwinner model was rapidly transformed by the increasing participation of women in the paid labour market, by the increasing financial independence of women (from men at least if not from the state) through the introduction of the welfare system, and by the transforming influence of the women's movement on gender attitudes and culture.

RESTRUCTURING THE AUSTRALIAN GENDER ORDER IN THE 1980s AND 1990s

With the onset of economic crisis in the 1970s and the subsequent period of economic, political, and social restructuring that followed in the next two decades, the Australian post-war gender order has come under even greater pressure. This pressure has taken two forms in particular, each of which raises important questions for understanding the restructuring process itself. First, further significant changes occurred in the position of women and men in the labour market. This poses an important question: to what extent have these changes affected the commodification of women's and men's labour? Conversely, to what extent have decommodifying processes, which ameliorate the raw impact of the labour market, increased or decreased in the context of neoliberal restructuring? Second, the old "father and Ford" social compact that existed between the market, the Keynesian welfare state, and the household has broken down, at least partially, as a result of the transformation of institutional and informal arrangements for care work and social reproduction (McDowell, 1991). A number of commentators referring to the experiences of various countries have noted that the neoliberal agenda has become even more radical by seeking to extend commodification to all aspects of human existence (Kofman & Youngs, 2003; Leys, 2003; Probert, 2002; Overbeek, 2002; Teeple, 1995; Acker, 1999). Ironically, however, while neoliberal policies have contributed to the commodification of many reproductive activities, many caring activities have also been reassigned to the realm of the family and household—a phenomenon that might be described as "re-familialization." The result is a quite contradictory dual movement towards the increased marketization or commodification of some social reproductive activities, on the one hand, and the re-familialization of others.

Against this broad backdrop, our concern here is to examine whether the male breadwinner/female carer model of gender relations within Australian households has undergone transformation over the past two decades and the extent to which a new "gender order" is emerging. While restructuring has undoubtedly had a profound effect on the labour market experiences of both men and women, its gendered impact on the Australian labour market has been complex and often misinterpreted. Recently, the Australian Bureau of Statistics (ABS) argued that, as a consequence of the dramatically higher labour force participation of women aged 24–54 years, there has been the "pervasive abandonment" of the traditional cultural norm that viewed a man's role primarily as "breadwinner" and a woman's as "home-maker" (ABS, 2000, p. 8). Women's labour market participation has certainly steadily increased while men's has declined, but the overall picture is more complex than that portrayed by the ABS. At the aggregate level, women's labour market participation rate in Australia increased significantly between 1966 and 2005—from 36 per cent to 54 per cent (ABS, 2003–2005b; ABS, 1986). By 2005, women represented 45 per cent of the total Australian workforce compared to 37 per cent in 1981 and 31 per cent in 1966. The labour market experiences of Australian men have also undergone fundamental changes under the impact of restructuring. The male labour market participation rate has declined significantly from 84 per cent to 71 per cent in the period 1966–2005. Most significantly, however, male full-time employment has dropped dramatically over the period 1976–2005 from 75 per cent to 55 per cent of the adult (aged over 15 years) male population. However, aggregate figures showing women's ever-increasing and men's ever-decreasing participation in the labour market disguise other important trends. Significantly, the percentage of adult women in full-time employment has actually remained steady over the period 1966–2005, with virtually no growth over that time in the percentage of women occupying full-time jobs (Broomhill & Sharp, 2004). Therefore, while Australian women's labour continues to be increasingly commodified, the so-called "feminization of work" is almost totally based upon increasing levels of insecure and part-time employment.

It is important to recognize also that for both women and men inequalities within the labour market have increased dramatically. The labour market, which formerly provided mostly permanent forms of employment, has increasingly been characterized by more precarious forms of work—including casual and part-time jobs. A variety of studies have documented that income inequalities substantially increased during the 1980s and 1990s as a result of labour market changes (e.g.,

Harding, 1997; Pappas, 2001). Rates of unemployment and underemployment rose well above the low levels experienced during the early post-war period. At the same time, hours of work and work intensity for those in employment increased. The overall impact of restructuring on the Australian labour market during the 1990s has been summarized as creating a polarization of households into work rich and work poor—with many households having access to several jobs and working long hours in total and an increasing number of others having little or no work (Borland, Gregory & Sheedan, 2001, p. 4).

The most important factor influencing the labour market experience of Australian women and men during economic restructuring was their class and socio-economic position. For the bottom 70 per cent of neighbourhoods (categorized by socio-economic status), average household incomes fell in absolute terms between 1976 and 1991. Household incomes in high-status neighbourhoods, however, increased markedly. The income gap between the top and bottom 5 per cent of neighbourhoods increased by 92 per cent (Gregory & Hunter, 1995, p. 5). While the labour market position of men has been strongly influenced by their class position, inequalities between the experiences of those from different socio-economic localities have been most extreme in the case of women. The pattern of employment change for women living in high-status socio-economic neighbourhoods was radically different from that of women in low-status socio-economic neighbourhoods. In fact, all the growth in Australian female labour force participation that occurred between 1976 and 1991 was experienced by women who resided in the top 50 per cent of neighbourhoods. Therefore, while many women from high-status neighbourhoods increased their labour market participation as a result of opportunities created by restructuring, working-class women's opportunities to gain paid work drastically shrank.

Importantly, these very different experiences of labour market restructuring had profoundly different consequences for gender arrangements in different types of socio-economic households. Women provided an increasingly important component of household income in working-class areas, not because their incomes were actually increasing but rather because working-class men's employment levels and incomes dropped so dramatically. While the male breadwinner model was clearly under threat in these households, it does not appear that women's employment opportunities provided an effective alternative model. In more affluent areas, increases in men's earnings only contributed marginally to the significant increase in household incomes that occurred, while the increased earnings of women in this socio-economic group contributed substantially to household incomes (Gregory & Hunter, 1995, p. 11). In these areas, women's economic role appears to have strengthened even though men's work role does not appear to have decreased in importance. There is evidence, therefore, of a shift towards a more symmetrical breadwinner model amongst some more affluent Australian households.

In summary, the labour market experience of women and men in a restructuring Australian economy is one of significant change, with an uneven distribution of the gains and losses. There does seem to be evidence of a decline in the dominance of the male breadwinner model within the structures of the labour market. The number of men in full-time employment has declined substantially while the number of women in part-time employment has risen. On the other hand, in spite of the increasing commodification of women's labour, there seems little evidence that a new gender order is emerging based upon increased equality for women in the labour market. While more women have undoubtedly gained part-time employment opportunities, an assessment of these gains needs to take into account the problems associated with part-time work. Significant also is the impact of restructuring on women's wages, working conditions, and their unpaid workload. It appears, on the whole, that restructuring and the so-called feminization of the labour market has been a liberating experience for only those women who have gained access to the core labour market and who have also been able to benefit from changes in the household sphere. Mostly, these are women from already privileged households. Although continuing to occupy relatively segmented positions in the labour market, men and women appear to be experiencing more similarity in working conditions. This does not so much reflect any significant improvement in women's position but rather perhaps a "harmonizing down" process whereby the decline in men's overall position has made many men's jobs more like women's jobs, with both incorporating less protection from decommodifying influences.

However, the impact of restructuring on the Australian gender order over recent decades extended well beyond changes to the levels of male and female participation in the labour market. Because business interests in the now dominant finance and service sectors were so intently focused upon achieving their own short-term economic goals, they largely discarded previous concerns for the maintenance of a stable workforce and the need to socially reproduce that labour force. On the contrary, capital became far more interested in enforcing greater labour market discipline within the economy, in particular by removing safety net and welfare provisions that were so important in underpinning the increasing bargaining power of workers, trade unions, and other groups (including women) during the post-war boom. Hence, the state also greatly reduced its traditional support for social welfare and reproduction resulting in the re-familialization of many of the tasks previously performed in the state sector. Unfortunately, restructuring simultaneously also brought changes to the nature and conditions of work for both women and men in Australia, changes that have severely affected the capacity of households to undertake the social reproduction and care work that has been re-familialized. During the 1980s and 1990s, there occurred an enormous increase in persons holding multiple jobs—an increase of 66 per cent over that period. An Australian Bureau of Statistics study showed that over half of multiple job holders in 2000 were women, and over 40 per cent of multiple job holders worked full-time in one of their jobs (ABS, 2000, p. 116). Invariably, the increased stress resulting from increasing hours of work was felt mainly by women as a result of their double workload (Pocock, 2003; Wooden, 2001, p. 42; Broomhill & Sharp, 1999).

The different and unequal labour market outcomes for men and women under restructuring also need to be understood in the broader context of changes occurring within the organization of family life and households. Gender relations within households comprise an important component of the mode of social regulation. Gender relations socially structure the work of households and the relationships between households and the formal economy. The "private" realm of the family and household is taken as a given and not subjected to scrutiny by conventional economic analyses of restructuring and by policymakers. The organization of the family and households has, amongst other things, a marked impact on the capacities of men and women to participate in paid work (Pocock, 2003). Being disproportionately responsible for the unpaid activities of households, women enter the labour market with "domestic baggage," with the result that the "labour market is no level playing field" (Humphries, 1998, p. 223). Understanding of the impact of restructuring on men and women in the "public sphere" will be very limited without an equal focus on the profound changes simultaneously occurring in the "private" spheres of the household and gender relations. An examination of what is happening to gender relations within the household, therefore, tells us something about the capacity of the social regulatory regime to sustain both capital accumulation and social reproduction.

The unpaid reproductive and productive work undertaken by Australian households is significant in size and remains, as elsewhere in the world, highly gendered. Unpaid household activities and voluntary and community work in 1997 was conservatively estimated at 48 per cent of the value of total measured GDP. Unpaid work grew 15 per cent from the previous national time use study in 1992 (ABS, 2000). More telling is Duncan Ironmonger's calculation that the volume of labour hours used in the household economy was 40 per cent greater than that for the formal economy (Ironmonger, 1996, p. 47). National time use studies show that, between 1992 and 1997, women's and men's relative unpaid work contribution overall remained relatively unchanged. Women contributed 65 per cent and 64 per cent of unpaid work activities in 1992 and 1997 respectively (ABS, 2000). Men increased their hours of childcare, but overall their hours of unpaid work did not change markedly. The main source of change in the gender division of labour between 1987 and 1997 occurred as a result of women (on average) doing less, rather than men doing more (Bittman & Pixley, 1997, p. 90; Baxter, 2002, p. 420). In other words, women substituted their time by buying market services or by simply not doing the housework because they seemed either unable or unwilling to negotiate substantial increases in men's unpaid work. As a result, neoliberal policies that re-familialized or re-privatized social reproduction tended to increase women's unpaid work burdens and undermine the capacity and resilience of households to carry out their productive and reproductive roles.

An important source of change in the gender relations of Australian households is the series of demographic changes in the structure of Australian families that accompanied labour market restructuring. Demographic trends included a decline in marriage rates, a rise in divorce rates, an increase in the average age for the birth of a woman's first child, and a declining fertility rate. These trends indicated a significant decline in traditional families. They also implied that women would spend less time during their lives engaged in household work (Baxter, 1998, p. 59). The decline in the fertility rate, from 2.9 per cent to 1.7 per cent between 1971 and 1998, reflected the tension faced by Australian women, tension between a family caring role and a worker role (MacDonald, 2000). The number of persons living in couple families with dependent children declined substantially during the 1990s—from 59 per cent of the population in 1991 to 52 per cent in 2001, with the number of lone person and one-parent families being the fastest growing types of household in Australia (ABS, 2002; ABS, 2003). The rise in gay and lesbian households and in lone person households and the doubling of single parent and de facto family households in the decades of the 1980s and 1990s also potentially provided a challenge to the traditional male breadwinner/female carer gender order. Unfortunately, the challenge to the male breadwinner gender order that arises from these demographic changes has not led to the emergence of more equitable alternatives. There is as yet little evidence of a cultural change that would allow women or men to make a choice to adopt a homemaker and carer role without experiencing economic and social disadvantage.

Nevertheless, there is evidence of significant differences in household gender arrangements according to place, class, and other socio-economic factors. Australian research on the impact of labour market changes on gender relations within households has emphasized the importance of class. Belinda Probert (1996), in a study of Melbourne households, demonstrated that the social reproductive activities of households and strategies for survival under restructuring have varied significantly by social class, reflecting a growing polarization of experience within different households. Working-class households in which the male breadwinner was in a low-skilled job and the female was engaged in full-time, unpaid household work appeared to be holding on to a male breadwinner model of gender relations based upon a strict sexual division of labour. In contrast, further up the socio-economic scale, women were more likely to combine work with parenting. In these cases, an increasing degree of negotiation around household work occurred, resulting in a less rigid sexual division of labour (Probert, 1996, pp. 42–44). Indeed, it appears that the scope for transforming the male breadwinner gender model underpinning men's and women's paid and unpaid work within working-class households was frequently less than that of their higher social status counterparts. These contradictory aspects of gender culture are interpreted in different ways by different households and are also significantly influenced by the state's policies. As neoliberal policies increasingly resulted in the withdrawal of support for social reproduction, those high-income households and professional women who could afford to purchase increasingly privatized childcare, education, health, and elder care services have done so. Less well-off women have used family networks of aunts and mothers. In short, restructuring has resulted in a "growing polarisation" of experience and gender attitudes particularly between the rich and poor (Probert, 1996, p. 44).

CONCLUSION: THE END OF THE MALE BREADWINNER GENDER ORDER?

Different feminist political economy theories have contributed to our understanding of the relationship between gender and the processes of commodification/decommodification. One approach has been to extend Esping-Andersen's theory by engendering the classification of welfare state regimes. Others have sought to extend the analysis beyond welfare states by examining the broader role of gender relations within social reproduction regimes. These analyses have demonstrated the crucial role of gender in linking the spheres of the labour market, state, and the household. We have sought to build upon these theories with a feminist regulation analysis that provides an historical and class perspective on the significance of changes occurring in the gender order resulting from neoliberal restructuring in Australia. Since the institutional and informal arrangements that define gender roles and relations within a society play a vital role in both capital accumulation and social reproduction, changes currently affecting the gender order have great significance. A feminist regulation perspective indicates that a significant restructuring of the gender order has implications for other elements of the global restructuring process and will be a very important factor in determining the shapes of all post-neoliberal societies.

There have been enormous and complex changes to the Australian gender order in the past few decades. A strong male breadwinner/female carer gender order was an important component of the mode of social regulation in the post-war era in Australia, but this gender order has been disrupted by the recent neoliberal restructuring process. The male breadwinner household structure has been transformed—not only because of the decline of the nuclear family but also because of women's significantly increased labour market participation and men's declining participation. However, while there is certainly evidence that recent changes to the breadwinner model have created opportunities for a progressive redefinition of the gender order, the neoliberal character of the restructuring process has ensured that many aspects of that model remain intact within households. One of the key characteristics of the neoliberal response to global restructuring in Australia, as elsewhere, has been a dramatic shift towards the (re)marketization of many of the aspects of economic and labour relations that had been decommodified during the post-war Keynesian era. At the same time, important changes have occurred in the structures of social reproduction. Some welfare provisions and state-organized care activities were shifted from public services to commodified market services as key aspects of the post-war Australian welfare state came to be perceived by capital as outmoded and no longer desirable, or necessary, for capital accumulation. However, new patterns of decommodification, or perhaps rather "re-familialization," have also developed as elements of social reproduction have been devolved from the state back to the household.

These changes and continuities in the patterns of household gender relations have not been experienced evenly. We have also sought to recognize more fully the complexity and diversity existing within restructuring gender arrangements resulting from the interaction of gender with class. Some of the differences in these experiences can undoubtedly be explained by individual choice. However, there is clear evidence of the role of place, class, culture, and other socio-economic differences in structuring those experiences. The combined impact of restructuring and neoliberal policies has put enormous pressures on the capacity of some households to undertake productive and reproductive activities effectively. For some households, on the other hand, restructuring has provided opportunities and benefits. The forces of neoliberal global restructuring are dramatically restructuring class, gender, and social arrangements—and, in so doing, are also restructuring the system of social reproduction.

These contradictory processes of increased female labour commodification, reduced decommodification, and re-familialization raise the question of the capacity of a neoliberal agenda to ensure a sustainable set of social arrangements for the future. In fact, rather than producing a new gender order, the restructuring process is producing increased instability and inequalities in gender arrangements—a gender (dis)order. Furthermore, any future neoliberal gender order, to the extent that such a phenomenon is possible, will not foster gender equality. The market, in the absence of state intervention or community solutions, will place more and more of the responsibility for social reproduction onto individuals and the family. Those that can afford to buy childcare, elder care, education, and so on in the marketplace will have opportunities and choices. However, for the majority of families, the burden of social reproduction will shift to them.

Is this scenario sustainable? To reiterate Polanyi's observation, ultimately, capitalism is not sustainable without a stable process for social reproduction, one that is invariably supported by the state. The neoliberal agenda that relentlessly pursues the commodification of every aspect of human existence cannot adequately ensure a sustainable set of social arrangements, even as a "temporary fix." This contradiction ensures that a space will continue to exist for challengers to neoliberal restructuring to pursue alternative strategies within and outside the state. A feminist regulation approach highlights that effective resistance to the negative effects of neoliberal restructuring should also include strategies to support social reproduction and the establishment of a new, progressive, and more equitable gender order.

CHAPTER EIGHT

Water is Life!
The Debate over Private Sector Participation in Water Supply

Karen Bakker

On a rainy Friday in March of 2000, the world's Water and Environment Ministers were meeting in The Hague to discuss the global water crisis. The statistics with which they were presented were alarming: water scarcity had been growing in many regions, and over 20 per cent of the world's population was without access to sufficient supplies of potable water for the most basic daily needs.

The government delegations had been invited to meet together with international financial institutions, bilateral aid agencies, and private water companies to discuss solutions to the world's water problems. Yet many of the governments represented at the conference had themselves been accused of irresponsible water management by their citizens. Representatives of the government of India, which continued to sponsor its Narmada dam project after the World Bank withdrew, were in attendance. The South African government, already planning for its role as host of the World Summit on Sustainable Development in Johannesburg in 2002, sent a large contingent. Little was said at the meeting about South Africa's continued support for the Lesotho Highlands Water Project, despite the participation of its then-Minister for Water Affairs, Kader Asmal, in the high-profile World Commission on Dams, which comprehensively reviewed—and condemned—the social, environmental, and economic record of large dams around the world.

As World Water Council Chairman Mahmoud Abu-Zeid, Egypt's minister of public works and water resources, began his inaugural speech, few surprises were expected from the carefully planned meeting—much of which had been scripted during exhaustive advance preparatory meetings. Given tight security at the event, the appearance on stage of members of the group *Solidarios con Itoiz* took the audience by surprise. Two members of this group approached the Presidential Table, removed their clothes, and handcuffed themselves to each other. On their bodies were painted the following slogans: "Stop Itoiz Dam" and "No to Water Privatisation." As security guards moved in to remove the protesters, Abu-Zeid continued with his speech, but the audience was repeatedly distracted by protesters, positioned throughout the room, who hung a banner from the balcony reading "stop water privatization" and shouted out information and slogans from seats in the audience. Few in the audience had heard of the proposed Itoiz dam in the Basque country, but the group's overall message was clear: the corporate takeover of the world's water, from building dams to privatizing water supply systems, had to be stopped.

The actions of the Itoiz protesters were indicative of a broader shift in the politics of dam protests in the Basque Country and elsewhere. In the long campaign against the Itoiz dam in the Pyrenees, campaigners had engaged in policy dialogue, bringing their case before regional, national, and European governments. Protesters had engaged in direct action and media-friendly protest tactics, with supporters scaling both the Vatican Dome and London's Millennium Wheel. Much of this earlier protest had been directed against governments, but by protesting against water privatization in The Hague, the anti-dam campaigners highlighted a central issue of concern to an emerging global alliance of water activists—the involvement of private companies in water supply management.

An emblematic reference for the protesters had been the protests in the Bolivian city of Cochabamba a year earlier. In September 1999, a 40-year private sector participation contract was signed between the municipality of Cochabamba and a consortium led by International Water—a subsidiary of the United States corporation Bechtel. The consortium was new to Bolivia; the local subsidiary of International Water, Aguas de Tunari, was domiciled in the Cayman Islands, and its upper-level management employees were largely British and American. In return for a yearly fee, the contract gave the company rights over not only the city's networked water supply system but also the water supply within the entire watershed. In the intensively farmed Andean mountain valley in which Cochabamba sits, well water and streams are essential sources for drinking and irrigating. As the company raised water rates and attempted to install water meters on private wells, a coalition of unions, farmers, and environmental groups emerged in response. Demanding the cancellation of the contract, the Cochabamba marches, roadblocks, and protests lasted for several months, at times bringing the city to a halt. After the central government brought in the army to suppress the protests, civil unrest spread, inflamed when one protester was killed when troops fired on demonstrators. As the *Coordinadora* coalition continued to report events in Cochabamba to the international press, with coverage from the *Economist* and CNN, union leader Oscar Olivera was spirited out of the country to Washington where he addressed the April 16th anti-IMF/World Bank rally. In response to internal protest and international pressure, the city cancelled the contract, in one of the few examples of successful grassroots resistance to private sector participation in water supply in countries of the South.

The Cochabamba protest is emblematic of potential and tentative alliances between organized labour, environmentalists, anti-globalization protesters, and community organizations, collectively mobilizing around defence of water resources, communities, and livelihoods. As a non-substitutable resource essential for life, water is a highly emotive issue. Water is a flow resource, which connects ecosystems and communities in material as well as symbolic ways. Essential for livelihoods, water is a potential source for alliance building among diverse groups, as a potential focal point for constructive approaches to what Brecher, Costello, and Smith term "globalization from below" (2000). A common thread to the many campaigns and protests on water issues around the world has been the issue of corporate versus community control, in which the need to resist commodification, or to decommodify water, serves both as a political tactic for mobilization and as the basis for alternative management strategies for water resources. In many instances, these alliances have emerged in response to the participation of private, for-profit corporations in local water supply management. In other instances, resistance by communities to corporate control of water—by the state as well as by private corporations—has been the focus of community mobilization.

CORPORATE VERSUS COMMUNITY CONTROL

The debate over how responsibility for water supply should be shared between state, private sector, and citizens centres on three idealized models of resource management: the public utility (or municipal) "services" model, the private sector "commercial" model, and the community "cooperative" model (Bakker, 2003; Budds & McGranahan, 2003). In practice, these models overlap; some communities run private corporations; some governments choose to retain ownership while corporatizing water services. In France, for example, private sector management of municipally owned water supply infrastructure via long-term management contracts is widespread. Other countries such as Denmark, with a long tradition of co-operative management of the local economy, prefer the co-op model—provision by a non-profit users' association in which local accountability is a key incentive. The Bolivian city of Santa Cruz runs its water supply as a not-for-profit co-operative, and the majority of residents have access to the water supply network.

The emergence of corporate control over water supply must be understood in the historical context of urbanization and the associated industrialization of water supply. As cities grow, some means of supplying large amounts of water and removing large quantities of sewage becomes increasingly necessary. In nineteenth-century European cities, universal water and sewer networks emerged as the preferred model. Water was to be mass produced, abstracted in large quantities, and treated at plants before being distributed through networks in densely urbanized areas where economies of scale made supplying water feasible.

In many cities, private corporations built and operated the first water supply networks. Private companies operated in cities like Boston, New York, London, Paris, Buenos Aires, and Seville, typically supplying water to wealthier neighbourhoods (e.g., Hassan, 1998). The poor had to rely on public taps, wells, rivers, or, in the most desperate cases, they stole water. The terrible cholera and typhoid epidemics of the nineteenth century, combined with an apparent inability or lack of interest on the part of the private sector to finance universal provision, led municipal managers and "gas and water socialists" to take over the business of providing a water supply infrastructure. In places where private companies continued to operate—as they did in France, England, and Spain—they were tightly regulated. Private water companies in the UK, for example, had dividends capped and were required to reinvest any remaining profits in the water supply business.

THE GOVERNMENT OR STATE MODEL

The "public utility" model of network water supply provision was, in many cases, a direct response to experiences with private provision of water supply in the nineteenth century. For much of the twentieth century, governments built, owned, and frequently managed water supply systems, particularly in industrialized countries and urban areas. With the aim of providing universal access and the protection of public health, governments created public utilities that owned the infrastructure and, in most cases, provided services to consumers on a subsidized basis. Water was regarded as a public service, often run at the municipal level, and it was frequently not metered.

The justification for government control of water supply systems rested on twinned economic and ethical arguments. On ethical grounds, drinking water supply was conceived of as a public good, a necessary precondition to participation in public life and, as such, a material emblem of citizenship. In economic terms, the high capital costs of water supply development projects and the monopoly characteristics of water supply networks were used to justify state involvement. In most industrialized countries and urban areas, governments dominated supplying water through much of the twentieth century.

THE COMMERCIAL MODEL

The private sector water supply model is characterized by the management, and sometimes ownership, of infrastructure by private, usually for-profit corporations. There are many different types of private sector models (Bakker & Cameron, 2004). A privatized water supply utility, such as those created in England and Wales in 1989, owns the assets and manages the infrastructure; this model is quite rare. Private sector participation in water supply usually involves private corporations in the management of various aspects of municipally owned infrastructure; for example, about 70 per cent of the French population is served through these "private sector partnerships" or "PSPs." Over the past decade, a rapid increase in "private sector partnerships," contractual arrangements under which private companies operate, manage, or even build water supply networks on behalf of government owners, has occurred. The majority of formal water supply systems around the world remains, however, municipally owned.

Privatization usually entails commercialization, in which markets and market norms are applied to water supply management. Commercialization frequently involves the introduction of metering and associated changes in water rates. The principles of full-cost pricing (prices should reflect the full cost of the service) and economic equity (consumers should pay for what they use) are usually applied, in contrast to the subsidized pricing and social equity principles that frequently characterize public utility systems, whereby consumers should pay according to their ability and prices should be affordable. Commercialization can also occur under public ownership; municipalities in the Netherlands, for example, have created publicly owned commercialized water supply corporations.

THE COMMUNITY MODEL

Community-run water supply systems are most frequently managed as co-operatives. Many types of co-operatives exist; a simple definition is "an enterprise owned and democratically controlled by the users of the goods and services provided." Users can be consumers, employees, or producers of products and services. In most co-operatives, users are actively involved in aspects of management and decision making. Effective, not necessarily efficient, management, in line with community norms, tends to be the goal of water supply co-operatives.

Co-operatives are widespread in developing countries, particularly in rural and peri-urban areas and in smaller villages and towns. In OECD countries, this model is most widely used in rural areas. About 200 water supply co-operatives exist in Canada, mainly in Alberta, Manitoba, and Quebec. In developing countries, the model is widespread. Water co-operatives are prevalent in Denmark. Water co-operatives are also common in Finland, where there is a long-standing tradition of private participation in water services through not-for-profit and self-sufficient "water associations" and co-operatives owned and managed by the consumers, especially in rural and sparsely populated areas. In Wales in 2001, the regional water and wastewater company, which had been privatized in 1989, was restructured into a non-profit corporation owned by its members and prohibited from diversifying or operating outside of Wales. The Bolivian city of Santa Cruz runs water supply as a not-for-profit co-operative, to which the majority of residents have access. The case of Santa Cruz contrasts with that of many cities in the South, where the poor obtain water from private vendors who deliver water to households by jugs or tankers, usually at a cost several multiples of that charged for water delivered via public water supply systems to the middle and upper classes.

FROM PRIVATE TO PUBLIC: THE GROWTH OF STATE CONTROL OF WATER SUPPLY NETWORKS

Private participation in water supply is not new. The many varieties of systems of water supply management and ownership worldwide—along a continuum between fully public and fully private—bear witness to repeated shifts back and forth between private and public ownership and management of water systems (Batley, 1996). The first companies to supply London, England with water were privately owned, typically serving only the wealthier areas of the city. Some companies briefly competed for customers by laying parallel networks of pipes down city streets. In cities such as Paris, New York, Buenos Aires, and Seville, private water companies created the first water supply networks. Over the course of the twentieth century, in most industrialized countries, municipal governments extended direct control of water supply systems until the private sector occupied a minor role, or ceased to operate altogether. The growth in involvement of the public sector coincided, particularly in industrializing countries, with an increase in connection rates. In mid-nineteenth-century England, fewer than 10 per cent of households had piped water connections (Gregg, 1950). Municipal involvement in water supply began to increase after 1850, and municipalities dominated the water supply sector by 1900. By the 1950s, over 90 per cent of the English population had access to piped water (Sleeman, 1953).

Despite the increasing importance of government involvement in water supply, private sector participation continued to exist in many places. In countries such as France and Spain, private sector management of municipally owned water supply infrastructure via long-term management contracts continues to be widespread. In France, municipalities own the water and wastewater networks, which they are legally prohibited from selling, but they frequently contract out operation and maintenance to private companies. In most cities of the global South, private water vendors—delivering water to households by jerry can or tanker—have long been the means by which the poor obtain water. In the vast majority of countries in the world, however, governments own water supply networks, where they exist, and either operate or delegate their operation.

Why did water supply shift from the private sector to government control? Intense conflicts arising between upstream and downstream users were important justifications for government regulations. Water, as a flow resource required to fulfil multiple functions, such as agricultural, industrial, drinking water, and environmental, is invariably a subject of conflict. Moreover, the need in industrializing, urbanizing societies to mobilize large volumes of water—invariably at a high cost relative to the economic value generated—was used, particularly in the twentieth century, to justify public sector involvement.

Concerns were often raised about the tendency of private companies to "cherry-pick"—choosing to supply only wealthier neighbourhoods or classes of consumers, where consumption was greater and profit margins higher. With rapid rates of urbanization came cholera and typhoid epidemics, which regularly swept through London and Paris in the nineteenth century. Concerns about public health, combined with an emerging consensus on the germ theory of disease and an awareness of the links between water pollution and public health, were key factors justifying the increase of state involvement to ensure universal provision. Private sector provision was not regarded as a likely vehicle to achieve universal provision. The standards of service being formulated by public authorities—universal provision of clean water 24 hours per day—would not be met without a significant increase in regulation, to control not only standards but also prices.

Moreover, water supply networks were usually operated as monopolies. Water is relatively expensive to transport relative to its value per unit volume, requiring expensive, large-scale capital investment in infrastructure networks, which act as effective barriers to market entry. Water supply is thus highly susceptible to monopolistic control, a condition economists often term "natural" monopoly. The pitfalls of a private monopoly supply of basic goods—most importantly, pricing issues—lent further support to moves to secure public ownership (Hannah, 1992). Typically, coalitions of municipal socialists, public health advocates, and philanthropists combined forces to lobby for the expropriation of private companies and for the creation of government-owned water supply utilities. In England, for example, advocates from a variety of backgrounds supported universal provision and strict government regulation of water supply; these advocates included the "gas and water socialists" of the small but influential Fabian Society, utopian socialists, philanthropists, and public health campaigners such as Dr. John Snow, who proved the link between polluted water and cholera in the 1850s (Fraser, 1973; Goubert, 1986).

In many countries, over the twentieth century, water supply came to be recognized as "a public utility that was important not only for reasons of health and hygiene, but also for economic, agricultural and industrial reasons" (Goubert, 1986, p. 185). Indeed, long before the advent of antibiotics and "modern" medicine, simple hygiene practices—water-borne disposal of sewage and hand washing—began the dramatic reduction in deaths from diseases such as cholera, typhoid, and dysentery witnessed in most countries in the "West." Clean water was recognized to be a critical element for continued industrial production and a functioning labour force. Universal provision was thus an economic as well as a social imperative (Bakker, 2003; Hassan, 1998). In less industrialized countries, and in rural areas, community control continued to play a central role in water supply; this remains the case in much of the global South.

FROM PUBLIC TO PRIVATE: PRIVATIZATION AND PRIVATE SECTOR PARTICIPATION

At the beginning of the 1980s, the private management of water supply was the exception. Two decades later, the water supply systems of many capital cities of developing countries are now managed by one of a handful of multinational corporations. Private sector participation in water supply is actively advocated by most multilateral financial institutions and by some bilateral aid agencies. Changes in legislation in many jurisdictions, in addition to trade liberalization agreements, have provided more enabling environments in which the private sector may participate more easily in the business of water supply than at any time over the past century.

The current phase of privatization can be distinguished from previous phases of water privatization by four characteristics. First, the scale of involvement of multi-utility, multinational companies is unprecedented. The three largest companies—France's ONDEO/Suez-Lyonnaise des Eaux and Vivendi/Générale des Eaux and Germany's RWE—are amongst the largest 100 companies in the world and dwarf their few credible competitors. The activities of these companies are facilitated by new trade rules (both international treaties and bilateral accords) that permit, and in some cases require, governments to open up to foreign companies access to domestic water supply services. Second, the amount of finance being mobilized via these corporations, as well as by multilateral lending and bilateral aid agencies, is frequently larger than that which often heavily indebted states can access. Third, private companies receive both ideological and financial support from key mediators of international finance, such as the International Finance Corporation and the Asian and American development banks, and key sources of bilateral aid, such as England's Department for International Development. The role of these international facilitators is crucial. For example, bilateral agencies provide technical assistance to governments considering privatization, and, in some developing countries, IMF conditionality requiring privatization and/or commercialization of the water supply sector has been imposed (Grusky, 2001).

Between 1987 and 2000, 183 water and sewerage projects with private participation were initiated in "developing" countries (Table 8.1), with a total investment of over $33 billion USD. These capital flows are being mobilized to stave off what the World Bank portrays as the possibility of "severe water shortages" in "developing" countries and to meet tougher environmental standards in "developed" countries (McGuinness & Thomas, 1997, p. 329). A significant proportion of this finance, insist multilateral credit organizations like the World Bank and bilateral agencies like DFID, must come from the private sector. The level of required investment in water supply is predicted to increase, given a combination of increasing pressure on water resources and increasing demands, particularly in conurbations experiencing rapid rates of urbanization (Winpenny, 2003).

These statistics include both water *resources*, or "raw" water, and water *supply*. Water companies may be involved in the construction of large-scale infrastructure developments, such as reservoirs or canals, to supply raw water, or they may also be involved in the management, rehabilitation, and extension of "clean" potable water and "dirty" wastewater networks. The majority of projects undertaken to date involve both "operation and maintenance" of the infrastructure, together with the construction and/or rehabilitation of infrastructure. In the case of water supply, private sector participation may take a variety of forms (Bakker, 2003). To date, the majority of contracts have been granted on a "concession" basis, in which a private company obtains the exclusive right to operate the water supply infrastructure for an extended period of time, usually 20 to 30 years. The vast majority of contracts have been granted in urban areas. Given economies of scale associated with con-

TABLE 8.1	Water and Sewerage Projects with Private Participation in Developing Countries (1987–2000)
Year	**Number of Projects reaching financial closure (cumulative)**
1987	2
1988	2
1989	5
1990	5
1991	7
1992	13
1993	22
1994	37
1995	57
1996	75
1997	105
1998	124
1999	158
2000	183

Source: Silva, Tynan, and Yilmaz (1998), World Bank, personal communication.

cession contracts, rural areas or even conurbations with a population of fewer than 500,000 are unlikely to attract private sector interest.

Privatization advocates argue that private sector management of water supply infrastructure increases efficiency. They point to the failure of governments and aid agencies to achieve the goal of universal water supply during the United Nation's International Water and Sanitation Decade (1981–1990) and to the low efficiency and low cost-recovery levels of public utilities. Private sector proponents argue that, through efficiency gains and better management, private companies can lower prices, improve performance, and increase cost recovery, enabling systems to be upgraded and expanded and that these are critical in a world in which one billion people lack access to safe, sufficient water supplies (e.g., Shirley, 2002). Privatization (the transfer of ownership of water supply systems to private companies) and private sector "partnerships" (the construction, operation, and management of publicly owned water supply systems by private companies) have, it is argued, worked well in other utility sectors. Proponents of privatization argue that the private companies motivated by profit can produce greater efficiency gains than the public sector, if the profit motive is properly harnessed. This harnessing requires the state to change roles—from a provider of services to a regulator of those services, and to a champion of choice, competition, and efficiency (Johnstone & Wood, 2002). Water, in this market-led scenario, is recast as an economic good, not a public good (Winpenny, 1994). Users are characterized as customers and rate-payers rather than citizens and voters. Lines of accountability flow from boards of directors to individual customers, rather than from elected representatives to voters.

This view has been strongly critiqued by those who argue that privatization entails the transformation of water from a commons into a commodity, an act of dispossession with negative distributive consequences that is emblematic of "globalization from above." The involvement of private companies invariably introduces a pernicious logic of the market into water management, which is incompatible with guaranteeing citizens' basic rights to water. Private companies—answerable to shareholders and with the overriding goal of profit—will manage water supply less effectively and sustainably than public sector counterparts. Opponents of privatization point to successful examples of public water systems, and they argue that private sector alternatives are not necessarily more efficient, and often much more expensive for users, than well-managed public sector systems (e.g., Estache & Rossi, 2002). They assert the effectiveness of democratic accountability to citizens when compared to corporate accountability to shareholders. This argument is less easy to refute following the collapse of Enron, which by the late 1990s had become one of the largest water multinationals through its subsidiary Azurix. Privatization opponents also point to high-profile cases of corruption, such as the conviction of two Lyonnaise des Eaux executives in Grenoble, France or the recent arrest of the former CEO of Wessex Water (a one-time Enron subsidiary) on suspicion of accepting $ 2.3 million (CDN) in "corrupt payments" during takeover negotiations; the payment, made in advance for unspecified "consulting fees," was later declared to be legal.[1]

Anti-privatization campaigners point to studies such as that conducted by the United States General Accounting Office (GAO), the investigative arm of Congress that examines the use of public funds, on the involvement of the private sector in water supply infrastructure. An extensive GAO study recently found that "a privatization agreement's potential to generate profits is the key factor influencing decisions by private companies that enter into such agreements with publicly owned utilities or the governmental entities they serve" (United States GAO, 2002, p. 5). The profit motive, it argues, will lead companies to under-invest in water supply infrastructure and to "cherry-pick" wealthier customers unless carefully regulated. Moreover, anti-privatization campaigners argue that introducing private sector management of water supply undermines the nature of public participation in a deliberative democracy (e.g., Barlow & Clarke, 2001). This claim rests on the understanding that water supply is an element of the public domain, a modern "commons" enacted through the welfare state, and not a commodity.

IS WATER A COMMONS OR A COMMODITY?

As outlined, the water privatization debate is often phrased as a struggle between two competing worldviews, one that sees water as a commons and the other that views water as a commodity (Figure 8.1).

A related question is often asked: who should manage water resources, communities or corporations? These are pressing questions given that private corporations are playing an increasingly important role as builders, owners, and operators of water supply systems.

At the risk of over-simplification, the commodity view asserts that private ownership and management of water supply systems, as distinct from water itself, is possible and indeed preferable. Water is no dif-

FIGURE 8.1	Two Competing World Views	
	Commons	**Commodity**
Definition	Public good	Economic good
Pricing	Free or "lifeline"	Full-cost pricing
Regulation	Public policy-based	Market-based
Goals	Social equity & Livelihoods	Efficiency & Water security
Manager	Community	Market
Access	Human right	Human need

Source: Lachman (1987, p. 17).

ferent from other essential goods and utility services. Private companies, who will be responsive both to customers and to shareholders, can efficiently run and profitably manage water supply systems. Water conservation will be incentivized through pricing—users will cease wasteful behaviour as water prices rise with increasing scarcity. Water must be treated as an economic good, as specified in the Dublin Principles[2] and in the Hague Declaration.[3]

In contrast, the commons view of water asserts that water is a resource essential for life and that the conversion of water supply into a business opportunity is unethical. Collective management—whether by communities or the state—is not only preferable but also necessary; private ownership of water supply will invariably conflict with the public interest. Conservation is more effectively incentivized through an environmental ethic, which will encourage users to refrain from wasteful behaviour. The real "water crisis" arises from socially produced scarcity, in which a short-term logic of economic growth twinned with the rise of corporate power, and, in particular, the ascendency of water multinationals, has "converted abundance into scarcity." Increasingly, anti-privatization campaigners in the North and South are making strategic alliances. Defence of water supply is a unifying theme, which rallies defenders of the welfare state, of public services, of ecological justice, and of community livelihoods.

The alliance-building potential of water supply is also visible at the local level. In many instances, threats to water supply—and in particular the perception of threats from private sector companies—motivate alliances between organized labour (water supply workers), social justice groups, consumers' organizations, and environmentalists. In Toronto, Canada in 2002, for example, an alliance of local public sector unions, environmental groups, and social justice campaigners created a "WaterWatch" coalition that opposed a municipal proposal to corporatize water supply management—the first time that these groups had worked together in a sustained way at the municipal level. Water supply is a potentially unifying site of resistance, enabling the "red-green" or "turtle-teamster" alliances mooted at Seattle and at other anti-globalization fora. These alliances tend to fuse different scales of struggle: local communities, regional and national governments, world water policy fora, and sites of global governance such as free trade agreements and the Bretton Woods institutions. Often, red-green conflicts pit jobs against environmental protection and the defence of resources from extraction. Water supply is not characterized by the usually false paradox between economic goals and environmental protection that plagues attempts to bring together social justice and environmental justice concerns.

Central tensions in these alliances are tactics and the role of the state. In places where water supply is largely controlled by governments, usually local, defending the public sector as a site of production of public goods is a key factor in alliance building. However, the state has, in some cases, rationally administered massive environmental degradation and systematic under-provision of environmental goods. Some of the great gains in human welfare during the twentieth century associated with the "state hydraulic paradigm" were made at the expense of the environment—as in the case of large-scale water resources development. Attitudes toward the state become more ambivalent, and conflating the "state" with "public" interest more obviously erroneous when the environment is factored into the re-distributive equation. This is particularly relevant to "developing" countries, where community-led resource management remains widespread and, in many cases, a more viable option to state-led development models, which are frequently more accurately described as the territorialization of state power through an imposition of control over local resources.

The perspective of Vandana Shiva on what she terms "water wars" hints at this tension (Shiva, 2002). In Shiva's view, the increasing corporate control of water resources and supply is predicated on an increasing commercialization of water— which entails treating water as an economic good—by assigning monetary values and requiring users to pay the "full cost." She critiques the argument that commercialization is the only means of promoting water conservation. These are the key points differentiating Southern water activists from some Western anti-privatization campaigners: an insistence on water's cultural dimensions, a critique of the state as well as the private sector, and an emphasis on water's spiritual significance as the source of life. From this perspective, the real "water crisis" arises from socially produced scarcity, and current "water wars" pit citizens against corporations and governments against communities in a battle to preserve the water commons against privatization, corporate control, and a logic of short-term profligacy. While refuting the argument that the private sector should manage water, which is the dominant rhetoric of development banks and some bilateral aid agencies, anti-privatization campaigners simultaneously critique state-led models of development that deprive communities of water rights and undermine local ecosystems in the short-sighted drive to modernize. Some, such as the International Forum on Globalization and the Group of Lisbon, assert that corporate control— whether by the state or private sector—is incommensurate with the sustainable, equitable management of water.

Many anti-privatization campaigners rely on a discourse of rights when articulating a defence of water supply. A focal point of the international debate has thus been the question of whether water supply is a human right or a human need.

Water as a human right would be enshrined in legislation, as in South Africa's constitution, placing a duty on governments to ensure its fulfilment.[4] If water is a human need, on the other hand, governments would have no such duty. In the mid-twentieth century, international debates stressed the importance of water for health and sanitation in basic need requirements. In recent decades, the argument for treating water as a human right has been advanced, drawing on the Universal Declaration of Human Rights (1948), and made explicit in the Convention on the Rights of the Child (1986). The Water Supply and Sanitation Collaborative Council's "Vision 21,"[5] the Cochabamba Declaration,[6] the Group of Lisbon's Water Manifesto,[7] the Declaration of the fourth P7[8] summit (2000), and the UN Covenant on Economic, Social and Cultural Rights[9] have supported the inclusion of water as a "third generation" right into international law (Gleick, 2000; Petrella, 2001). In practical terms, this would imply a basic volumetric allocation per person per day, an allocation, in Gandhi's phrase, "sufficient for everyone's need, but not for anyone's greed." To date, only South Africa has attempted to implement a "basic right to water" through a policy of free minimum water supply for all citizens, although the South African government's failure to implement this policy quickly and in a manner responsive to the needs of poorer communities has been critiqued (Bond 2002b; MacDonald, 2002).

The debate over the control and management of water supply has a long history. The latest phase is intertwined with broader issues, such as trade rules and development policy, and with social movements, in particular, the shared strategies of those who group themselves around the banner of "anti-corporate globalization." One point of agreement between positions that seem otherwise diametrically opposed is the belief that the traditional models of state control of water supply should be reformed. Questions about the respective roles to be played by communities, states, and private corporations raise broader issues of environmental sustainability and deliberative democracy; in debating private sector participation in water supply, we are also debating the relationship between markets, states, the environment, and one another. This is a properly political debate about our worldviews of water, and of society. Making space for this collective debate is necessary if we are to move beyond what risks becoming a stale confrontation between market fundamentalists and ardent defenders of the state.

Notes

1. "Wessex boss cleared over bribery claim," BBC News On-line, February 4, 2003.
2. The 1992 International Conference on Water and the Environment set out what became known as the "Dublin Principles": Fresh water is a finite and vulnerable resource, essential to sustain life, development and the environment; Water development and management should be based on a participatory approach, involving users, planners and policy-makers at all levels; Women play a central part in the provision, management and safeguarding of water; Water has an economic value in all its competing uses and should be recognized as an economic good. The Dublin Principles have been adopted by many international, multilateral, and bilateral agencies, including the World Bank.

NOT FOR SALE

3. The Ministerial Declaration of The Hague on Water Security in the twenty-first century followed the inter-ministerial meeting known as the "Second World Water Forum" in 2000. See <www.world waterforum.net>.

4. The Constitution of the Republic of South Africa guarantees to citizens the right of access to sufficient water (Act 108 of 1996, section 7(2)).

5. Funded by governments and multilateral agencies, the Water Supply and Sanitation Collaborative Council, located in Geneva, is a non-profit organization, which acts as an "international policy think tank" on water management.

6. The Cochabamba (Bolivia) declaration followed a meeting of several hundred people concerned about the involvement of private sector corporations in water supply management. See <http://www.canadians.org/blueplanet/cochabamba-e.html>.

7. The Group of Lisbon is a group of distinguished scholars from around the world who analyse globalization, call for a new type of economic governance, and advocate new forms of social contracts.

8. The P7 (now P8) annual conference was convened for the first time in June 1997 by the Green Group in the European Parliament, as an alternative Summit to the G7 (now G8). Representatives from the world's poorest countries attend the conferences, which focus on the structural causes of and solutions to poverty.

9. The UN Covenant on Economic, Social and Cultural Rights, which entered into force in 1976, has been signed and ratified by 145 states, and signed but not ratified by seven states (including the United States). In November 2002, the UN's Committee on Economic, Social and Cultural Rights adopted a "general comment" on the right to water, according to which "States party to the International Covenant ... have the duty to progressive[ly] realize, without discrimination, the right to water" (CESCR, 2002).

part three
DEMOCRATIC STRUGGLES FOR DECOMMODIFICATION

CHAPTER NINE

Commodification and Decommodification in Mexico under NAFTA

Teresa Gutiérrez-Haces

Until the 1980s, Mexico's economy was marked by a significant amount of state intervention. This feature enjoyed such a long life for two reasons. First, Mexico's Constitution had originally established, in articles 27 and 28, state interventionism as a guarantor of national wealth and sovereignty.[1] Second, the Party of the Institutionalized Revolution (PRI) was identified with interventionism. This party ruled the country uninterruptedly for seventy years.

The constitutional establishment of state directives for national economic development meant, in practice, the intervention of various government agencies to support economic growth and employment, as well as unilateral selection of criteria for fairly distributing income and wealth.[2] Over time, these practices imposed one line of thought regarding the management and meaning of the public interest and wealth for Mexicans.

This paternalistic and corporatist formula worked fairly well until the mid-1970s. The economic development strategy had mainly consisted of protectionism, import substitution industrialization, state intervention, and control of the working class under an alliance between official unions and the PRI. Then, the political hierarchy concluded that it needed to switch to a new current model that would prolong the PRI's political and economic power and enact economic structural changes demanded by new globalization currents.

Beginning in 1982, a current of thought grew within some PRI and government sectors that invalidated many past economic measures. This criticism was backed by the long-reaching vision, announced worldwide, of the "market evangelists," who gradually convinced many governments and individuals that the welfare state and Keynesian policies were to blame for the economic crisis (Dixon, 1998).

Without disavowing the importance of ideas associated with Reaganism about economic and political changes in Mexico, it is vital to introduce a different interpretation. This perspective explains both economic changes after Mexico's external-debt crisis in 1982 and accelerated commodification in Mexico, which was consolidated by NAFTA, the North American Free Trade Agreement.

Commodification in Mexico should be viewed as the central component of a political and economic struggle amongst social forces within a larger vision in time and space. This struggle, known in Mexico as the "*nation in dispute*," swirled around a nationalist economic development model.[3]

Both the Mexican Revolution (1910) and the Political Constitution of the United States of Mexico (1917) confirmed a vision in which the nation was the owner of public wealth—the land, the subsoil, the natural resources, and the infrastructure of public goods. The fight over the nation was, and still is, an ideological and political struggle about the right of the state and groups associated with the PRI, including the top levels of the state bureaucracy,[4] to determine the uses of the nation's wealth in the context of the growing commodification ushered in by economic liberalization.

Mexico has experienced an internal political and economic process to adjust to the rhythm imposed by the fight over commodification. For example, *ejidos* are political entities in which land is constitutionally recognized, in Article 27, for peasants to use from generation to generation, without being able to sell or lease it. *Ejidos* were created in 1910 to protect peasants against the rapacity of private interests. This disposition reflected the Mexican Revolution's agrarian character and its war against big landowners. However, over time, successive governments distorted the original purpose of *ejidos*, and this distortion resulted in peasants being bound to a piece of land they could exploit but not sell. In 1992, as a part of measures to adjust Mexican law to the new, neoliberal economic environment brought in by NAFTA, Article 27 of the Constitution was modified regarding land ownership. Disputes about *ejidos* before and after 1992 should be understood as part of a struggle over land use, in which government and peasants have different perspectives on the right to commodify land.

Until the late 1960s, Mexico applied a nationalist policy, which in its social aspects followed the "Welfare State." This conferred significant political and social support for the government and the PRI and had important consequences for official social policy.

In 1985, the political elite, including the President, openly decided to change the nation's economic development, as well as the tradition of government intervention. Such changes were launched without an accompanying shift toward greater democracy. This meant that government members, including most bureaucrats and PRI unions, assumed the right to make changes, even constitutional changes, as defenders of the nation's best interest.[5]

Economic changes reflected Mexico's anti-democratic climate. Decisions to liberalize the commercial and financial sectors, sell state enterprises and banks, as well as partly privatize social programs were decreed from the top, with the unconditional support of official unions.[6] Social and economic decisions were made hierarchically and supported by the PRI-dominated legislature.

Mexico's incorporation in 1986 into the GATT (General Agreement on Tariffs and Trade) to lower tariffs, and later into trade and foreign capital protection treaties such as NAFTA, consolidated "free trade" in Mexico. These agreements, particularly NAFTA, give crucial new rights to foreign corporations from North America, treating them as if they were "national" actors, who have a right to change the political and economic course of Mexico.

A minority of citizens, who were regarded as third-rate members of society, disagreed with the exclusive nature of economic liberalization. Among this group were the Mexican Action Network to face Free Trade (Red Mexicana de Acción frente al Libre Comercio, RMALC), founded in 1990, and the *indigenas* (aboriginals) who participated in the uprising in Chiapas in 1994.

Taking advantage of an economic crisis in Mexico, supranational entities imposed structural adjustment policies on the government to control inflation through low salaries, cutting social programs, high interest rates, a radical reduction in the state's role, and privatization of state owned companies. Mexico's economy was liberalized through a badly regulated economic transition, which consisted of pushing macroeconomic changes without anchoring them solidly in the existing microeconomic environment. The transition was delegated to supranational entities such as the GATT, the IMF (International Monetary Fund), and the World Bank. Second, the transition to democracy was postponed to an uncertain future. The assumption was that changing the old economic model would automatically take care of the political adjustments and perhaps bring the alternation of political parties in power.

The forced coexistence of new economic practices with old, anti-democratic practices resulted in considerable political and economic instability, which has not yet been overcome. The PRI and the government stubbornly insisted on carrying out macroeconomic changes and privatizing many state functions without giving up its share of political and economic power.

In combination, these factors gradually drained the government of its power as the social administrator and distributor of national wealth and forced it to become even more authoritarian in order to guarantee the permanence of the economic changes begun in the 1980s.

This is the context in which the commodification of important segments of the social fabric and the physical and economic space of Mexico took place. In the past, articles 27 and 28 of the Constitution had defined ownership of land, the exploitation of natural resources, and the establishment of monopolies in ways that favoured "social benefit" and with the goal of "achieving a fair distribution of public wealth." To remove obstacles to greater commodification, especially those related to land and agriculture, it was necessary to change those articles in Mexico's Constitution. The result was that economic liberalization left unprotected large social sectors, such as traditional agriculture, and allowed the commodification of economic space that was attractive to private corporations and transnational businesses.

When approved in 1994, NAFTA became supranational legislation regarding trade, investments, intellectual property, and services. Many of the state's existing commitments on national wealth, the common good, and their possible commodification were officially ignored.

The purpose of this chapter is to analyse how Mexico's state has gradually transferred most of its power to transnational corporations. Sheltered under NAFTA, the latter have made decisions about geographic space using commercial criteria that affect negatively Mexican citizens' interests. We have chosen three case studies about economic liberalization and NAFTA. Each provoked social protest against commodification.

The first case was the protest against a toxic waste plant belonging to US-owned Metalclad and located in the municipality of Guadalcázar in the state of San Luis Potosí. When Metalclad was unable to install the plant, it sued the Mexican government, citing Chapter 11 of NAFTA. The suit cited a violation of Metalclad's right to invest in the municipality, according to the "National Treatment" clause in NAFTA, which confers rights on American and Canadian investors as if they were Mexican citizens. The company accused the government of "expropriating" Metalclad's investment.

The second case is the political struggle over US-owned Costco's actions in Cuernavaca. Costco acquired a huge property of enormous ecological, historical, and cultural value in the city centre. It contains the ruins of a pre-Hispanic town, and an old hotel building, with valuable murals.

The third case analyses resistance against the expropriation of land to build a new international airport in Atenco, Texcoco, and Chimalhuacán, three municipalities in the State of Mexico near Mexico City. The expropriation responded to the demands of economic modernization and NAFTA.

The case studies show how commodification has disturbed social and cultural values related to the commonwealth, well-being, and what is considered public space. These values affect the governability of the three levels of political power: federal, state, and local governments. The federal government and the media have bombarded the public with the negative effects of the previous development model, and this has resulted in the values and the criteria of the market economy becoming reference points for all that is good, useful, and necessary for the people. While governments are concerned about efficiency, profitability, and competitiveness in the short term, they do not realize that, by tirelessly undermining the public interest, they also undermine the foundations supporting the social understanding between state and citizens.

The shift from an authoritarian regime to one of alternation between governing parties is very recent. Within this context, efforts, however isolated, to recover social control over the economy are part of a world tendency against corporate tyranny.

MECHANISMS OF COMMODIFICATION

Structural adjustment, privatization, and liberalization of foreign investment have hardly responded to citizens' common interests, but have satisfied the demands of international corporations and markets.

For more than twenty-five years, competitiveness was most frequently invoked to justify such policies. Defined officially as Mexico's national interest priority, competitiveness is a demand of big corporations and international institutions. It has been imposed on a Mexican government cornered into an economic liberalization strategy that has not yet shown sustainable growth.

The priority of market values and criteria reflects the recent, dominant international perspective. This perspective, the dictatorship of a single economic way of thinking, understands the dynamics of the international economy as about conquering the markets of most developed countries and imposing globalization demands on them. This perspective also considers individuals and geographic spaces, whether private or public, as economic resources, like nature and financial and technological resources. In this perspective, public or private goods imply monetary expenses, earnings or losses, and can be used or discarded by their owners (Petrella, 1998).

This perspective, imposed by big corporations and, to a certain extent, governments, has undermined the foundations and principles that have ruled most contemporary societies, including Mexico.

Elevating competitiveness to the status of a natural logic that should rule society and the economy results from a quiet war to undermine the state's role and to discredit political agencies originating from the people and the state, at all levels.

A central feature of commodification is the lack of clear policies by governments to defend the common good. Because the state has retreated from protecting the common wealth and the common good, citizens are choosing more violent forms of protest against commodification in Mexico. Generally, citizens' protests, at various levels of violence, have been the only resistance that has partially stopped commodification. This was the case with the expropriation by decree of *ejido* lands to build an additional international airport near Mexico City. This was stopped in 2002.

THE COMMODIFICATION OF SPACE AND TERRITORY

NAFTA has created an unprecedented dynamic in which the central government encourages local governments to commodify their regions in response to corporate demands. This dynamic has had three immediate consequences: first, the automatic subordination of local spaces to the rules of NAFTA; second, the need of governments and citizens to compete against US and Canadian corporations over Mexican territory, national resources, and human capital; and third, the emergence of more governability conflicts resulting from the violation of the federal pact, a consequence of greater commodification unleashed by NAFTA's Chapter 11 on states and municipalities (Gutiérrez-Haces, 2002, 2004).

Chapter 11 of NAFTA gives corporations and investors from North America important rights and privileges, not extended to other foreign investors, to operate in the three NAFTA countries. Apart from allowing foreign ownership, it responds directly to the interests of investors under a market perspective, penalizing any type of legal or political intervention that might encumber it. The main objective of Chapter 11 is to guarantee investor rights to private property of space, resources, and means of production acquired outside the country (Bachand, 2001, p. 15).

Chapter 11 marginalizes all laws originating from public rights. It places suits and arbitration under international trade law. Articles 1115 to 1139 define *expropriation* and *compensation* as investors' legal resources against the opposition of local governments and citizens. Thanks to these clauses, a court in British Columbia, Canada, decided in favour of Metalclad in 2001 and against the government and citizens of San Luis Potosí, who opposed the reopening and enlargement of the toxic waste plant.

Two important aspects of Chapter 11 led to several conflicts, which affected negatively the relationships amongst the federal government, some state governments, and their civil society. The first are the limitations and extent of what is defined as foreign investment in NAFTA, a particularly loose definition that not only encompasses companies but also invested capital, concessions, intellectual and industrial rights, property titles, debt titles, shares, common stock, voting stock, and loans to enterprises. This means a larger range of legal protection for alien investors. The second aspect that led to increasing complaints is the existence of a legal disposition that forces the losing country in a Chapter 11 dispute to compensate financially the country that wins the suit. This measure, the only one of its kind within NAFTA, has aroused speculative attitudes in many companies, which often look for controversial investment spaces in order to then sue governments and obtain compensation (Gutiérrez-Haces, 2004, pp. 44–45).

Articles 1116 and 1117 in NAFTA require companies to file a suit within three years of the company first detecting an alleged violation of its investment rights and learning of losses or damage suffered. If we consider that NAFTA began in January 1994 and that the company cannot go over the three-year limit to file a complaint, it means that any investment period cannot have been very long.[7] Nevertheless, in the cases presented to date, the numbers of claims for compensation in US dollars are visibly inflated relative to the amount invested, which in many cases does not even cover the initial stage of the project.

Citizens' organizations discovered that, in some cases, plaintiff companies were bankrupt before beginning the investment.[8] They probably sought the conflict to better their financial standing by collecting compensation. This was true in the case of the Robert Azinian Company, which in 1997 sued the federal government for 19 million dollars before the manoeuvre was discovered and the suit dismissed (Public Citizen, 2001, p. 34; Gutiérrez-Haces, 2004, p. 41).

Chapter 11 disturbs the three levels of political power (federal, state, and local) by demanding governments pay compensation from their public budgets. If this sort of mechanism is multiplied in the future, governments will face considerable budgetary losses, with negative effects on citizens. This was the case in the decision favouring American-owned Metalclad against Mexico, which after prolonged negotiations paid 16.5 million US dollars to Metalclad. The original assessment was 90 million (Gutiérrez-Haces, 2004, p. 42).

Initially, Mexico's federal government offered to cover the compensation. However, in May 2002, it decided the debt belonged to San Luis Potosí, because the state and the municipality of Guadalcázar obstructed Metalclad's investment. This unexpected federal decision is an important precedent for how social protest that provokes international conflicts will be treated in the future. The Metalclad case sends a clear message to civil society: local protests will bring costs that affect the budgets of rebellious municipalities. San Luis Potosí cannot pay the compensation from its own resources, so the federal government will take the amount out of federal transfers to states and municipalities.[9]

Metalclad's case has been studied a lot for its NAFTA implications for Mexico. However, little has been said about how NAFTA established the mechanisms of commodification through many clauses which guarantee corporations full freedom of operation in all three countries.

NAFTA has rules whose only objective is to discipline governments that favour the interests and demands of civil society. This was the case when the governor of San Luis Potosí tested Metalclad's strength, and federal government support, by declaring land around the toxic waste dump a protected ecological zone. This declaration prevented Metalclad from continuing to build the plant. The state's decree achieved its goal, but San Luis Potosí paid the political costs, to the detriment of social spending. The Metalclad case shows the conflicts that can arise when a company uses NAFTA and fails to consider the impact of its investments on citizens, the environment, and culture.

THE COMMODIFICATION OF PUBLIC AND PRIVATE SPACE IN THE AREA OF NATIONAL PATRIMONY

In 2001–2002, conflicts grew in Mexico around the commercialization of certain spaces. This is evidence of international capital's attack and the subordination of Mexico's government, and of the growing protest of civil society, which resists the commodification of its spaces. Two cases are illustrative: first, the construction of the mega commercial centre Costco in Cuernavaca and second, the Decree of Expropriation of thirteen parcels of *ejido* land in the State of Mexico to construct an international airport. In both cases, cultural and spatial components of commodification played a central role.

Cuernavaca, a city famous for its climate and green areas, opposed the destruction of the Casino de la Selva hotel to make way for Costco. The hotel had gone bankrupt seventeen years earlier and was acquired first by the Banamex-Accival financial group and then by the Fondo Bancario de Protección al Ahorro (Fobaproa—Bank Fund for the Protection of Savings). In 2001, the Secretaría de Hacienda sold the installations and more than four hectares of green area, at the bargain price of ten million pesos, without declaring the cultural wealth it contained: mural paintings by Reyes Meza, Renaud, González Camarena, and Dr. Atl; a cupola constructed by Felix Candela; and the ruins of a pre-Hispanic settlement. The sale raised suspicions, since the land is valued at four thousand pesos per square metre, much more than Costco paid for the whole land.

Protests began with the news of the felling of the first trees and the destruction of part of the building containing the paintings. Years before, the town of Tepoztlán had also carried out a violent protest against the construction of a golf course, which was finally cancelled after a harsh repression of townspeople (Starr, 2000, p. 87).

The Costco-Casino de la Selva case is an interesting lesson on how mega corporations, under the cover of NAFTA and commercial liberalization, have destroyed the traditional networks between local communities, small businesses, and public markets. Recently, mega corporations began moving from the fringes of cities to more central spaces without cars, to capture a greater urban clientele. This trend contributes to commercial mega-centres substituting for traditional parks and public plazas as places for community gatherings.

In their eagerness to attract foreign investment, authorities have sacrificed parks, plazas, and green areas. This reduces municipal expenses for public services. The Casino de la Selva case raises new questions over citizens' rights to enjoy nature within the city and to consider environmental services provided by trees as a social and public function rather than a private one, as Costco insists. The demolition of the Casino de la Selva symbolizes the disappearance of a public good with a cultural component tangible to the community, and the end of a symbolic reference to Cuernavaca's daily life traditions. The prefabricated construction with some green areas that was substituted for this recreational place will never be able to replace this natural lung for the city. The ensuing protest sparked debate over public and private space in Mexico.

Beginning with commercial liberalization in the 1980s, land use planning obeys the law of supply and demand in a global market more than social or political criteria responding to citizens' needs. Investment plays a central role, and this operates within the context of NAFTA's foreign investment measures.

The governor of the state of Morelos offered facilities for the company to build the commercial centre, but when social conflict broke out, he declared that the troubles were the responsibility of the Cuernavaca City Council. Subsequently, the conflict followed the same steps that occurred with Metalclad. The problem was dumped on local authorities, who shielded themselves by saying they authorized demolition but not construction.

Meanwhile, the protest movement has grown in numbers and in creativity, offering alternatives to the destruction of the land, which possesses an important number of trees that are becoming extinct in the state of Morelos.

The *Frente Cívico Prodefensa del Casino de la Selva* (Casino de la Selva Civic Defence Front) brought together other groups defending other areas considered public goods. One example is the *Comité Prodefensa de Fomento Cultural Banamex* (Banamex Cultural Promotion Defence Committee), which protects cultural and architectural assets located mainly in the historic centre of Mexico City. This historic centre was bought by Citigroup as part of the assets of a private bank, Banamex. Another example is the *Frente Nacional de Defensa del Patrimonio Cultural* (National Front for the Defence of Cultural Heritage), which opposes the growing commodification of archaeological zones such as the El Tajín and Teotihuacán pyramids, currently being commercialized by entertainment companies.

In September 2002, the municipal authorities declared that Costco had received government and administrative support for their investment project calculated at 40 million US dollars. The authorities had carefully documented the process to avoid being sued before an international tribunal set up under Chapter 11 of NAFTA. To show how much the authorities favoured the Costco project, police brutally repressed protesters and jailed their leaders.

THE DOUBLE COMMODIFICATION: GOVERNMENT AND PEASANTS

Our last case, the 2001 decree to expropriate 13 *ejido* lands to make way for an airport, is very different from the others in that Mexico's federal government, not foreign businesses, attempted to commodify space. The land to be expropriated is located in the municipalities of Texcoco, Chimalhuacán, and Atenco. The latter would be most affected, since 70 per cent of the expropriated land belongs to this municipality. The remaining 25 per cent and 5 per cent belong to Texcoco and Chimalhuacán respectively. Within Atenco, the *ejidatarios* [residents of the *ejido*] of San Salvador Atenco would lose 80 per cent of their lands to expropriation, virtually wiping out the community.

Nineteen decrees of expropriation in the three municipalities were signed by the Secretary of Agrarian Reform (SRA) and the Secretary of Natural Resources and the Environment (SEMARNAP). This provoked a judicial response by the *ejidatarios* and a provisional suspension of the decree until the Judicial Power of the Federation resolves the expropriation's constitutionality.

The social protest that took place brought to the surface important elements linked to the first part of our chapter in which we analysed the partial retreat of the Mexican State in protecting public goods and the imposition of NAFTA as a supranational constitution. The long process of protest, negotiations, and repression initiated by the expropriation decree displays the precariousness of reforms to Article 27 (1992) of the Constitution. Although the reform made the *ejidatarios* owners of their land, in practice, the peasants were left trapped in a legal morass requiring them to show, with documents, that they were entitled to the parcels. This means that the advertised massive transfer of parcels to private hands did not take place.

Up to the year 2000, close to two and a half million peasants received titles of property. Sixty million hectares were measured for private individual ownership.[10] Despite this, the legal sale of *ejido* land to agribusiness has been minimal: 0.28 per cent to 2.4 per cent, according to various official sources. And many of the sales were of lands already invaded by cities and only regularized by this procedure (Esteva, 2000, pp. 106–08).

The decree of October 22, 2001, expropriating the thirteen *ejidos* that formed close to 5,383 hectares, shows that commercial liberalization of *ejido* lands through constitutional reform and presidential decree is not automatic. The *ejidatarios*, especially those in Atenco, decided that their land would not be expropriated at any price, considering that this meant the economic and social destruction of their communities. Fixing the price of land at an extremely low price of 25 pesos per metre for irrigated land and 7.20 for seasonal land first roused the ire of the peasants. But as the protest took form, it became clear that they would accept no economic compensation for the expropriation of their lands. Protests were violent from the outset. Peasants advanced on horseback and foot, armed with machetes, through the centre of Mexico City, an action reminiscent of the times ninety years ago when Zapata and Villa marched in with similar armies.

This expropriation attempt demonstrates two opposite visions of commodification and its actors. This is not only a case in which one party tries to commodify a space while the other resists. This is a dispute about the use of land in which each party has a specific viewpoint about how commodification should be carried out.

The first is the perspective of the federal government. Using its right to administer public-interest goods, the government took the initiative to expropriate a considerable extension of land to build a public project from which corporations would derive great direct and indirect benefits. The government's point of view uses strictly economic considerations, among them, the chance of buying land very cheaply, land with which it will later speculate and let others speculate. Social and cultural criteria do not exist in its commodification vision, and the potential political problems that may arise from the affected communities are ignored, since the government considers that it knows better "what is a public good than do the *ejidatarios*."

The *ejidatarios* espouse a second perspective, using a discourse that, for social and cultural reasons, rejects expropriation, arguing that the community's existence would be endangered. This discourse grows as public protest increases, and it is kept in the media by national and international social organizations. But this viewpoint also has a less publicized current, one present in the minds of *ejidatarios* as the government raises its offers. The *ejidatarios* do not think that the lands should be appraised according to their original use as irrigated and seasonal lands. According to *ejidatarios*, these lands have received strong pressures from urbanization because of the use the peasants have given them over the years. Proximity to

Mexico City creates pressures on these lands that had become space for small businesses and workshops, an added reason not to consider them exclusively as harvest lands. A final consideration is the role the *ejidatarios* and their families would play as potential workers in the future airport as luggage carriers, cleaners, or security guards. The conclusion is that, if the *ejidatarios* are to commodify their living and working spaces, they had better do it as citizens and not as outcasts.

A second element in the protest is who represents the *ejidatarios*, a question the government tried to exploit. Due to the antiquity of the *ejidos*, the certification of deeds was difficult in many cases because the land had passed from generation to generation within the same family for over half a century. In negotiations, the government tried to converse only with those *ejidatarios* who had obtained official, up-to-date property deeds according to the reforms of Article 27 of the Constitution. The strategy of using the politically co-opted was not successful and only hardened the conflict.

Finally, the position of the *ejidatarios* against expropriation is complicated by the fact that some of the lands had been illegally rented prior to 1992. Strictly speaking, the *ejidatarios* had already commodified part of the *ejido*. This aspect could entangle the social networks of the community. If expropriation went ahead, it would imply relocating all inhabitants and changes in ways of life linked to the *ejido*.

As the protests grew, the federal government raised the offer to 50 pesos per square metre, without making a distinction between irrigated and seasonal lands. This amounted to about one million pesos, not really a valuable deal for the peasants but impressive for most because they live in poor conditions and with precarious incomes through agriculture.

After this offer in July 2002, the public speculated that the case was not yet closed, because the peasants could not possibly resist such an offer. But they did. Finally, the project to build the new metropolitan airport at that precise location was abandoned by the federal government, and the decision to increase operations in the existing airport, with improvements of the facilities, was taken by Fox's government. The rejection by the *ejidatarios* showed the failure of presidential power, confused between its political responsibilities, its entrepreneurial background, and its undeniable loyalty to business community interests.

CONCLUSION

In Mexico, commodification still has pending issues: oil exploitation and its commercialization by the state and pressures to privatize electrical power. Those are the most visible aspects of the drive of transnational corporations, which are looking for further commodification spaces.

Despite weaknesses and contradictions, Mexican economic nationalism has nurtured generations of Mexicans who struggle for a national project that rejects the wholesale commodification of the nation. The everyday struggle of individuals and communities to recover social control over the market when the government has abdicated is remarkable.

Notes

1. "The ownership of lands and water within the national frontiers correspond originally to the Nation, and the Nation has the right to transmit ownership to private persons, thus constituting private property.... The Nation will have at any time the right to impose on private property the modalities that it deems are in the public interest, as well as the right to regulate, in favour of social benefit, the use of natural resources susceptible to appropriation with the objective of achieving a fair distribution of public wealth" (Article 27).
2. "It corresponds to the State, the regency of national development.... The state will plan, conduct, coordinate and guide the national economic activity, and will be in charge of regulating and supporting activities demanded by the interest of all" (Article 25).
3. The name came from a book with the same title. It analysed the fight between nationalists and monetarists inside Mexico's government since the 1970s (Tello & Cordera, 1985).
4. Mexico's government was able to transform itself into a large business structure, controlling the exploitation and commercialization of sectors such as oil, electricity, mines, and railways.
5. These included changes over peasants' long-standing right to cultivate land in the *ejido* system.
6. Most unions and union confederations are members of the PRI. Unions were always important in the political life of Mexico. Without their support, initiatives such as Mexico joining NAFTA never could have had workers' support. Independent unions (not affiliated to PRI), such as the Frente Auténtico del Trabajo, played an important role with the NGOs in opposing NAFTA.
7. Metalclad was the first company to file a suit against Mexico. It was January 1997, three years after NAFTA began. This meant that with difficulty, Metalclad could invest $90 million US dollars, the price that initially determined the amount of damages sought.
8. Two of these citizens' organizations are the Public Citizen's Global Trade Watch in Washington and the Defence of Canadian Liberty Committee.
9. In March 2004, the Federal Supreme Court decided that the federal Ministry of Finance could not take this amount from the money the federal government gives to the states each year (Gutiérrez-Haces, 2004, pp. 46–47).
10. The old *ejido* titles are being given to specific private persons. Once this is done, the Mexican government no longer owns the land.

CHAPTER TEN

Forging New Democracies
Indigenous Struggles for Autonomy

GERARDO OTERO & HEIDI JUGENITZ

For more than five hundred years, indigenous peoples in Latin America have been the victims of enclosure, forced from their land and livelihood by colonists, non-indigenous farmers, and extractive industries. In the current era of neoliberal globalism, industry and international economic entities have taken the enclosure trend to a new extreme, joining forces with supportive or complicit Latin American governments to commodify what few elements of society have not yet been commodified, namely communal indigenous lands. This drive to privatize communal lands and "rationalize" their use is a looming threat to the physical and cultural survival of Latin America's indigenous peoples. Far from resigning themselves to the inevitability of the "new global order," Indian peoples are fighting back. They have launched major campaigns for survival by forming new organizations for struggle and mobilization. Their key demands are contained in the notion of autonomy and include issues of self-determination, land, and territory. In Latin America, such Indian demands can only be accommodated by transcending the weak liberal-democratic regimes that began to emerge in the 1980s, by moving into broader forms of societal democracies.

"Autonomy" can be defined in two ways, only one of which can address Indian demands (Díaz Polanco, 1997). The first is the liberal definition of autonomy, conceived as the "permission granted" from above by the ruling classes to indigenous communities to tend to their own affairs and retain at least some of their customs. In this case, the specific definition of autonomy depends on the whims of the ruling classes. The second definition of autonomy, by contrast, involves a "political juridical regime, agreed upon and not merely granted, that implies the creation of a true political collectivity within the national society" (Díaz Polanco, 1997, p. 95). We posit that arriving at such an agreed upon regime of autonomy requires that indigenous peoples become politically formed actors who assert their rights and demands.

The purpose of this paper is to do a comparative analysis of two movements that include a central Indian component, both in their key demands and their constituencies. One is Mexico's Zapatista National Liberation Army (*Ejército Zapatista de Liberación Nacional* or EZLN), and the other is Ecuador's Confederation of Indigenous Nationalities of Ecuador (*Confederación de Nacionalidades Indígenas del Ecuador* or CONAIE). Our main argument is that Indian struggles for autonomy are non-capitalist (although not necessarily *anti*-capitalist) in the sense that they aim to decommodify nature and labour power, at least in Indian territory. Indian struggles thus challenge one of the main tenets of neoliberal globalism: the attempt to privatize whatever resources remain in the public domain. Another argument is that Indian struggles at the turn of the twenty-first century constitute a challenge to the emerging liberal democracies in Latin America. Based on the principle of individual equality for all and centred on the electoral process, liberal democracy can hardly accommodate Indian demands for identity recognition as Indian peoples. Their resolution requires a transition into a post-liberal, societally democratic regime that respects both equality and difference. A similar argument has been advanced by various scholars (e.g., Zamosc, 1994; Selverston-Scher, 2001; Stavenhagen, 2000; Van Cott, 1994; Yashar, 1998, 1999), but we provide additional evidence from the CONAIE and EZLN movements, in conjunction with our central argument about the non-capitalist nature of Indian struggles.

The chief paradox or contrast of the two movements' quest for Indian autonomy is as follows. CONAIE started out its organizing at the local and regional levels as an Indian movement, which then developed into national-level class struggles involving non-Indian sectors and supporting the creation of the Pachakutik Movement (*Movimiento de Unidad Plurinacional Pachakutik-Nuevo País*) in January 1996. In Mexico, what the EZLN started in 1994 as a classic national-popular revolutionary movement was eventually reduced to a regional Indian struggle. The EZLN-sponsored *Frente Zapatista de Liberación Nacional* (Zapatista National Liberation Front or EZLN) in 1996 became a political organization whose members would act only in civil society, but would not directly seek political power in the state. We will use Gerardo Otero's theory of the political-cultural formation of groups, communities, and classes to understand the ways in which CONAIE and the EZLN have challenged the limitations of liberal democracy, and how their demands are non-capitalist (Otero, 1999, 2004a; Otero & Jugenitz, 2003). The theory will also help us to resolve the paradox of their diverse emergence, trajectories, and development.

In the remainder of this introduction, we present some central similarities and differences between CONAIE and EZLN and outline our main concepts. Next, we look at regional cultures to determine how the two movements' demands have been shaped. We then analyse the pattern of state interventions vis-à-vis the indigenous movements in Mexico and Ecuador over the past two decades. Leadership types, organizational structure, and governing norms of both organizations are then explored. We show how their internal dynamics have enhanced their ability to challenge the hegemony of neoliberal globalism with differing degrees of success. Finally, we sum up the main similarities and contrasts between the EZLN and CONAIE, and we review how our theory helps one understand their different trajectories.

CONAIE-EZLN COMPARISON

A comparison around organizational genesis, structure, tactics, and strategies will help establish the chief similarities and differences of these organizations. CONAIE was formed as such in a 1986 public event inaugurating the confederation of a multiplicity of Indian local and regional organizations, which had been taking shape for a couple of decades. This organization eventually became officially recognized by the government of Ecuador in 1993. While the EZLN took about a decade to organize in the state of Chiapas in south-eastern Mexico, throughout this period, it was a clandestine military organization until its insurrection on New Year's Eve of 1994. Even though the Mexican Congress issued laws to enable the EZLN's leadership to negotiate with the government, it is still not legally recognized and remains a military organization. Yet it is an army commanded by the civilian authorities of the EZLN's base communities, and, since early 1994, it privileges a peaceful approach to redressing its grievances.

CONAIE is not only legally recognized but a pan-Ecuadorian confederation that rests upon the regional and local indigenous organizations from which it was constituted. It unites diverse and free-standing organizations with agendas, strategies, and organizational dynamics of their own, which leaves them more susceptible to co-optation on the basis of their immediate corporate-economic interests. CONAIE was formed out of the merger of the country's highland (peasant and artisan), Amazonian (hunter-gatherer societies), and coastal (peasant and fishing) indigenous organizations (Selverston-Scher, 2001, p. 38). The EZLN emerged as a region-specific organization of indigenous peasants, artisans, and rural semi-proletarians, but it also became a national symbol of Indian struggles: most Indian peoples have publicly recognized and supported the EZLN as representing their interests (Gilbreth & Otero, 2001).

While both organizations struggle primarily on behalf of their Indian constituencies, the paradox discussed previously remains: that CONAIE moved decisively from an Indian-identity-based organization to one involving broad alliances with other popular struggles in pursuit of "re-founding the state" while the EZLN, which initially called for the generalization of a national-popular liberation struggle with primarily class-focused grievances, has become increasingly isolated in its struggle for indigenous rights and culture on a national level and now fights to implement such rights at the local level in Chiapas. The similarities of these organizations around their Indian core will help us understand their challenges to liberal democracy and neoliberal globalism, while their differences will help explain the relative failures and successes of each organization.

THE THEORY OF POLITICAL-CULTURAL FORMATION (PCF)

PCF is a theory about how civil society "thickens" and becomes strengthened vis-à-vis political society or the state in the strict sense (Otero, 1999, 2004a). Civil society "thickens" when subordinate groups, classes and communities increase their organized presence and political action to advance their interests (Fox, 1996). PCF contrasts with class-reductionist perspectives in Traditional Marxism (TM) and identity-based theories emerging from new-social-movement (NSM) theories. While the former see a direct causal link between class position and expected political behaviour, the latter abstract from material demands to focus on processes of identity formation. PCF theory attempts a systematic synthesis that transcends the reductionism in both approaches. (See Otero & Jugenitz, 2003 for a critique of TM and NSM.) PCF's central research question is this: how can subordinate classes achieve hegemony, or at least the ability to advance their interests, by promoting state policies in their favour? It proposes regional cultures, state intervention, and leadership types as the mediating determinations between class structural processes and political-formation outcomes. The main political outcomes are "bourgeois-hegemonic," when the state or the ruling classes co-opt the resulting organization; "oppositional," when the state is unresponsive to or repressive of subordinate-class struggles; and "popular-democratic," when favourable state interventions are the result of strong, organized mobilization and bottom-up pressure. Regional cultures form the basis to articulate an organization's demands. State intervention shapes the initial contours of the resulting character of a class organization. Finally, leadership types and grassroots modes of participation determine the organization's chances to remain independent from the state and autonomous from other political organizations, as well as its alliances with other movements (Otero, 2004a, pp. 331–35).

REGIONAL CULTURE AND THE SHAPING OF DEMANDS

Regional culture shapes the object(s) of an organization's struggle. Anthropologists and historians have shown that humans reshape values and traditions through interaction with people from other ethnic groups, and particularly by resisting dominant groups or classes (Kearney & Varese, 1999; Stern, 1987; Wearne, 1996). Latin America's indigenous peoples, who have sustained cultural differences for centuries, have framed their contemporary struggle in terms of indigenous identity based on indigenous "peoples" or "nations." Hence CONAIE, for instance, strives to achieve a truly "plurinational state" and an "intercultural society" (CONAIE, 2004a). As Wearne has put it, "It is vital for indigenous people to be seen as 'nations' and 'peoples' rather than simply 'ethnic groups' and 'people'" because this terminology has major implications in international law regarding collective rights and self-determination: "'Peoples' have a right to self-determination; ethnic groups merely the right to minority rights" (Wearne, 1996, p. 20). The drive to decommodify themselves and their cultures—expressed through the values of collectivity, community, and ethnic survival as peoples that require land and territory—is the essence of the movement's ideological challenge to neoliberal globalism. It also forms the basis of the central indigenous demands on the state, such as the recognition of rights to communal territories for indigenous nationalities, autonomy from the state, official recognition of indigenous languages, and the right to self-determination. These demands have been so prevalent throughout the world among indigenous peoples that, in 1989, the International Labour Organization recognized them in Convention 169. However, fewer than 20 governments, including Mexico's and Ecuador's, went on to sign this convention (Van Cott, 2000). Indian peoples have taken this Convention very seriously and attempted to make it a reality in their countries.

In Ecuador, the struggle to maintain and enhance Indian identity has been at the forefront of the Indian movement, but it is inseparable from the struggle for land and territory. CONAIE's founder and first president, Luis Macas, noted,

> We believe that a fundamental cause [of the 1990 indigenous uprising] was the existence of mobilizing axes like the defense and recuperation of land and territory, as well as a clear unity forged by the revitalization of the ethnic identity of the Indian people. (Macas, 1991, p. 5)

Although the EZLN's Subcomandante Marcos stated in a press interview on 1 January 1994 that NAFTA was a death sentence to indigenous ethnicities in Mexico, material demands were centrally framed in the First Declaration of the Lacandón Jungle. It focused on economic and political demands: "work, land, housing, food, health care, education, independence, freedom, democracy, justice and peace" (EZLN, 1994). It was only later on, once indigenous organizations from Chiapas and throughout Mexico showed their solidarity toward the EZLN, that the symbolic fight for the right to Indianness became a key rallying point in its struggle. Dialogue with these organizations became so critical for the EZLN that it called for a National Indigenous Forum to be held in January 1996, in preparation for the final stage of negotiations with government representatives on the theme of "Indian rights and culture." This was the first of four major themes to be negotiated with the government, the others being economic and land issues, women's rights, and democracy and reform of the state. The consensus reached at the National Indigenous Forum, which included the central demands of autonomy and self-determination, was eventually reflected in the San Andrés Accords of 16 February 1996 (Gilbreth & Otero, 2001).

While there are some discursive differences between the demands of the EZLN and those of CONAIE, their essence is the same. In Mexico, the object of struggle is the recognition of "*pueblos indios*" with territories, new jurisdictions, and competencies in accord with their specific social, political, and cultural realities (Ruiz Hernández, 2000). In Ecuador, CONAIE struggles for recognition of politically autonomous "*nacionalidades indígenas*" within a plurinational state. Both movements envision nations that recognize and appreciate indigenous peoples in place of the current reality, which seeks to assimilate them to a "national culture" and reduce them to labour commodities within free-market hegemony. The objective of political autonomy is to establish a new relation between the state and indigenous peoples. This challenge implies a new conception of citizenship, one that goes beyond the recognition of individuals as subjects of rights. A plurinational state would be a new political enrichment, the first deep and true integration of the states rather than their weakening or fragmentation (Kymlicka & Norman, 2000).

By framing their common grievances as indigenous peoples and transforming these into a collective identity of Indianness, the members of the Mexican and Ecuadorian indigenous movements have been able to define what unites them, name their collective demands, and envision a society in which their cultural rights are recognized and appreciated. This process has both unified the members of the indigenous movement and reinforced the ideological distance between the post-liberal vision of the movements and the liberal states they challenge. This ideological division has been an integral source of the indigenous movement's success in rallying for social change and constitutional rights. The responsiveness of the Ecuadorian and Mexican states, however, has been mostly in the form of liberal constitutional legislation that grants limited views of autonomy, which is not accompanied by the proper enabling laws to implement or protect Indian rights as these actors see them.

STATE INTERVENTION

In PCF theory, state intervention may assume either a favourable or an unfavourable character from the perspective of subordinate groups, communities, and classes. Favourable state policies tend to occur for at least two reasons, each with different consequences: (1) Because the state wants to co-opt the movement or (2) because the movement has shown enough strength, alliances, and/or public support to extract gains from the state. It is the latter result that can be said to have a popular-democratic character. We argue that both EZLN and CONAIE have assumed this character, even when tangible state interventions in their favour are sparse (although greater for CONAIE); the construction of sustainable organizations in the face of state-sponsored repression or government unresponsiveness or betrayal, however, is a substantial political achievement in its own right.

Mexico

The EZLN captured international attention on January 1, 1994, when it launched an armed uprising in the south-eastern state of Chiapas. Carried out on the day that the North American Free Trade Agreement (NAFTA) went into effect, the uprising was a statement against the neoliberal policies that were threatening the survival of indigenous peasants. The participants in the insurrection—overwhelmingly Mayan peasants—explained their rebellion in terms that were both anti-neoliberal and pro-indigenous. State intervention had been so systematically exploitative and oppressive toward Indians in Chiapas that their only resort was to form an oppositional organization. Having exhausted all legal means of redressing its grievances, the EZLN had no way out but to rebel, as it stated in The First Declaration of the Lacandón Jungle:

> To prevent the continuation of the above [exploitation, exclusion, etc.], and as our last hope, after having tried to utilize all legal means based on our [Mexico's] Constitution, we go to our Constitution, to apply Article 39, which says: "National Sovereignty essentially and originally resides in the people. All political power emanates from the people and its purpose is to help the people. The people have, at all times, the inalienable right to alter or modify their form of government." (EZLN, 1994)

Only after 12 days of armed struggle in 1994, and under tremendous national and international pressure for a peaceful response to the uprising, did the government propose an armistice to initiate peace talks. The government's first proposal to resolve the EZLN's grievances was rejected by the Zapatista base communities in June after a long process of democratic consultation and decision making. In early August 1994, two weeks before the national presidential elections to be held on the 20th, the EZLN sponsored a national convention of the political and social left. It managed to assemble more than 6,000 representatives of left political parties and other democratic civil-society organizations in what came to be known as the National Democratic Convention. Its goals included defeating the ruling Institutional Revolutionary Party (PRI) in the coming elections, or getting ready to mount a civil-society opposition in case of electoral fraud. Nevertheless, the PRI still won the presidency by the narrowest official majority in its 65-year history. An exception must have been the previous presidential election in 1988, widely considered to have been stolen by fraud (Chand, 2001).

The new president, Ernesto Zedillo, started his term with a pro-peace discourse. Yet, fewer than three months later, on 9 February 1995, he launched a military offensive to capture the EZLN's leadership, which he labelled as "terrorist." Instead of confronting the federal army, the EZLN withdrew into the jungle with more than 22,000 people from its base communities. The army ransacked the empty homes of the indigenous peasants. While such state aggression generated divisions, and a few turned to the state for assistance, the core of the Zapatista base communities remained firmly in support of their organization. The negative state intervention against indigenous peasants strengthened their determination to stay an oppositional force. Later in 1995, thirty-eight municipalities in Chiapas were declared "rebel municipalities" by the EZLN and its constituents, where autonomy and self-government were put into practice (Van der Haar, 2001; Burguete Cal y Mayor, 2000).

In March 1995, the Mexican Congress passed a law of "Accord and Pacification," which granted amnesty to the EZLN leadership so that it could negotiate a peaceful settlement. From then on, the government followed a two-pronged policy. On one hand, it began to negotiate with the EZLN. It was first agreed that the four central themes to be negotiated were as follows: indigenous rights and culture, economic and land issues, women's rights, and democracy and state reform. On the other hand, the government turned a blind eye to the formation of a series of paramilitary groups formed by local ruling-class members of the PRI (Centro de Derechos Humanos Fray Bartolomé de Las Casas, 1996; Human Rights Watch, 1997).

On February 16, 1996, representatives of the government and the EZLN reached the first agreement on indigenous rights and culture in San Andrés. Part of the Constitution and a number of state and federal laws would have to be modified in order to enable the implementation of these accords. By August of 1996, and in view of the fact that no advancement was taking place to implement the San Andrés Accords, the EZLN suspended talks on the remaining issues mentioned previously. By November of 1996, the Congressional Commission for Concord and Pacification (*Comisión para la Concordia y la Pacificación*, COCOPA) had elaborated a concrete proposal of legislative changes to implement the San Andrés Accords. The COCOPA decided that the EZLN and the government had to either agree to the entire package or reject it. After a brief consultation period with its support bases, the EZLN accepted COCOPA's proposal even though it was below its expectations. President Zedillo, however, requested a 15-day period to "study" the proposal and then made a counterproposal, thus derailing the negotiation process (Hernández Navarro & Herrera, 1998). In sum, state intervention during Zedillo's administration granted a concession on paper (the San Andrés Accords) on which the government later reneged, but its primary policy was repressive by allowing the proliferation of paramilitary groups that increasingly harassed Zapatista base communities.

In July 2000 Mexico, Vicente Fox, an opposition candidate of the centre-right National Action Party (PAN), managed to oust the PRI from the presidency after 71 years of continuous rule. Several factors contributed to Mexico's electoral democratization, including the continuous thickening of civil society after the student movement of 1968, the struggle of democratic teachers and electricity workers, the peasant movements of the 1970s and 1980s, and the civic organizational upsurge in the aftermath of Mexico City's earthquake of 1985 (Otero, 1995; Chand, 2001). Crucially, the EZLN's pressure as an actor external to the political system forced the Mexican Congress and the Zedillo administration to introduce a series of democratic reforms that made for a more competitive system. These included new rules for the state's financing of political parties, the creation of an independent Federal Electoral Institute to operate and monitor elections, and even the introduction of primary elections within the ruling PRI (Gilbreth & Otero, 2001; Prud'homme, 1998).

One of Fox's first acts of government was to send the COCOPA legislative proposal to Congress, but then he pursued an ambiguous policy toward the EZLN. The EZLN announced three conditions for the reinstatement of negotiations with the newly elected government of Vicente Fox: the withdrawal of seven military positions from Zapatista base communities, the release of presumed Zapatista sympathizers from jail, and the passage of the San Andrés Accords (Henríquez & Aponte, 2000).

Initially, Fox fulfilled these conditions only partially. He withdrew four military positions (out of 30) and released 20 political prisoners (out of more than 90). He also lobbied members of congress to pass the indigenous legislation emanating from the San Andrés Accords, but this specific item was now out of his hands. The main difficulty for Fox and Congress in fulfilling the Zapatista demands rests with economic interests that oppose Indian autonomy, for its repercussions on decommodification. According to Héctor Díaz Polanco, part of the obstacle to real change is the Plan Puebla-Panamá, a mega-project that intends to appropriate natural resources in the Zapatista regions and commodify indigenous communities. The latter would be considered only as a source of labour power (cited in Correa, 2001, p. 22; Carlsen, 2004). For Díaz Polanco, the San Andrés Accords "would have the effect of turning these indigenous peoples (*pueblos indios*) into [social] actors that could become obstacles in these [economic] projects" (cited in Correa, 2001, p. 22).

By mid-2001, the federal Congress had passed a watered-down version of the San Andrés Accords that did not satisfy the EZLN. Failing to recognize autonomy to Indian peoples federally and to consider them subjects of public rights perpetuates the commodification of Indian labour power, lands, and territories, leaving them vulnerable to capitalist development and exploitation without any say in the matter (Harvey, 2002). After almost two years in silence as a protest against this spurious legislation, the EZLN support bases launched a massive demonstration, taking over the highlands city of San Cristóbal de Las Casas, Chiapas on 1 January 2003. More than 20,000 indigenous men, women, and children, many with machetes in hand, filled the central plaza for more than three hours, during which seven EZLN commanders spoke to the masses (Bellinghausen, 2003).

By August 2004, the EZLN decided to wait no longer for Congress to correct its legislation along the lines of the San Andrés Accords. Instead, it set out to implement de facto autonomy in its base communities. Any socio-economic advancement has been achieved mostly without any help from state agencies. Instead, Zapatista communities have resorted to support from NGOs, which may decline at any time. A more substantial legislation will have to pass before the military conflict in Chiapas is resolved. Any legislative or other achievements for Indian peasants will have to be primarily their own, the result of bottom-up initiative, solidarity, and mobilization, rather than a concession by the state.

Ecuador

The 1980s marked the consolidation of Ecuador's contemporary indigenous movement. In the context of greater political space proffered by the country's first democratic civilian administration, indigenous groups from the Amazon and the
highlands consolidated their struggles at regional and national levels. Of CONAIE's
creation in 1986, Luis Macas said,

> CONAIE's creation marked the emergence of what had been an invisible
> social sector in the national and international scene for many centuries.
> CONAIE was the realization of the indigenous people's dream of uniting all
> indigenous people, overcoming all political and religious differences....
> (quoted in Selverston-Scher, 2001, p. xv)

Macas's testimony about achieving a common indigenous dream may be over-
stated, but its underlying thrust—that CONAIE has supplied indigenous peoples
of various backgrounds with a common means of pursuing social change—is accurate. Since CONAIE's formation, its membership and name recognition have
grown rapidly, and the organization has assumed a position of considerable political influence. In contrast with the EZLN, CONAIE has retained a solid presence in
civil society, and, by supporting the formation of the Pachakutik Movement in
1995, it started to act in the realms of political society and electoral politics in
1996 (Mijeski & Beck, 1998).

When Rodrigo Borja took office as Ecuador's President in 1988, CONAIE had
been functioning as an umbrella organization for the country's indigenous groups
for two years. In contrast to the unabashedly repressive administration of Febres
Cordero (who had preceded Borja), the democratic-left Borja government
(1988–92) displayed a willingness to converse with indigenous leaders. During
Borja's first year in office, indigenous and government representatives met on an
almost weekly basis (Selverston-Scher, 2001, p. 45). These overtures by the state,
though largely superficial, created a political opening that the indigenous movement exploited by staging its first major *levantamiento*, or uprising, in 1990. With
the exception of an armed confrontation in the province of Loja, the national
mobilization was completely non-violent.

The immediate outcomes of the 1990 uprising were mixed. The uprising provoked the instant militarization of indigenous communities and accusations that
foreign subversives had infiltrated the movement, but it established the movement
as an enormous social and political force while sparking a series of dialogues
between the state and indigenous leaders. Although these dialogues were not
nearly as fruitful as indigenous activists had hoped, they provided a forum for the
concrete articulation of the indigenous struggle against commodification, including
demands for territorial rights, constitutional recognition of Ecuador as a plurinational state, rights to self-governance, and executive control of the nation's
bilingual, multicultural education program. Furthermore, as a result of his con-

versations with indigenous leaders, Borja began to incorporate elements of their discourse (such as the concept "plurinational state") into his language, lending it a new validity within the realm of institutional politics (Egan, 1996, p. 133).

The next major indigenous mobilization came two years later, while Borja was still in office. Whereas the vast majority of the participants of the 1990 protest had been highland Indians, the 1992 mobilization was organized and carried out primarily by indigenous people from the lowlands. The march was completely non-violent and almost celebratory in nature, as indigenous people (many of them dressed in costume and carrying banners or flags) made their way through the highlands to the capital. Upon their arrival, and in what was perhaps the most clear-cut case of a favourable state intervention in the history of the contemporary movement, Borja granted two million hectares of communal territory to the OPIP, the *Organización de Pueblos Indígenas de Pastaza* (Egan, 1996, p. 134). He later granted an additional 1.5 million hectares of land to the Huaorani, the most isolated of Ecuador's indigenous peoples. These were significant achievements for OPIP and the Huaorani, but they also planted the seeds for future divisiveness and infighting in CONAIE's leadership.

The positive state interventions that took place during the Borja administration raised indigenous people's expectations of the state and inspired additional mobilizations in coming years. Borja, however, departed from office in 1992, and his successor, Sixto Durán, was far less amicable towards the indigenous movement. A 1993 protest against elements of the National Agrarian Law resulted in a confrontation with the military and the clubbing of CONAIE founder and President Luis Macas. Durán also revoked the bilingual education programs that had been implemented under Borja and attempted to undermine the land grants implemented by his predecessor. Even in the face of these repressive measures, the indigenous movement managed to continue growing on the basis of its reputation with the public.

In 1998, a National Constituent Assembly was planned to make revisions to the Ecuadorian Constitution. Participants of the indigenous movement, seizing the opportunity to enact into law its long-articulated demands for autonomy and a plurinational state, joined forces with other social organizations and proposed to the state that the members of the National Constituent Assembly be elected not according to majority rule but through nomination by different popular organizations (Andolina, 1998). Under this arrangement, popular groups (such as CONAIE) would select their own representatives to sit on the National Assembly. In this context, the term "nation" refers to the country, rather than an indigenous people. Congress quickly suppressed this proposal in favour of a traditional election based on majority rule. Yet Pachakutik, the indigenous-backed popular movement, had 7 representatives in the 70-member assembly in addition to 3 more seats through alliance. Nevertheless, in response to what they judged to be a display of exclusionary lawmaking, indigenous activists convoked their own alternative assembly (the National Popular Assembly) prior to the meeting of the official

Assembly and presented their proposed changes to the official government-appointed body.

The official Assembly's response to the Popular Assembly's recommendations was less than enthusiastic. Even so, input and pressure from indigenous leaders and the Popular Assembly resulted in a constitution that codified the hemisphere's then most advanced regime of indigenous rights. It recognized collective rights and laid the foundation for regional autonomous governance of indigenous territories:

> Regional autonomous government will be exercised by provincial councils, municipal councils, parochial boards and other organisms determined by the law for the administration of indigenous and Afro-Ecuadorian territorial units. Provincial and county governments will enjoy full autonomy and will be able to dictate ordinances, and to create, modify and eliminate taxes and special contributions. (Asamblea, 1998, p. 122)

In January 2000, amidst a national economic crisis, CONAIE engaged in what was arguably its most aggressive and internationally visible act of protest to date. Just days after President Jamil Mahuad announced his plans to adopt the US dollar as Ecuador's currency, CONAIE initiated a march to the nation's capital. On January 21, 2000, its members proceeded to "takeover" the Congressional building, the Supreme Court headquarters, and the Presidential Palace, forcing Mahuad to flee the country. As indigenous peoples flooded into the Presidential Palace, CONAIE President Antonio Vargas, military officer Lucio Gutierrez, and a former Ecuadorian supreme court justice joined hands and proclaimed themselves a junta of "national salvation." Their time in power was short-lived. Under intense pressure from the United States, the triumvirate rescinded its control and allowed Mahuad's vice-president, Alvaro Noboa, to take office as the new president.

Mahuad's abdication—essentially a non-violent coup—stirred great controversy on the national political scene on the normative value of democracy and military rule (Valpy, 2000). Since the ousting of Mahuad, CONAIE through Pachakutik was a strong supporter in Lucio Gutierrez getting elected Ecuador's president in a broad coalition in 2002. Luis Macas was initially appointed Minister of Agriculture. After a few months in office, however, it became clear that Gutierrez would not fulfil his promises to the indigenous peoples, so Pachakutik withdrew from the governing coalition, and Macas and another indigenous minister stepped down from office. Gutierrez had merely continued to push the previous neoliberal agenda.

Several problems for the indigenous movement resulted from this political alliance. On one hand, there was an internal division between those who opposed and those who supported direct participation in the institutions of the state. On the other, part of Gutierrez's strategy included the co-optation of several regional leaders of indigenous organizations. In fact, the II Congress of Indigenous Nationalities and Peoples of Ecuador, led by CONAIE and held in December of 2004, denounced this co-optation and Gutierrez's attempt to also take control of the congress through spurious local leaders from the Amazon region (CONAIE, 2004b).

Luis Macas become CONAIE's president once again for a three-year period as of January 2005. Since taking the organization's helm once again, CONAIE busily mobilized its constituency to oust the Gutierrez government: Says Macas,

> We must recover the spaces that were achieved by the indigenous movement and we warn our enemies to take care; they owe us the greatest respect because we have been respectful in this country for 512 years. We have been respectful of our diversity and plurality, and we want to construct our autonomy, but this autonomy is today usurped and intervened by Lucio Gutiérrez, by this servant of the oligarchy and by this butler of imperialism. (Macas, 2005)

On 20 April 2005, CONAIE and many other popular organizations and urban protesters achieved their goal of ousting Gutierrez. The former vice-president assumed the presidency and promised to initiate a process to "re-found the state," one of CONAIE's major goals (Cano, 2005).

In sum, the 1990 indigenous uprising marked the beginning of a pattern of some favourable state interventions for Ecuador's indigenous population, although there have been a number of unfulfilled promises by opportunist politicians. Since the 1990 uprising, state interventions—both favourable and unfavourable—have had a variety of implications. Their ultimate meanings for indigenous people and for the state have changed due to the movement's new found power. As a politically-formed actor, CONAIE has proven its ability to (1) impose its will on the government to force at least some favourable interventions; (2) improve its own reputation and strength when the government successfully carries out a negative intervention; (3) respond to negative interventions in such a way that they are effectively nullified or, at least, use them to further consolidate the movement's organization; and (4) maintain alliances and promote political action with other popular sectors. CONAIE's and Pachakutik's withdrawal of support for the Luis Gutierrez government, for instance, has been critical for his ultimate downfall. (See Destituye [2005] for a chronicle of the 2005 crisis.) It remains to be seen to what extent the promised "re-founding of the state" will include substantive Indian autonomy and decommodification measures.

LEADERSHIP TYPE AND MODES OF PARTICIPATION

The final intervening variable in PCF is leadership type and modes of participation, which affect the process of political-cultural formation in at least three ways. First, leadership strength, which depends in turn on its level of responsiveness and accountability toward its constituency, is critical for the organization to retain its independence from the state and resist co-optation attempts. Second, leadership shapes the alliances that organizations establish with other groups or classes, how broad or narrow they become. Third, by resisting state co-optation, the leadership influences the ability of organizations to move beyond a mere oppositional stance to become "popular-democratic." In sum, a democratic-participatory leadership, as opposed to a corrupt or opportunistic one, involves the highest degrees of internal democracy and accountability, as well as the lowest likelihood for its co-optation and/or corruption. A democratic-participatory leadership type also enhances the likelihood for an organization to become popular-democratic (Otero, 1999, 2004a, pp. 334–35).

Established democratic processes are crucial to an organization's ability to sustain effective mobilizations against the state, as they both indicate and bring about a strong sense of solidarity and provide a microcosmic vision of the participation they are seeking within the nation-state (Brysk, 2000, p. 298). The expression of democracy within the EZLN has been more consistent than within CONAIE, as there have always been real and occasionally serious differences between the Eastern (Oriente) and Highland (Sierra) factions of the latter. Moreover, the post-2000 and pre-2002 fractures within Ecuador's indigenous movement around national electoral processes were, in some cases, less regional than personal in nature. In addition, the serious cleavages that emerged after the removal of President Mahuad in 2000 included differing strategic views not only within CONAIE and Pachakutik but also between the two organizations. Despite such internal divisions, however, the leadership of CONAIE has continued to emphasize the centrality of dialogue and participation to the advancement of both the organization and reform of the state (CONAIE, 2004a, 2004b; Macas, 2005).

Mexico

The EZLN leadership has excelled in promoting a "dialogical" relationship with its constituency, in the sense given to this term by Brazilian educator Paulo Freire (1970) (Johnston, 2000). Freire used this term to describe a relationship in which students are assumed to already possess considerable information and knowledge, and the teacher's role is to help students bring out and systematize such knowledge.

As is common in the history of village uprisings in indigenous communities, leadership tends to be collective (Taylor, 2000). Subcomandante Marcos has been the key spokesperson for the EZLN from its first public appearance, but the organization has made every attempt to divert attention from this figure. In fact, the very symbol of the ski mask indicates that, to the Zapatistas, *"todos somos Marcos"* ("we are all Marcos"). This means that anyone else could take the leadership position, as all remain faceless. The consistent modelling of a bottom-up, dialogic leadership style within the EZLN has lent legitimacy to the organization's goals and agenda.

In regards to political alliances, it was a very consistent choice in 1997 for Subcomandante Marcos to reject the "help" offered to the EZLN by the new Popular Revolutionary Army (EPR), which launched a classic guerrilla offensive against the state in that year, with the goal of taking over state power. Subcomandante Marcos responded that the only help needed by the EZLN was that from civil society organizations (Le Bot, 1997). With this response, the EZLN was giving at least two messages: (1) It had no intention to take over state power but wanted to consolidate itself within civil society, and (2) its main partners in dialogue to change society's power relations with the state are the organizations of other subordinate groups, communities, and classes that make up civil society and whose strategies and tactics are peaceful.

All in all, then, the EZLN's collective leadership is holding up well, has not been corrupted or co-opted, and continues to practice its most central democratic principles after a decade of varying degrees and intensities of oppositional confrontation with the state. Its constituency has not achieved any of its express demands to any significant extent. However, 38 municipalities took it upon themselves to implement the San Andrés Accords of 1996, and became "autonomous municipalities" (Burguete Cal y Mayor, 2000a; Van der Haar, 2001). Therefore, at least on an organizational level, the EZLN has had considerable successes both among its own support bases and by promoting the widespread organization of other subordinate groups, communities, and classes in civil society. The question that emerged after more than a decade of struggle was whether the EZLN's leadership had focused too much on Indian demands, to the detriment of its class demands, and whether it had become isolated from other popular-democratic struggles in Mexico (Bartra & Otero, 2005).

This apparent isolation was broken by the EZLN in mid-2005, when it launched the Sixth Declaration of the Lacandón Jungle (CCRI-EZLN, 2005). Among other things, this declaration acknowledges its previous isolation, reiterates its focus on civil society as the main locus to strengthen democracy, and calls for the organization and alliance of all subordinate groups, communities, and classes against capitalism. This declaration comes in the midst of the conjuncture leading to presidential elections in 2006, so the EZLN is said to be waging its "other campaign." Although all other political parties in their own campaigns try to posit themselves as being at the political centre, the EZLN has criticized them for actually being on the right and for being traitors to indigenous demands. While a bridge is being constructed toward other poor and oppressed peoples, then, another cleavage is being opened in EZLN's relation to the State and to the political parties of the Left.

Ecuador

CONAIE's internal workings reflect the alternative democratic-participatory model it seeks to apply in Ecuador. Where most democratic institutions utilize majority rule in determining their courses of action, CONAIE's decisions are based on consensus (Dávalos, 2000, p. 2). Similarly, CONAIE departs from the Western democratic tradition of representation by promoting direct participation in decision making. CONAIE has promoted a bottom-up method of decision making as a national solution to the shortcomings of Ecuadorian democracy:

> CONAIE and other social organizations drew selectively on various ideas and practices: indigenous, socialist, radical democratic, corporatist, and that of "grassroots development." The goal [was] to generate a system that emphasizes bottom-up, participatory politics rooted in consensus, social equity, development that meets basic needs and generates self-sufficiency, cultural and social diversity, and protection of the environment and human rights. They called their model a plurinational, participatory democracy with a social (communitarian) economy. (Andolina, 1998, p. 4)

CONAIE's leadership, however, has been criticized for being out of touch with its base membership, and there has been much contention about how to advance the plurinational agenda. As mentioned, the decision to support Gutierrez's presidential candidacy in 2000 was a major bone of contention, as was direct participation in the state. Given the strong link between an organization's internal politics and the politics it promotes, it is likely that CONAIE's own decision-making and participation mechanisms will prove to be the single most important (controllable) factor in its future ability to elicit state interventions on behalf of its constituency.

CONCLUSION: RESOLVING THE PARADOX

The struggles of both CONAIE and the EZLN focus on the quest for autonomy for indigenous peoples, which centrally includes decommodification of Indian land, territory and, labour power. The successful struggle against neoliberalism and toward a post-liberal, pluricultural and popular-democratic society, however, requires alliances and coalitions well beyond indigenous organizations. The challenge for Indian organizations is contained in three dilemmas. First, how can they assert Indian-identity struggles without diluting class grievances and anti-commodification struggles? Second, because indigenous peoples have been the most politically marginalized groups in Latin American societies, launching themselves directly into electoral and governmental politics may entail grave risks. The dilemma for indigenous organizations is how to do this without compromising their independence, or risking leadership co-optation. Finally, the third dilemma is related to the second: whether the organization focuses its struggle in civil or in political society, how narrowly or broadly will it attempt to build alliances? Confining themselves to their immediate indigenous constituencies ensures that their main demands will not be diluted in broader struggles, but without broader alliances they risk becoming isolated and, ultimately, defeated or ignored by the state.

CONAIE and the EZLN have both pursued essentially the same goals, but they have each favoured slightly different approaches to pursue them in terms of their focus on civil and/or political society and in regard to alliances. Returning to the chief paradox noted in the introduction, CONAIE framed its initial struggles more centrally around Indian identity, and yet it has expanded into building a broad national-popular coalition through the Pachakutik movement, which includes a wide range of popular sectors. CONAIE has also entered the governmental realm, at least temporarily. In contrast to this, the EZLN set out to launch a broad national-popular insurrection, but has ended up as a rather isolated, regionally localized Indian movement attempting to implement autonomy in its immediate midst. The EZLN, in contrast to Pachakutik, has been rather tightly controlled by the EZLN and has not managed to encompass a very broad spectrum of the population; it is mostly concentrated in Mexico City and limited to a few intellectuals and students.

How can this paradox be resolved from the vantage point of the theory of political-cultural formation? Let us briefly outline a resolution to this paradox. Given that their objects of struggles are essentially the same, we focus on the state and leadership types. First, each organization has been acting within rather different states. Mexico has a much stronger network of corporatist organizations that, even after the PRI's electoral defeat in the presidential elections of 2000, continue to represent a central feature of this state's authoritarianism and bourgeois-hegemonic control (Otero, 2004b). In contrast, Ecuador has a much weaker state that had resorted to authoritarian rule until the 1980s, although without being overly repressive. Therefore, not only has CONAIE been able to make a strong contribution to thicken civil society with its broad-based alliances, but also it has ventured to attempt state reform from within, from the top down. The EZLN, by contrast, has adamantly opposed both electoral politics within an essentially authoritarian state or, at best, an electoral democracy of elites. Furthermore, given the lack of implementation of the San Andrés Accords, the EZLN has also refused to seek or accept any socio-economic-development funds from state agencies. This approach has sheltered the EZLN from divisiveness, corruption and co-optation, but it depends on the weak socio-economic support of NGOs.

CONAIE's involvement in the mobilization to oust three of Ecuador's presidents since 1998 has been received with ambivalence by society. Furthermore, CONAIE's electoral or governmental participation since 1998 (mostly through supporting Pachakutik) put it in a vulnerable situation—several of its constituent organizations and members became susceptible to divisiveness and co-optation. This trend may have been corrected by the end of 2004, when CONAIE's congress retrenched back into civil society. Once again, after sustained mobilization in a broad alliance with other popular sectors, with the left opposition, and even with left municipal presidents of Ecuador's main cities, President Lucio Gutiérrez was ousted by Ecuador's Congress in 2005 (see Ecuador's main online news dailies—*El Universo*, www.eluniverso.com and *El Comercio*, www.elcomercio.com—and CONAIE's web page, conaie.nativeweb.org). Given the greater weakness of the Ecuadorian state, then, CONAIE and the popular sectors may be closer to their goal of "re-founding the state" along the lines of a plurinational society.

In contrast, the EZLN's guarded position against co-optation has resulted in its relative isolation from society, particularly since the passing of the spurious Indian legislation in April 2001. Such a guarded position likely responds to the very fact that the Mexican state is comparatively a much more formidable enemy. Proof of this is the fact that, in 2003 and 2004, one of the greatest peasant mobilizations, called *"El campo no aguanta más"* (The Countryside Can Bear no More or ECNAM), was finally divided by state intervention in October 2004 (Celis Callejas, 2005). ECNAM's central demand was the re-negotiation of NAFTA's agricultural chapter and a new agricultural pact from the state, but its sixth and final point also demanded the resolution of indigenous rights and culture contained in the San Andrés Accords. The EZLN, however, remained isolated from this peasant mobilization. Ironically, then, it seems as if the Mexican state managed to isolate the EZLN by confining its struggle to Indian rights and culture. Because of this "Indianizing," the EZLN, for a long time, lost sight of its original class struggle and its drive to build a broad, pluricultural and popular-democratic front against neoliberalism and for humanity. And yet, given Mexico's strong corporatist culture and institutions, ECNAM collapsed in divisiveness among the leadership of its multiple organizations after two years. In the meantime, the EZLN has been patiently constructing Indian autonomy from the bottom-up. Patient struggle is what it may take, ultimately, to debilitate the Mexican leviathan. Indian autonomy and decommodification struggles will be resolved only within an agreed upon political collectivity and a pluricultural national society. Now that the EZLN has launched itself to construct a national-popular coalition, its main demands may have to be heeded by the state, to the extent that such a coalition becomes consolidated from the bottom up.

CHAPTER ELEVEN

In Defence of the Environmental State
NGO Strategies to Resist the Commodification of Nature

ANITA KRAJNC[1]

Expectations were raised following the 1992 Rio Summit in Rio de Janeiro that the 1990s would be a "turnaround decade." Governments, societal institutions, businesses, and citizens around the world were supposed to redouble their efforts to promote environmentally sustainable development. Instead, we saw the unprecedented commodification of nature, enhanced profits for multinational corporations, the blatant anti-environmental bias of international trade agreements, and the rollback of the environmental state. Although nature has been subject to intense commodification throughout the history of capitalism, neoliberal globalism is facilitating an unparalleled objectification and commodification of nature in terms of its intensity and reach into previously unimagined realms. This process is evident, for instance, in the patenting of individual life forms, including mammals like the so-called Harvard mouse (genetically altered to be predisposed to develop cancer),[2] and in the aggressive push by multinational corporations to privatize the world's water.

Alarmed at corporate attempts to commodify water and other basic necessities, Maude Barlow (1999), the head of the Council of Canadians and founder of the Blue Planet water project, states,

> At the heart of the WTO is an assault on everything left standing in the commons, in the public realm. Everything is now for sale. Even those areas of life that we once considered sacred like health and education, food and water and air and seeds and genes and a heritage. It is all now for sale. Economic freedom—not democracy, and not ecological stewardship—is the defining metaphor of the WTO and its central goal is humanity's mastery of the natural world through its total commodification.

Environmental and other public interest groups are currently engaged in a battle of ideas over what has inherent value, moral standing, and rights, and what can be legitimately objectified, commodified, and hence *devalued*. In this epic ethical and democratic struggle, there is a growing recognition among activists and concerned citizens of the key role the state can and should play in combating the commodification of nature.

In this chapter, I argue that Canadian governments have, for the most part, taken the "wrong turn" since the early 1990s by rolling back the "environmental state"; shifting environmental responsibilities to lower levels of government, the private sector, and NGOs; or simply terminating environmental programs by expanding the rights and power of corporations and by decreasing opportunities for democratic citizen input. Rather than achieving a workable model of sustainable development, such a restructuring of the state and society will very likely lead to the "death of nature" and greater social inequity (Merchant, 1982). According to the International Forum on Globalization (2002), history is likely to view the past twenty years as a historical anomaly, a time when a single dominant model was promoted despite its inherent social and ecological unsustainability. Environmental groups have reacted by shifting their repertoires of collective action. Traditionally, environmental organizations have focused their efforts on public education and lobbying in order to persuade governments to adopt more progressive environmental policies. Now, growing numbers of environmentalists in Canada and abroad have adopted an additional role: to defend and renew the environmentally activist state itself as a means of decommodifying nature.

THE "VALUE" OF NATURE: CHALLENGING INSTRUMENTALISM

At the most fundamental level, the battle over the commodification of nature is a battle over worldviews, moral principles, and the appropriate distribution of benefits and costs. This difference is illustrated in how different actors view a forest. Take, for example, the boreal forests that encircle the Northern Hemisphere like a halo. A handful of giant forest and mining companies and neo-conservative governments see the forests as nothing more than standing fibre to be clear-cut and converted into pesticide-strewn and mono-cultured tree farms, lands to be mined, rivers to be dammed, and wildlife to be commercially trapped or shot for blood sport. Alternatively, environmental and social justice activists look at the rich ecosystems as not only the ancestral home of many First Nations peoples who have lived in exemplary harmony with their surroundings for thousands of years, but as the habitat for a variety of species such as woodland caribou, martens, wolves, and countless of bird species. What's more, they appreciate the important ecological functions the boreal's wetlands and bogs provide in cleaning air and water and acting as a carbon sink (putting a brake on global climate change), and they value the aesthetic and spiritual purposes of the place as immortalized in the works of the Group of Seven in the Algoma Highlands, for instance.

The first perspective, deeply embedded in the mindset of today's economic and political elite, is emblematic of a crudely instrumental attitude towards nature with a much broader history in modern Western culture. Part of its lineage derives from the philosophy of John Locke, the seventeenth-century philosopher who brought forward a theory of the enclosure of the commons and the commodification of land that attempted to justify the progression of capitalism. In his *Second Treatise of Government*, Locke declared that land without human labour attached to it had no value: "Land that is left wholly to Nature, that hath no improvement of Pasturage, Tillage, or Planting, is called, as indeed it is waste, and we shall find the benefit to little more than nothing" (quoted in Miller, 1997, p. 51). Moreover, according to Locke, the "ownerless" commons would have to be privatized to extract the full benefits of its natural resources. For Peter Miller (1997), one of "Locke's mistakes" was that he attributed value to nature based solely on its utility to humans, not recognizing its inherent value (p. 52). In this instrumental view, whose echoes still reverberate today, everything in nature—animals, species, natural features like the Grand Canyon, and so on—is seen and evaluated in terms of its commercial potential. This extremely anthropocentric (also androcentric and classist) view assumes that humans are separate from and superior to nature rather than a part of nature. It encourages the attitude that humans have the right to dominate and ultimately destroy nature.

Locke's ideas are indicative of a broader problem embodied in today's intensive commodification of nature. For instance, today's biotechnology—from xenotransplantation to genetically modified organisms (GMOs) and other forms of exploitation and manipulation of animals and plant life—is in many ways a prime example of Western culture's traditionally mechanistic and instrumental view of nature: non-human life-forms are conceived of as unfeeling machines and non-holistic entities that can be taken apart and reassembled at will according to human purposes. Human relations with nature in the contemporary world are exploitative and manipulative in large part due to anthropocentric ideas that set humans apart from and above nature, combined with the rise of the idea that we can know the natural world only by fundamentally distancing ourselves from it. As ecofeminist Barbara Noske (1997) puts it, nature is being reduced to "an exploitable and useful *thing*, removing comprehensive moral status and leaving it value-free" (pp. 53–54). If the environmental crisis is at least in part related to our predominant belief system, culture, and way of thinking, then we clearly need to re-examine our worldview critically and develop an alternative (Evernden, 1991). The new worldview ought to be ecological and holistic. Instead of depicting nature as a machine or clock, the new metaphor in the holistic, ecological paradigm might be that of an organism. Living beings are not machines that you can take apart and put back together again (they die!), and the unit of survival is the organism *and* its environment (Sterling, 1990). Nature and animals need to be valued for both their intrinsic and instrumental values. Switching from a mechanistic worldview to an ecological or systemic, holistic perspective and ethos would be akin to a "religious conversion" or "cultural rebirth" (Berman, 1981; Sterling, 1990, p. 86). However, more is needed than a major shift in individual and societal consciousness and values. Defending a non-commodified vision of nature will require political action and fundamentally different state priorities and policies than those espoused by neoliberal globalists.

NEOLIBERAL GLOBALISM UNDERMINES THE ENVIRONMENTAL STATE

The battle against neoliberal globalism is not only one of highly contested ideas about nature but also one of competing interests and institutions. In the latter part of the Keynesian era in the early 1970s, Canadian federal and provincial governments, like other governments around the world, created environment ministries in response to multiplying environmental problems, growing scientific concern, and a "green wave" of public concern and pressure that originated in the 1960s. Over the next twenty-five years, these governments strengthened the environmental state in recognition of the necessity to develop an adequate state capacity to address growing local and global environmental concerns. Another green wave of public interest and concern occurred in the mid-1980s and early 1990s following a series of environmental crises, many having a global reach, including the Bhopal industrial accident in 1984, the Chernobyl nuclear disaster in 1985, the discovery of the ozone hole in the Antarctic in 1987, global climate change, and deforestation in the Amazon and massive clear-cuts in British Columbia's ancient temperate rainforests. Governments responded by adding new environmental laws, regulations, and programs; increasing environmental budgets and staff; implementing and enforcing environmental laws against recalcitrant industries in a more proactive and assertive way; incorporating environmental concerns in the work of other government departments besides environment ministries; and significantly increasing the opportunities for democratic participation in decisions affecting the natural environment and public health and safety.

In a sharp reversal, major decreases in public expenditures on environmental protection occurred in the mid-1990s at the federal level and in a number of provinces. For example, the Chrétien government cancelled the $3 billion Green Plan in 1995 and then launched two program reviews, cutting the Department of Environment's budget by about a third (from $737 million in 1995-96 to $503 million in 1997–98) and the staff by a quarter (1,400 of 5,700) across the country (Toner, 1997). The cuts were even more severe in Ontario, where the neo-conservative Harris government, elected in 1995, cut the Ministry of Environment budget by almost one half and the staff by more than 40 per cent from 2,430 in 1994 to 1,277 by the end of 1999 (Krajnc, 2000). These and other reductions can be explained in part by the historical rise and decline of environmental departments closely following the ebb and flow of "green waves" (Harrison, 1996). Green waves are periods of intense public awareness and concern about environmental issues, which arise due to factors such as environmental crises, growing media coverage of environmental issues, and the work of scientists, environmental groups, and policy entrepreneurs. Governments tend to respond to heightened public concern by introducing new environmental legislation and programs. On the flip side, governments are often inactive or engage in minor retrenchment when the environment is no longer a top-of-mind issue for the public and gets bumped off the political agenda.

The unprecedented retreat of the state on environmental matters can be explained by a confluence of domestic and international forces that have given primacy to the market and economic growth and have further spurred the commodification of nature. First, the rise of neo-conservative ideology has played a central role. In the 1980s, neo-conservative ideology gained political expression at the federal level, particularly after the 1984 election of Brian Mulroney's Conservative government. The Tories, inspired by Reaganism and Thatcherism, were determined to privatize crown corporations, deregulate, reduce government intervention in the market (by cutting the Foreign Investment Review Agency and the National Energy Program), cut the civil service and various social programs, and negotiate a free trade agreement with the US (Ayres, 1998). New right ideologues also appeared in two provinces—the Social Credit government in British Columbia in the early 1980s, which cut the public service by 25 per cent, and the Conservative Devine government in Saskatchewan. Immediate threats to the federal environmental state—at least with respect to downsizing and environmental deregulation—were averted by the green wave of environmental concern in the mid-1980s to early 1990s. However, the longer term erosion of the environmental state was inherent in the Canada/US Free Trade Agreement, signed in 1989, which began the process of limiting the ability of the Canadian state to introduce regulations to conserve its natural resources and provided the US guarantees of market access to the country's resources (Swenarchuk, 1988).

Since the mid-1990s, with a drop in salience of the environment in public opinion polls, the federal government and neo-conservative governments in provinces like Alberta (under Premier Ralph Klein), Ontario (Mike Harris), and, recently, British Columbia (Gordon Campbell) have been able to reverse many of the institutional gains environmentalists had made in the last two and a half decades. The key principles of neo-conservatism are less government, a move away from government intervention towards an increased reliance on the market, and a redistribution of wealth from the lower to the upper classes (Jeffrey, 1999). In addition, neo-conservatives promote the commodification of nature by rejecting the very notion of public goods and the implicit role for government in protecting these goods on behalf of society as a whole. In partnership with groups in the Wise Use Movement, they have also striven to further exploit and commodify wildlife and the natural environment by pushing for sport hunting and fishing, commercial trapping, snowmobiling, mining and logging-road development even in parks and protected areas (Weis & Krajnc, 1999; Krajnc & Weis, 2000). This drive towards commodifying nature was accompanied by drastic cuts to the Ministry of Natural Resources (MNR) budget and staff: 2,170 people were laid off between 1996–97. The MNR's monitoring and legislative capacities were slashed, all in an effort to move towards "self-regulation" in forestry, mining, and fur industries—meaning privatization has made it more difficult for the public to know what is going on and to do something about it.

Neo-conservative governments in Canada have undertaken a very systematic approach to environmental deregulation. In Ontario, the Harris government set up a Red Tape Review Commission in December 1995, which was made a permanent body in May 2000. The Commission, comprised of nine Conservative MPPs, a secretariat attached to the Cabinet Committee on Regulations, and an External Advisory Committee of business representatives, reviewed new and existing environmental, health, and safety safeguards with a view to eliminating regulations that "unnecessarily" hinder business. Alberta also set up a Regulatory Reform Task Force in April 1995. In British Columbia, the neo-conservative Gordon Campbell government promised in its 2001 election campaign to reduce government regulations by a third over three years—a bizarre *a priori* target for reducing environmental, labour, and other regulations, avoiding even the pretence of a rational evaluation of what existing regulations may be necessary. To undertake this task, the Campbell government created a new Minister of State for Deregulation and set up a 13-member advisory committee comprised entirely of representatives of business, thus excluding labour, public interest groups, or experts in government (Goldberg, 2001; McInnes, 2001a, 2001b). There was a similar, deregulatory initiative at the federal level, the Regulatory Efficiency Act, which was withdrawn after protests by environmentalists in the mid-1990s—perhaps revealing a slightly softer, more responsive version of neoliberalism at the federal level.

Another factor undermining the environmental state, particularly the federal government's role in environmental policy, was Chrétien's so-called devolution or disentanglement strategy. In 1998, the federal government, all the provinces except Quebec, and both territories signed the new Canada Wide Accord on Environmental Harmonization and three sub-agreements on inspections, Canada-wide environmental standards, and environmental assessment. With this Accord, the federal government devolved many of its environmental responsibilities to the Canadian Council of Ministers of the Environment (CCME), an intergovernmental body, and to the provinces. The federal transfer of power to the CCME and the provinces tends to drive environmental standards to the lowest-common-denominator, since the CCME operates based on a consensus decision-making process in which each of the governments (i.e., ten provinces, three territories, and the federal government) have a veto power. Environmentalists generally oppose disentanglement because they believe that checks and balances are needed, and they oppose devolution to the provinces since provincial governments are generally less environmentally friendly than the federal government because resource industries tend to have more clout at the local level.

Finally, increasing corporate globalization is threatening state sovereignty in indirect and direct ways as well as promoting the commodification of nature. The globalization of capital creates competitive pressures on states to cut taxes, deregulate, and lay off public servants, thus indirectly undermining an activist role for government. At the same time, international trade agreements (ITAs) contain provisions that directly limit governments' ability to regulate corporate activity and foreign investment. NAFTA's investor-state provision, for example, gives corporations new rights to sue governments for environmental regulations that lower their profits (Mann, 2001). ITAs also reduce the freedom of governments to use various trade tools to implement national and multilateral environmental goals (Marchak, 1998; Conca, 2000). Various trade challenges and rulings on environmental policies highlight the way in which trade agreements are becoming corporate rights agreements, in which capital gains new power at the expense of government. To date, ten out of the seventeen cases involving the investment chapter of NAFTA, Chapter 11, have involved environmental or natural resource issues, including management of hazardous waste, clean drinking water, and gasoline additives (Mann, 2001).

The mechanism by which the commodification of nature is enhanced in NAFTA's Chapter 11 is through the introduction of the notion of "regulatory takings." Ironically, this is something the right-wing, US property rights movement sought and failed to obtain at the national level in the US. Canada and US law recognizes the difference between expropriation of land and land use regulations. The property rights movement has unsuccessfully attempted to demand compensation for costs imposed on property owners as a result of land use regulations, such as the prohibition of development on environmentally sensitive shorelines (Weisbrot, 2001; Swenarchuk, 1998). Ironically, what the property rights movement failed to achieve at the national level, multinational corporations succeeded in obtaining in NAFTA's Chapter 11. For example, the Ethyl Corporation of Virginia was the first to threaten to use the expropriation provisions of Chapter 11 to challenge Canada's ban of MMT, a gasoline additive that is an expected neurotoxin and leads to an increase in air pollutant emissions. It filed a $250-million claim arguing that the regulatory ban was tantamount to an expropriation, but settled for $13 million in damages after the Canadian government (fearing it would lose the case) withdrew its 1997 import ban and apologized to the company.

Furthermore, the WTO is limiting the use of various trade tools in new agreements and undermining existing international environmental regimes. Trade measures are an important tool for many environmental regimes, including the Convention on the International Trade in Endangered Species (CITES), which bans trade in endangered species; the Montreal Protocol, which uses trade measures to promote compliance with the regime; and the 1994 amendment to the Basel Convention, which bans North-South trade in hazardous waste. The use of such tools in new environmental agreements is now severely limited by trade treaties (Conca, 2000). Further, in the S.D. Myers case, the appointed NAFTA arbitration board made a ruling in November 2000 that appears to threaten existing environmental treaties that employ trade measures. S.D. Myers, an Ohio-based waste company, sued the Canadian government for $50 million (US) under NAFTA's Chapter 11 following Canada's nine-month-long ban on the export of PCB-contaminated waste. The company launched a suit even though NAFTA specifically lists the Basel Convention as one of three international environmental treaties exempt from the general restriction of using trade measures to protect the environment. Canada sought a judicial review of the award through its own Federal Court.

These internal and international aspects of neoliberal globalism lead to the creation of a climate of regulatory chill and a growing democratic deficit. Regulatory chill occurs when governments (elected officials and/or civil servants) become reluctant to introduce environmental laws and policies due to fears of reprisal. For example, civil servants may be fearful of introducing necessary environmental regulations in the face of a neo-conservative government's aggressive deregulatory drive, as occurred in the Walkerton tragedy (discussed in the next section). Moreover, governments may not introduce new environmental regulations if they fear potentially having to pay compensation to investors for costs they incur as a result of new laws. NAFTA's expropriation provision very much reverses the "polluter pays principle" to "pay the polluter." The state-investor provision not only potentially forces states to roll back environmental regulations, but also has a negative impact on government's capacity to introduce new environmental policies. The chilling effect often takes place not in open ways, thus making it hard for environmental activists to challenge government inaction or "nondecisions."

Neoliberal globalization also creates a democratic deficit, defined by the absence of democratic safeguards such as access to information, public accountability, and public participation in the policy-making process. At the domestic level, neo-conservative policies, such as privatization, deregulation, budget and staff cuts, and the elimination of public advisory boards, tend to substantially reduce public accountability, transparency of decision-making processes, and democratic input. Internationally, the negotiations and implementations of international trade agreements involve notoriously secretive, imbalanced, and opaque processes (Mann, 2001). Such procedural and substantive concerns exacerbate environmental problems and create the perception that the process lacks public legitimacy, making neoliberal globalism highly contestable and unstable.

NGO STRATEGIES AND TACTICS

Canada's environmental movement has had to adapt its repertoire of collective action in response to new rules in the neoliberal globalism game in which the playing field has been tilted much further in favour of capitalist interests. Just as trade agreements and neoliberal governments are giving multinational corporations new rights and opportunities, NGOs are ironically faced with fewer instruments at their disposal to effect policy change. Previously, environmental groups had used public pressure strategies aimed at the state as a means of forcing governments to adopt new or better environmental policies. Such strategies presumed that the state was competent, responsive, and capable of acting. These assumptions worked when the state was underpinned by Keynesian values, but they were thoroughly undermined with the combined forces of neo-conservative ideology and corporate-oriented globalization. The number of political vehicles for environmentalists to pursue their agenda was reduced as state capacity declined dramatically and many regulatory tools were lost. Ken Traynor (2002) of the Canadian Environmental Law Association believes that, in the near term, there are "very few places where the state is available to come into play," primarily due to cutbacks and deregulation at the domestic level. Cecelia Lynch (1998) focuses on international forces: "There is a developing understanding among some 'progressive' contemporary social movement groups that economic globalization poses the primary obstacle to the fulfilment of their goals" (p. 149). John Willis, a board member of Greenpeace Canada, worries that "as international trade agreements handcuff politicians, activists may be gaining access to an increasingly impotent system" (quoted in Falconer, 2001, p. 41). The environmental movement must now add to its list of tasks plans to defend the state and its primary role in protecting the environment against these reinforcing, inside-outside effects of neoliberal globalism. Environmentalists are confronting the increasing scope of the market aimed at enhancing private profitability by ensuring that certain "public goods" are preserved from pure market logic and regulated in the name of non-economic values as well.

On the domestic front, provincially based organizations analysed and protested cutbacks to environment ministries and worked through the Canadian Environment Network (CEN) to oppose attempts by the federal government to devolve environmental responsibilities to the provinces. Also, environmental organizations turned their attention to trade matters and organized international protests against corporate attempts at commodifying nature worldwide. In the 1980s, only a few environmental groups were intimately involved in the opposition to the Free Trade Agreement between the United States and Canada. By the early 1990s, the threat posed by international trade agreements was becoming more apparent to environmental groups, which were galvanized into fighting NAFTA, though there was some disagreement among environmental groups about whether NAFTA's side deals on the environment and labour were commendable or toothless agreements—the anti-environmental implications of NAFTA's Chapter 11 were not understood then. The Sierra Club of Canada and the Canadian Environmental Law Association were among the 500 NGOs rallying against the proposed Multilateral Agreement on Investment (MAI) in 1997, environmental groups were a major force in the collapse of the WTO's Millennium Round in Seattle at the end of 1999, and environmentalists helped organize protests and workshops at the April 2001 "Summit of the Americas" in Quebec City.

In the late 1980s, the Canadian Environmental Law Association (CELA), a legal clinic and public interest environmental group based in Toronto, played a catalytic role in developing an environmental critique and raising public awareness of the environmental consequences of the General Agreement of Tariffs and Trade (GATT) and the Canada-US Free Trade Agreement (FTA). As the FTA was being negotiated in 1987-88, CELA staff worked closely with the Toronto-based Anti-

Free Trade Coalition, created in 1985, and later the ProCanada Network—a country-wide network of over 20 national organizations opposed to free trade created in 1987. The anti-free trade campaign adopted an organizing strategy that involved advancing an overall Canadian nationalist perspective on the dangers presented by the FTA to Canada's sovereignty, as well as a host of issue-based perspectives, including those of labour, social justice advocates, women, housing activists, and environmentalists. In 1988, CELA added an environmental critique to other sectoral critiques when it published a report documenting the potential impacts of the FTA on resource conservation, acid rain policy, pesticide regulations, waste, and standard setting. Working with the Canadian Environmental Network (CEN), CELA was able to get over 90 environmental organizations across the country to endorse its report, which it released on September 22, 1988 in a series of 15 simultaneous media conferences held in every province and in the Northwest Territories. However, the Tories were re-elected in late 1988 (despite losing the popular vote) and promptly proceeded to ram through the FTA.

By the early 1990s, opposition to NAFTA within Canada, Mexico, and the United States was gaining ground and increasingly alerting the North American public to the environmental implications of emergent trade regimes. However, a number of more conservative environmental groups in the US with close ties to the corporate elite were supportive of the NAFTA agreement, once the side deals on environment and labour were attached, and even helped promote it (Audley, 1997). More grassroots-oriented environmental groups in the US, including Greenpeace, Friends of the Earth, and the Sierra Club, opposed the deal, and Canadian groups worked closely with these groups by exchanging information and analyses. In Canada, the issue of the merits of NAFTA and its side agreements was also divisive, with groups like Pollution Probe commending the agreement. Most other environmental groups, including Greenpeace Canada, Transport 2000, and CELA, opposed NAFTA because it tied government's hands with respect to natural resource conservation, it created downward pressure on environmental standards by facilitating capital flight to jurisdictions with low standards, and its negotiations and administration were anti-democratic.

The targets of Canada's environmental movement protests have depended, in part, on the relative threats posed by domestic and international forces. In the 1980s, protests were aimed mainly at the US-Canada Free Trade Agreement. By the mid-1990s, many of the same ENGOs fighting the FTA and NAFTA now had to contend with the downsizing and devolution of environmental responsibilities at the federal level and with significant cutbacks to environmental programs in Ontario, Canada's most populous province. In 1998, the Canadian Environment Network (CEN) sent a letter to the Prime Minister signed by more than 50 ENGOs from across the country asking the federal government not to proceed with the Harmonization Accord, fearing the erosion of the federal government's role in environmental protection (Winfield, 2002, p. 128). In Ontario, the Canadian Institute for Environmental Law and Policy (CIELAP) and CELA took the lead in providing research and analyses of the implications of the environmental cutbacks facing the province following the election of the neo-conservative Harris government in 1995. Opposition to the Harris government, however, was less coordinated than existed in British Columbia in the early 1980s, when trade unionists, anti-poverty activists, and women's groups formed an umbrella organization called Operation Solidarity, later named Solidarity Coalition, and organized a series of strikes and protests. In Ontario, for example, conservative environmental groups, in particular the World Wildlife Fund Canada, praised the Harris government prior to the 1999 election on its Ontario's Living Legacy policy, a highly compromised land use strategy (Weis & Krajnc, 1999).

However, environment groups, such as CELA, were able to attribute the May 2000 Walkerton crisis to the severe cuts to the Ministry of Environment's budget and staff, a result of the Harris government's neo-conservative ideology. The Walkerton tragedy put the national spotlight on the neo-conservative policies of the Harris government after seven people died and more than 2,300 people became severely ill because of E. Coli contamination of their drinking water from a nearby cattle farm. Prior to the outbreak of this environmental crisis, environmentalists had repeatedly brought the issue of cutbacks to the attention of the government and the public, but it was not enough to shift public opinion or government policy. Sustained research and analysis allowed environmentalists to use the occurrence of the crisis to demonstrate the effects on public health and the environment caused by the rollbacks to the environmental state. On July 31, 2000, Canada's national paper, the *Globe and Mail*, declared in an editorial entitled "Water and Big Government" that "Ontario's water problems likely mark the limit on the limitation of Big Government." The Walkerton Public Inquiry, established on June 12, 2000, learned of the severe cuts to budget and staff levels at Ontario's environment ministry since 1995, the privatization of water-testing laboratories, and the fact that civil servants were fearful of introducing new environmental regulations in a numbing climate of "regulatory chill." The crisis has spurred growing calls from opposition parties, the public, and the media for the provincial government to rebuild Ontario's public services. The Ontario Public Service Employees' Union's (OPSEU) new slogan is "Learn from Walkerton ... Rebuild the Public Service."

By the late 1990s, more attention was paid to international campaigns, and environmental groups were joining both the Council of Canadians and the Polaris Institute in developing transnational advocacy coalitions (TANs) (Johnston & Laxer, 2003). However, Gordon Laxer (2003) argues that national campaigning and domestic popular mobilization are crucial to successful campaigns. The campaign against the Multilateral Agreement on Investment (MAI), for instance, comprised a network of country-based campaigns with Canadian NGOs such as the Council of Canadians taking the lead in countering this neoliberal globalist initiative. Mass mobilization took place primarily at the domestic level, involving municipal, provincial, and federal targets. This mobilization was combined with a top-down TAN approach in which activists intervened at international negotiations at the OECD. Michelle Swenarchuk of CELA and Elizabeth May of the Sierra

Club of Canada went to Paris in late 1996 to warn OECD delegates about Chapter 11 cases under NAFTA, thus providing critical information to foreign negotiators, many of whom were unfamiliar with Chapter 11. Activists felt they could have more influence by going to Paris than by protesting or lobbying in Ottawa. In part, this shift in targets was due to the 1993 federal election of the Liberal Party, which represented "a dramatic closure of national opportunity structures" (Ayres, 1998, p. 130) because of the right turn of the Liberal Party and a divided opposition. At the same time, the Internet expanded international political opportunity structures (Smith & Smythe, 1999).

With the defeat of the MAI, activists decelerated the expansion of the deregulatory agenda. The WTO became an increasing concern. The Common Front against the WTO (CFWTO), co-chaired by organizers from the Canadian Union of Public Employees and the Council of Canadians, was formed in 1996 to promote public education and support direct action events. The CFWTO developed a large membership, including labour, health, education, culture, human rights, women's, antipoverty, faith, civil society, and environmental groups looking at a broad range of issues. Participating environmental organizations in the CFWTO include the Sierra Club of Canada, CELA, CIELAP, Sierra Youth Coalition, Mining Watch Canada, International Fund for Animal Welfare, and Greenpeace Canada. A number of members decided to set up a subgroup, the Canadian Alliance on Trade and Environment (CATE), in 1998, to focus on trade and environment. CATE consists of the Canadian Labour Congress, the West Coast Environmental Law Association, the Council of Canadians, the Polaris Institute, and the Sierra Club of Canada. The coalition undertakes legal analysis and actions concerned with the WTO trumping multilateral environmental agreements, as happens under the Basel Convention and NAFTA challenges citing Chapter 11. In the S.D. Meyers case, CATE applied for intervener status at the federal court level, but was denied even though the Sierra Club in the US had been instrumental in banning imports of PCBs (Rickman, 2002).

By the mid- to late-1990s, the Sierra Club of Canada played a lead role in developing an international campaign against corporate globalization. The national office of the Sierra Club of Canada was formed in 1989, and the regional chapters in Canada, formerly part of the Sierra Club in the US, were made into separate entities and part of the Sierra Club of Canada. (The Ontario and BC chapters, set up in 1969, predated the national office by 20 years.) The group's work with CATE informed other Sierra Club campaigns, for example, their work on pesticides, climate, shrimp aquaculture/turtles, and the labelling of GMOs. Environmental youth took a leadership role in grassroots direct action campaigns, including the APEC protests in 1997, the WTO protests in Seattle in 1999, and the Free Trade Area of the America (FTAA) protests in Windsor in June 2000 and Quebec City in April 2001. The Sierra Youth Club, for instance, a branch of the Sierra Club of Canada, worked with various labour and social justice groups to organize a WTO Caravan to Seattle. Activists, starting in Prince Edward Island

and joined by others along the way, took the train across the country, stopping at various cities to do teach-ins and demonstrations (Falconer, 2001, p. 101).

In sum, Canada's environmental movement refocused its strategy in the late 1980s with the negotiation of the Free Trade Agreement between Canada and the United States. In the 1980s, a few discerning environmentalists (especially legal experts) took the lead in working with the nationalist and popular sectors in issuing warnings about the Agreement's implications for the country's sovereignty. They played a key role in building coalitions and solidarity networks at the national and transnational levels. In the early 1990s, environment and trade issues were a source of dispute in the environmental community, which lacked consensus on the implications of NAFTA. By the late 1990s, the environmental implications of trade regimes became patently obvious with a litany of anti-environmental WTO rulings and NAFTA Chapter 11 challenges, and, as a result, there is a growing consensus on the environmental threats posed by international trade agreements. At the same time, unprecedented cutbacks to the environmental state in a number of provinces and at the federal level further encouraged environmental groups to refocus their strategy and to defend the state from neoconservative ideologues.

REBUILDING THE ENVIRONMENTAL STATE

Defenders of bureaucracy call for a reinvigorated state, noting that proactive policy options are available despite increasing economic globalization. However, the challenge is enormous. The role of government will need to be strengthened at local, national, and global levels. In their book *Globalization from Below*, Jeremy Brecher, Tim Costello, and Brendan Smith (2000) rightly call for a multilevel approach to opposing corporate-oriented globalism since rules at higher levels can enable or disable environmental policies at lower levels of governance. They write, "The empowerment of local and national communities and polities today *requires* a degree of global regulation and governance." At the same time, "national regulation that protects minimum standards and limits the race to the bottom actually strengthens, rather than undermines, the ability of people in local communities to control their own lives" (pp. 40–41). Views vary on how much emphasis to put on strengthening the environmental capacities of local communities, national governments, and global institutions.

At the international level, environmental organizations and think tanks have called for a moratorium on further trade negotiations, amendments to international trading agreements, enforceable codes of conduct for MNCs, and the creation of stronger international environmental regimes. The Sierra Club of Canada, the Council of Canadians, and other anti-globalization groups are calling for a moratorium on international trade negotiations until the full repercussions of these agreements are understood. In particular, there is concern about restoring political or state sovereignty over environmental and economic policies. The Winnipeg-based International Institute for Sustainable Development recommends that

NAFTA governments should issue an interpretive statement (e.g., on the meaning of expropriation) that would bind future Chapter 11 Tribunals. The NAFTA text should be reopened and its procedural rules amended to address democratic deficiencies. Moreover, the gross imbalance between the rule making and enforcement of international economic regimes as compared to international environmental regimes, whose role is mostly advisory and informational, needs to be addressed. Clearly, international environmental organizations and regimes are not well institutionalized at the regional and global levels, especially when compared to economic regimes.

In 1987, the Brundtland Commission made a number of recommendations to strengthen environmental bureaucracies and public input at the local, state, and international levels. They are even more relevant today. Six priority areas for institutional and legal change were identified:

i)   Getting at the sources by strengthening state capacity to monitor and evaluate sustainable development;

ii)   Dealing with the effects by strengthening "the role and capacity of existing environmental protection and resource management agencies" (p. 319);

iii) Assessing global risks of new technologies by collecting information systematically;

iv)   Making informed choices by increasing the roles played by the scientific community, NGOs, and the general public;

v)   Providing the legal means—instead of de-regulating, governments should re-regulate on environmental matters; as the Commission noted, "the accelerating pace and expanding scale of impacts on the environmental base of development is rapidly outdistancing legal regimes. Human laws must be reformulated to keep human activities in harmony with the unchanging and universal laws of nature" (p. 330); and

vi)   Investing in our future through environmentally sound policies, which makes long-term economic sense since a healthy economy ultimately depends on a healthy environment.

Much of the literature highlights the importance of the local level, though it is generally recognized that re-localization involves all levels of state(s) (Mander & Goldsmith, 1996). David Morris (1996) makes the case for a bioregional approach in which economic activities are rooted in place. He shows how worker control and green industries such as recycling, solar energy, and biological products (e.g., vegetable oil-based inks) promote economic and ecological sustainable development at the local level. At the same time, a strong national and international role is required to set minimum environmental standards that prevent pollution havens and a race to the bottom.

The development of an environmental state is premised on the idea that it is primarily the role of government to protect the environment. Only the state has the capacity to assemble and allocate substantial resources to address market failures in protecting the environment and addressing issues of social equity. Civil society is not seen as a replacement for government activism. Although environmental organizations can and do implement environmental projects, equally important are their efforts to increase public awareness on the importance of the environmentally activist state and the key role a citizen-oriented state can play in decommodifying nature. Richard Falk (2001), an international relations theorist, writes, "Only the state, among existing political actors, has the potential capabilities to implement a degree of environmental regulation that will be needed to safeguard the health and well-being of peoples now alive on the planet and discharge responsibilities to future generations" (p. 223). Similarly, Gordon Laxer (2001) notes that "... the state is a more equal adversary of transnational capital than any other institution. The crucial battle is whether citizens will succeed in turning corporate-oriented states into citizen-oriented states" (p. 7). The environmental movement is joining with other progressive movements to defend and re-orient the state towards democracy. Democratizing the state involves, for example, increasing the transparency of corporate lobbying and party finance reform and introducing proportional representation in Canada's electoral system. A strong and democratic activist state is an essential component of any plan to stem and reverse the commodification of nature.

Notes

1. I wish to thank the editors and Mike Gismondi for their most helpful comments on this paper and the SSHRC-funded *Neoliberal Globalism and its Challengers* Project and the Skelton-Clark Memorial Fund at Queen's University for their generous support.
2. Harvard researchers were granted a patent in the US in 1988, and in July 2004, the European Patent Office upheld a pan-European patent on the mice. Canada is exceptional in this case. It became the only industrialized country to ban patents on higher life forms when in 2002 the Supreme Court ruled in a 5-4 decision that the mice could not be patented under current Canadian law because the mice failed to meet the definition of an invention under Canada's Patent Act. Environmental, animal rights, public interest, and religious groups intervened in the case. Jerry DeMarco, a lawyer for the Sierra Legal Defence Fund, argued, "Mammals are the product of evolution, not invention. Harvard isn't inventing the whole mouse. They're just tinkering with the genes, and that does not constitute an invention" (Baglole, 2002).

CHAPTER TWELVE

From the Knowledge Economy to the Knowledge Commons
Resisting the Commodification of Knowledge

JENNIFER SUMNER

The "knowledge economy" has become a familiar phrase in government, academic, and business circles. Intellectual property rights, university research parks, privatized extension services, and a thriving knowledge industry are the outward signs of a growing acceptance of this burgeoning economic form. While the concept may have a certain surface cachet, it begins to lose its lustre on closer inspection, revealing the frontiers of commodification in the brave new world of corporate globalization.

Essentially, economies are concerned with the production and distribution of goods otherwise in short supply. Knowledge would not seem to be in short supply because people around the world construct it every day. So the idea of the knowledge economy appears to be an oxymoron, a contradictory concept that carries little meaning. To compound matters, heralds of the so-called knowledge economy generally make little effort to distinguish between knowledge and falsehood, knowledge and information, or knowledge and skills. In spite of this web of meaninglessness, the concept has caught on and spread as common currency among such diverse institutions as the World Bank, the Social Sciences and Humanities Research Council, and universities worldwide.

How does the uncritical acceptance of prevailing assumptions about the knowledge economy affect academics and society as a whole? Focusing on universities as sites of inquiry, this chapter will examine the commodification of knowledge in the age of corporate globalization and offer promising examples of resistance to this enclosure of the commons. While the commodification process may often appear overwhelmingly powerful, I suggest, it is important not to reify its seemingly totalizing character. By looking at commodification as a social relation, we can begin to better understand what non-commodified alternatives would look like. This understanding can help us not only to resist the commodification of knowledge that forms the basis of the knowledge economy but also to build the "knowledge commons"—co-operative human constructions that protect and/or enable universal access to knowledge.[1]

THE ESSENCE OF THE KNOWLEDGE ECONOMY: THE COMMODIFICATION OF KNOWLEDGE

As many other chapters in this book have emphasized, commodification is an essential aspect of corporate globalization. In tandem with consumption, it forms a twin dynamic that can produce the increased profits that investors restlessly seek. While by no means a new phenomenon, the process of commodification has intensified as the economy has gone global. According to Thrift (1994), this process has increasingly reached into every nook and cranny of modern life, both in Western and non-Western societies. In effect, as Vandana Shiva (1997) has argued, "all aspects of everyday life are being transformed into globally-traded commodities. Food, land, seeds, plants, and animals are now all commodities on international markets" (p. 22). Central to the expansionary dynamics of the global market system, the process of commodification is at the heart of many of the problems we face in the world today. From the oceans to the countryside, from human understanding to death itself, commodification has invaded all aspects of our lives by pricing the priceless: social services, personal experience, human bodies, family grief, and public knowledge.

Knowledge, understood as a set of shared, subjective, often taken-for-granted meanings and assumptions that are socially and historically constructed, is one of the hallmarks of human existence (Mezirow, 1995). Forbidden or otherwise, it has been central to our evolution as a species, as well as a key to the exercise of social power. Our basic assumptions about the origins of knowledge shape the way we see the world and ourselves as participants in it. In spite of the fact that "the human interest in knowledge is a plural one" (Morrow & Torres, 1995, p. 23), certain restrictive forms of knowledge have tended to dominate human social existence, taking on the seemingly unassailable mantle of "expert knowledge." This expert knowledge has, in turn, characteristically been understood as a kind of official knowledge that supports the dominant groups in society. Frank Cunningham (1988) explains the role of such official knowledge from a Gramscian perspective:

> All bodies of knowledge are not equal. The knowledge that supports the dominant paradigms in a culture is systematically produced, disseminated, and reified so as to become common sense to the average citizen. (p. 137)

One of the ways that official knowledge supports the "dominant paradigms" in a culture involves either the co-option or dismissal of knowledge that does not conform to this culturally entrenched notion of "common sense." All forms of knowledge—scientific or religious, formal or informal—have the potential to be co-opted into maintaining the status quo. For example, the indigenous knowledge associated with organic farming in California has been bent to the service of the organic-industrial complex so that organic farming "has replicated what it set out to oppose" (Guthman, 2004, p. 9). Those forms of knowledge that cannot be co-opted, such as the traditional knowledge system of ayurvedic medicine, are generally ignored, marginalized, or criminalized.

Official knowledge has excluded, co-opted, or marginalized other forms of knowledge throughout history. Indigenous knowledge, women's knowledge, experiential knowledge, transformative knowledge, situated knowledge, and local knowledge have all experienced the exclusionary power of the official knowledge regime. What is unprecedented, however, is the current range and power of official knowledge. The increased consolidation of the mass media, the advent of the Internet, and the introduction of satellite technology have all contributed to the spread of official knowledge. The foregrounding of marginalized forms of knowledge, such as what is available on media outlets like Al Jazeera, only serves to emphasize the powerful hold of official knowledge. Its breadth of reach and depth of penetration has been made possible by the commodification of knowledge on a global scale and the creation of the knowledge economy.

One expression of the logic of commodification is privatization. With the process of privatization, knowledge is moved from the public realm into private control, then priced, packaged, and profited from. Agricultural extension is a prime example of the privatization of knowledge. For decades, extension workers formed the link between cutting-edge university research and farmers. At no cost, they disseminated the knowledge generated from research to educate farmers and promote better farming practices. In the wake of neoliberal restructuring, extension services have been eliminated, and farmers now have to purchase the services of private agricultural consultants. Within the academy, researchers are constrained from freely offering the knowledge they produce either by privacy agreements with corporate funders or by changes in university policies, which no longer reward public outreach in the tenure and promotion process. And through the expansion of the global corporate market, such privatization of knowledge is increasing, with more and more knowledge formerly held in the public realm being transferred to a "corporate sector that views knowledge merely as another commodity to be bartered in the marketplace" (Berman, 1998, p. 230).

UNIVERSITIES AND THE COMMODIFICATION OF KNOWLEDGE

In many countries, universities have long embodied the contradictions between private and public knowledge. On the one hand, they have been sites of hegemonic knowledge production. For example, the problems in establishing feminist perspectives in academic teaching, publication, and research stem from the resistance of the dominant (male) knowledge producers who judged that feminist contributions were not "real" knowledge and shut them out of the academy. On the other hand, universities have also been one of the bastions of public knowledge, a role many of them acknowledge in their mission statements. According to Doherty-Delorme (1999),

> One of the purposes of a public system of higher education is to provide a haven where the exchange of ideas may flow, not only between teacher and student, but also among peers.... The knowledge created is shared freely for the benefit of all society. (p. xi)

Within the tensions of knowledge production for elite versus public interests, the free flow of knowledge is losing ground as defunding increases under neoliberal pressures. Indeed, universities increasingly provide a microcosm for investigating how, in the age of corporate globalization, the commodification of knowledge is being intensified through the process of privatization.

This process works in a number of ways. Knowledge can be generated by universities but owned, controlled, and sold by private companies. Countless animal experiments on some campuses involve the testing of products to bring animals to maturity faster, and thus ensure a quicker return for intensive feedlot operators. Institutions of higher education copyright distance-education course materials, which can then be sold to either private or public institutions. Products developed in university laboratories are patented by "entrepreneurial" faculty, in an academic environment where provincial and federal research grants increasingly require finding corporate partners.

Newson (1998) examines some of the assumptions involved in this privatization of knowledge:

> The idea that universities can enter into partnerships in which knowledge is traded off for money implies that "knowledge" can be bundled up into neat packages and a precise monetary value can be attached to them. To accomplish this end, knowledge needs to be quantified and measured in terms of its economic "exchange" value. (p. 116)

This packaging and pricing of knowledge goes against the vision many people have of universities. According to Noam Chomsky, for instance,

> Universities have a purpose. They are supposed to be pressing the boundaries of knowledge and inspiring student questioning; they are basically supposed to be subversive. That is their role in a healthy society. (quoted in Shaker, 1999, p. x)

But many universities today are not choosing to press the boundaries of knowledge, although some individual faculty members still partake in critical thinking. In the United States, however, faculty who question the increasingly repressive climate in American universities are threatened with job loss. And in Canada, few faculty need to avail themselves of the protections of academic freedom, precisely because they don't press the boundaries of acceptable knowledge. More often than not, they are following administrative dictates and producing knowledge that Polster (1996) describes as "increasingly narrow and oriented to serving the needs of industry," such as research funded by corporate think-tanks to disprove evidence of climate change or websites that champion the benefits of biotechnology (p. 109).

One of the reasons for this altered purpose is that universities, like other parts of the public sector, are targets for privatization. The first step in this privatization process involves the reduction of public funding for higher education.[2] Strategies like lowering taxes, diverting public money to service deliberately created debts, and discrediting the public service can virtually bankrupt higher education, thus eliminating the competition of low-priced or free public knowledge. Facing insolvency, universities have been forced not only to restructure but also to increase the cost of tuition fees, which threatens to turn post-secondary education into a highly priced commodity, accessible only to those with the financial means. In addition, they have been pushed into alliances with transnational corporations, euphemistically known as the private sector. In the wake of this "corporate turn" in higher education, the major product of the university—knowledge—becomes ripe for privatization.

Under such conditions, producing knowledge is no longer the issue; the issue becomes the capacity to *trade* in knowledge (Blunden, 1999). This explains the stampede to develop distance-education courses, which justifies Alexandra's (1999) critique of universities as "knowledge mongers," peddling their wares on the Internet. We also witness the rise of "market-model universities," where departments that make money, study money, or attract money are given priority (Warde, 2001, p. 13). In this way, economics departments, biotechnology laboratories, and computer science centres all become targets for selected funding. Blunden (1999) even goes so far as to refer to universities as,

> Faculties of Fastbuckery [that] now market degrees as an export commodity and ... model themselves organisationally and ideologically on commercial corporations. (p. 4)

This move toward the commodification of knowledge through privatization has fostered the rise of professor-entrepreneurs, who use their academic affiliations as a launching pad for lucrative ventures and often spend most of their time working on their private projects (Warde, 2001, p. 13).

Blunden (1999) has argued that the introduction of commodification into areas where value relations have not penetrated has consistently lead to social upheaval. For example, he describes the introduction of women's labour into the market system.

> There has always been women's labour; women have always worked ... when women's labour became *valued*, rather than something tendered within relations of *domestic servitude*, then enormous social upheavals followed. (p. 2)

Blunden continues that "there is good reason to believe then, that the commodification of knowledge is leading to major social change and upheaval" (p. 2). In the age of corporate globalization, academics experience this change and upheaval in a variety of ways: profit-driven research, selective funding, and a highly corporatized campus. In the larger world, those without "passports to the knowledge economy" will be lucky to find employment in low-pay sectors such as the service industry (Local Futures, 2001). Unlike regular passports, which are the right of every citizen, passports to the knowledge economy require having the money to buy your way in.

THE BASIS OF RESISTANCE: RETHINKING THE COMMODIFICATION PROBLEM

The intensification of the commodification of knowledge through privatization has far-reaching implications for the future of the academy, and for society as a whole. In the words of Newson (1998),

> These changes in university practices constitute a potentially, if not already realized, significant transformation in the *raison d'être* of the university: from existing in the world as a publicly funded institution oriented toward creating and disseminating knowledge as a public resource—social knowledge—into an institution which, although continuing to be supported by public funds, is increasingly oriented toward a privatized conception of knowledge—market knowledge. (p. 110)

This fundamental tension between knowledge as a public resource—social knowledge—and knowledge as a corporate resource—market knowledge—is the logical outcome of the commodification process. Market knowledge is knowledge that is privatized, priced, packaged, and profited from. All other forms of knowledge acquire a secondary or marginalized status as a result of this expression of commodification. In this age of corporate globalization, how can we effectively challenge the seemingly totalizing power of the commodification process?

In his investigation of commodification, McMurtry (2001) summarizes Marx's position with respect to commodities: "the commodity is a 'social hieroglyphic' in that it is not only an object, but a carrier of hidden social relationships" (p. 2). He argues that many schools of thought, from Marxism through the Frankfurt School to postmodernism have ended in a "commodity cul-de-sac" in which commodification is either totally demonized or totally ignored. After warning against lionizing its totalizing capacity, McMurtry proposes that we not view "the individual commodity as an enemy, as a thing in itself which is oppressing us, but rather as a key to a social relation which we must first understand and then replace" (p. 12). McMurtry goes on to remind us that a commodity is something that must be transferred to another by means of an exchange. Understanding this process and then looking for, and building on, alternatives to it help us to understand what a commodity is *not*, and what non-commodified relationships entail. McMurtry's analysis has far-reaching implications for our understanding of the commodification of knowledge.

To reify the commodification process is to confess a kind of impotence in the face of change. Instead of lionizing its totalizing capacity, we can understand the commodification of knowledge as a relationship that we can choose to continue or replace. Within universities, the commodification of knowledge establishes a complex set of relationships that are based on exchange. For example, academics can be seen as the knowledge producers, transnational corporations as the knowledge owners, and the public as the knowledge customers. Academics are paid to produce a product that corporations can sell to the public for a profit. Like other social relations, however, this set of relationships can be transformed through recognition and change.

Recognition is the first part of this transformation process. It is imperative to become aware of the ways in which the commodification of knowledge, legitimated through such terms as the knowledge economy, is changing how academics relate to knowledge itself, to each other, to students, to the university and to society at large. Change is the second part of this transformation process. Transformative change involves two steps: resistance to the knowledge economy and reaching out to build the knowledge commons. Academics must learn to build relations of resistance to the commodification of knowledge and to reach out to other knowledge producers, including those who have been left behind in the rush to privatize knowledge. While some other knowledge producers may even have been marginalized by academics themselves in their position as producers and bearers of "expert knowledge," they can contribute to building alternatives to the commodification of knowledge in the age of corporate globalization.

RELATIONS OF RESISTANCE

Resistance to the commodification of knowledge is part of the agenda for transformative change. Central to this resistance is the understanding that knowledge is a "social artefact" constructed by people in society (Raiskums, 2001, p. 49). As such, it is "irreducibly social" by its very nature (Barnes, 2000, p. 452). This understanding can form the basis of the knowledge commons.

Once produced, knowledge assumes a life of its own. It becomes "an entity in its own right, possessing an existence of its own and distinct from the knowers who produce it" (Wojciechowski, 2001, p. 1). As an entity in its own right, knowledge becomes something with which we have a relationship. Our relationship with knowledge has been described by Wojciechowski (2001) as the "ecology of knowledge." Just as ecology studies the relationship between organisms and their environment, the ecology of knowledge studies the relationship between humans and the body of knowledge that forms a distinct element of their environment and a rapidly growing factor in human life (p. 1). This relationship, however, is not fully understood, nor is it exclusively beneficial (Wojciechowski, 2001, p. 6). The increasing commodification of knowledge is just one example of our less-than-beneficial relationship with knowledge. But like all relationships, this one can change. Building relations of resistance to the commodification of knowledge can turn a harmful relationship into a beneficial one.

One of the sites for building relations of resistance is the university itself. Brown (2000) offers a rationale for academic resistance when he raises the question of accountability:[3]

> I do not for a moment believe we should be living in an ivory tower, indifferent to the world outside. The question is to whom we should be accountable—to use a favorite term of the privatizers. The answer is simple: the public. We owe it to them to keep knowledge free for all. (p. 1702)

Within the university, Brown (2000) advises that "regular academics must take up the cudgels" (p. 1702). At the individual level, academics can refuse to do contract research that requires nondisclosure and insist on keeping knowledge public; at the university level, academics can put pressure on their leading administrators to take decision-making power out of the hands of private interests, corporate or philanthropic; at the political level, academics can pressure government leaders to keep research and education as part of the public good.

Polster (1996) also provides suggestions for action by academics, along with relevant community groups. At the level of the state, they can work to reform, if not abolish, unelected and unaccountable advisory bodies as well as a host of federal programs, policies, and regulations that put control over university resources into private hands; and they can press for a range of new federal programs and policies that would promote closer research and other links between the university and a broad range of social groups. At the level of the institution, they can wage campaigns against particular university/industry research initiatives; they can oppose new decision-making procedures that marginalize community participation; and they can demand greater accountability and improved representation from the leaders of their institutions who sit on the various politically incorporated advisory boards and other bodies that are gaining greater influence over higher educational policy-making.

The Massachusetts Institute of Technology (MIT) provides a path-breaking example of resistance to the commodification of knowledge. By announcing in April 2001 that it was making most of its course materials available for free to the public through the Internet, MIT "swims against the current that sees knowledge as private property and the Internet as a way to make money by attracting on-line, fee-paying students" (Fine, 2001, p. A1). In a move intended to counter what it calls "the privatisation of knowledge," MIT sees itself as sharing its knowledge, especially with third-world countries that want to use its courses as templates for starting up their own (Naughton, 2001; 24). Based on a belief that access to knowledge is a right that should be available to everyone, MIT's body blow to the commodification juggernaut represents a watershed in the knowledge wars.

MIT's resistance to this enclosure of the commons has far-reaching ramifications for distance education. Described by David Noble (2000) as "an education racket," online learning has grown exponentially with the spread of home computers and the rise of the Internet (p.15). This growth has attracted transnational corporations like Disney and Microsoft, which see education as a profit opportunity and knowledge as a globally traded commodity. By decommodifying its course materials, MIT presents the ultimate competition to corporate globalization—the global public good that is free of charge.

Lowering tuition fees is also a form of resistance because it broadens the base of knowledge production within the academy. In the face of escalating tuition fees in countries like Canada, which increasingly ensure that only the children of the elite can afford higher education, both Ireland and Scotland have chosen to reverse the trend, making university tuition free of charge.

As a primary source of knowledge production within higher education, research can become a site of resistance. While some research has always served private interests, there has been a seismic change in university research priorities as a result of the intensification of the commodification of knowledge through privatization. The void of deliberate underfunding is being filled by the infusion of corporate influence. While corporate funding appears to revitalize cash-strapped universities, in reality it provides corporations with unlimited access to publicly funded resources such as research grants, laboratories, and highly educated personnel.[4] It also allows corporations to enclose the knowledge commons by controlling the research agenda and owning the knowledge produced. As a result of this corporate influence, the overall direction of research has changed:

> There is a cultural shift under way. This relates to the universities' attitude to their central product—knowledge. This used to be regarded as a "common good," but is in the process of being re-appraised as "intellectual property." ... This balkanization of knowledge, packaged for sale, will alter our universities and weaken them. (Polanyi quoted in Doherty-Delorme, 1999, p. xix)

Intellectual property involves the privatization of formerly public knowledge. It embodies the idea that knowledge can be "commodified and thus offered for sale and appropriated as the protected (even private) property of an owner" (Newson, 1998, p. 117).

Masked by euphemisms such as "technology transfer," such privatization of public goods widens the corporate influence in higher education:

> In Canadian universities, the trend has been to set up special offices to man-
> age the intellectual property generated on-site. The purpose of these offices is
> clear in the final report of the Expert Panel on the Commercialization of
> University Research, which states: these operations are often referred to as
> Business Development Offices, University-Industry Liaison Offices or
> Technology Transfer Offices. For the purpose of this report, we will refer to
> them as commercialization offices. (Makela, 2001, p. A11)

Polster (2000) describes how groups opposed to the development and extension of intellectual property regimes (IPRs) currently advocate two strategies of
resistance. The first involves claims that some forms of knowledge, such as information about the human genome, should be declared unprivatizeable because they
belong to the common heritage of humanity. The second involves arguments for
various forms of exemptions from IPRs in the name of the public interest. Polster
advocates including academics in these exemptions, arguing that such an exemption is crucial to the survival of the liberal university and hence vital to the public
interest. She also suggests additional measures, such as promoting efforts to
change government policies that promote the commercialization of university
knowledge and launching campaigns to get academics to voluntarily sign over to
the public the IP rights to their work.

Thesis defences also provide sites for resisting the commodification of knowledge. One of the spinoffs of the corporate research agenda now controlling universities is closed thesis defences. Traditionally open to the public as part of the
pursuit of public knowledge, some thesis defences are now closed to everyone
except those who are willing to sign a document promising they will not reveal
what they have heard behind closed doors without the express permission of the
researcher. This abrogation of the defining tradition of the academy—shared
knowledge and open debate—has been permitted because "from time to time a
student will develop significant intellectual property in the course of his or her
research and wishes, legitimately, to protect that property until it can be patented
or published in a particular format" (I.W. Heathcote, Dean of the Faculty of
Graduate Studies, University of Guelph, personal communication, 2000). Such a
departure begs the question of public ownership of knowledge produced at publicly funded institutions. And while some may find it "legitimate" to privatize public knowledge, academics should make it clear that such privatization not only
contravenes the mission of many institutions of higher learning but also contributes to the destruction of public education and undermines the public good.

RELATIONS OF PRODUCTION

Another route to overcoming the commodification problem involves building new relations of knowledge production. To say that knowledge is produced suggests "an active process of creative construction 'on site' according to specific local rules and conditions"; indeed, "producing knowledge entails a confluence of the right conditions of production: people, places, ideas and material artefacts" (Barnes, 2000, p. 452). One of the ways of achieving that confluence of conditions is to reach out to other knowledge producers—in effect, building the knowledge commons. A form of resistance in itself, reaching out begins with the understanding that knowledge reflects the social, political, and economic conditions under which it is produced and transmitted (Newson, 1994, p. 142). Cunningham (1993) argues that we must acknowledge the social production of knowledge and understand that, if knowledge is socially produced, then knowledge can be produced by any group of people. Working from Gramsci's notion of organic intellectuals, Cunningham poses a series of critical questions:

> Whose knowledge are we studying? Why? Is there an official knowledge? Why? Are some people privileged by the knowledge we study? If so, who? If knowledge is socially produced, am I a producer or consumer? Why? If knowledge is affected by the socially constructed culture and the context from which it arose, then whose culture is being celebrated? If social knowledge is not objective, then how does that affect the way we conduct research? If objectivity is not the only way of knowing, in what other ways can we know? (p. 11)

Cunningham's questions raise the issue of power and knowledge production. Who has the power to control and legitimize knowledge production? While this power used to reside with diverse elite groups, including academics, it is now being concentrated in the hands of transnational corporations.

Many academics suddenly find themselves in the position of other groups of disenfranchised knowledge producers, such as women, rural people, and indigenous people. To overcome this disenfranchisement, academics must reach out and build alliances with each other and beyond the university. To begin this process of reaching out, academics can develop what Polster (2000) refers to as "knowledge collectives" in which various academics pool their intellectual capital and use it as a lever to free up even more knowledge (p. 36). She suggests that people wanting to use the collective's knowledge would have to share their own knowledge in return, thus reversing the progressively limited access to knowledge while protecting and enlarging the knowledge commons.[5]

The next vital step in this process is to reach out beyond the academy to form alliances with knowledge producers in the larger community. These alliances begin with a fundamental understanding:

Knowledge is produced when people make sense of their world and knowledge is based on their experience as they construct tools, methods, and approaches to cope with the situations facing them. This meaning-making notion of knowledge production leads to an understanding of power imbalances in society. (Hill, 1998)

Understanding that knowledge is socially produced changes the way people relate to it, and changes the way they relate to those who have the power to control it. No longer merely the purview of experts or the private property of transnational corporations, knowledge can emerge from many locations. Reaching out makes the knowledge that is produced rich and varied, creating a kind of epistemic diversity that challenges the packaged homogeneity of commodified knowledge.

Alliances are already being formed in the field of knowledge production. For example, Miles (1996) describes how transformative feminists "clearly recognize that progressive change will involve drawing on the resources of many holistic, nondualistic, nonhierarchical knowledges which have been denied and destroyed by the colonial and patriarchal imposition of dualistic competitive values and structures on indigenous people as well as women" (p. 286).

While academics have been implicated in such colonial and patriarchal impositions, they can leave these practices behind and join as equals in the global resistance to corporate domination by participating in building communities of knowledge that reach beyond the walls of the academy.

Progressive social movements provide an opportunity for reaching out and building communities of knowledge. While social movements have long been known as sites of knowledge production, academics have traditionally shied away from association with them.[6] This aversion to dealing with issues affecting the public good and building alliances with groups that pursue these issues must be overcome if we are going to change the relations of knowledge production in the academy and in society at large. For example, the organic farming movement is a loose coalition of organic farmers, distributors, and consumers who are dedicated to a more holistic relationship with the earth and with each other. A small number of academics have already linked up with this movement, sharing research results and sabbatical experiences and helping the movement to become more aware of itself, its potential, and its challenges.

Another opportunity for reaching out involves universities sponsoring working groups and community forums. For example, a number of researchers from the University of Wisconsin facilitated a working-group session at a rural-urban conference that focused on how participants—consumers, producers, activists, and other food system practitioners—envisioned a sustainable food system. In addition to the seven attributes already formulated by academics, the participants came up with seven additional, distinct attributes. This infusion of new knowledge resulted in a set of attributes that can provide "more dimensions for distinguishing between competing visions" and "may prove resistant to co-optation by the proponents of a 'conventional' sustainability" who promote the industrialized global food system (Kloppenburg, Lezberg, DeMaster, Stevenson, & Hendrickson, 2000).

Hosting conferences that promote alternative visions of society can also be a form of reaching out. Such conferences create spaces where different kinds of knowledge can be shared, which mirrors the commitment to the dissemination of knowledge that has historically been the mandate of publicly funded universities. For this reason, striving to establish such alternative venues helps to build the knowledge commons.

One more example of reaching out involves the People's Free University of Saskatchewan (Woodhouse, 2003). It opened its doors in the fall of 2002 with six courses offered in different locations in Saskatoon. Retired professors and members of the community gave their services for free to almost two hundred students. Upon completion of the course, these students could obtain a certificate of learning. The People's Free University was created because of opposition among faculty, staff, and students to increasing privatization at the University of Saskatchewan, including a doubling of tuition fees and funding for research that increasingly serves the corporate market.

Reaching out could also involve appointing a community activist in residence. While many universities feature an entrepreneur in residence or a CEO in residence, such a choice does little to prevent enclosure of the commons. Inviting a community activist to be a vital part of academic life legitimizes alternative ways of viewing communities and builds alliances with community groups, not corporate "partners" who use the university affiliation as an opportunity for brand exposure.

Reid and Taylor (2000) offer a model that academics can follow when reaching out to form alliances with communities. Working with rural miners in the Appalachian Mountains of Kentucky, they recognize that the great value of local knowledge is its gift for particularity and a sense of place. From this recognition, they argue that "academics must resituate themselves into ontologies of the particular and the placed" (p. 462). Academics can join the grassroots globalization that is being embodied in notions like ecological citizenship. Reid and Taylor propose joining "local knowledge to expert knowledge-building partnerships between academics and community-based, citizen self-education and research" (p. 462).

The model Reid and Taylor (2000) put forward involves what they call "participatory reason," which

> requires thinking that is attuned to, and characterized by, emergence (rather than mechanical causality), the matrixical, and acceptance that the universal, as thought by humans, is always embedded in, emergent from, the local and concrete. New forms of alliance between "local" and "expert" knowledges could be a powerful site from which to unsettle these reifying dualisms. (pp. 462–63)

New forms of alliance between local and expert knowledges could also be a powerful site from which to unsettle the commodification of knowledge itself. These non-commodified communities of knowledge would be "off the grid" in terms of commodification, given the restricted market such local understanding would provide.[7] But they would be networked by a common understanding in the inherent use value of what they know in their particular ways—that life, in its wildly divergent forms around the world, does not exist to serve money, but that money exists to serve life.

Renowned educational theorist Paulo Freire (1996) captured the idea of communities of knowledge when he proposed that

> Knowledge emerges only through invention and re-invention, through the restless, impatient, continuing, hopeful inquiry human beings pursue in the world, with the world, and with each other. (p. 53)

Such knowledge is never scarce, can never be made scarce, because it is publicly owned knowledge that is produced every day through the lives of people who are working to resist the effects of corporate globalization. Whether their resistance involves fighting the takeover of common land, the closure of schools and hospitals, the clear-cutting of forests, the amalgamation of municipalities, the downloading of services, or the arrival of big box stores, these people produce knowledge that is vital to life, not the global corporate market.

As Maturana and Varela (1987) have argued, knowledge is effective action in the domain of existence. Resistance to corporate globalization and its knowledge economy produces knowledge that is local in nature, but universal in understanding. From their particular concrete forms of resistance, producers of this non-commodified knowledge reach out and embrace the world, helping to build the knowledge commons and providing hope and direction for others who, in their own diverse ways, also resist and reach out.

Notes

1. My formulation of the knowledge commons is based on the concept of the civil commons developed by John McMurtry (1998, 1999). The civil commons is any co-operative human construction that protects and/or enables universal access to life goods. As a life good, knowledge is a logical candidate for the protections and enablements of the civil commons.

2. According to Buchbinder and Newson (1991), a Canadian organization called the Corporate Higher Education Forum (CHEF), made up of university presidents and corporate executives, argued that universities could solve the problems of underfunding by tuning their curricula and research programs more directly to the needs of industry (p. 23). In a written report, members of CHEF strongly recommended that the provincial governments continue their underfunding policy—thus creating greater incentive in the university community to seek out corporate partners.

3. Newson (1998b) reminds us that "the call for accountability does not resound in meeting rooms wherein trade agreements are drafted that establish publicly *un*accountable bodies and assign them powers that supersede those of elected governments" (p. 309).

4. At the University of Guelph, it is estimated that the roughly $10 million (1998 figures) that industry invests annually to support proprietary research allows it to leverage a healthy chunk of the much larger (roughly $250 million) taxpayer investment at the university (Clark, 1999).

5. Such requirements would help to eliminate free-riding on the commons, a phenomenon that is clearly seen in, for example, the appropriation of taxpayers' money by corporate research "partnerships" with universities.

6. Academics have often shied away from association with social movements, but they have not shied away from association with corporations. This selective association provides a telling example of not only the self-censorship of academics but also the legitimation that corporate association confers.

7. Polster (2000) uses the term "alternative knowledge" to refer to knowledge that is not primarily oriented to the production of tangible, economically valuable goods (p. 38).

CHAPTER THIRTEEN

Decommodifying Daily Life
The Politics of Overconsumption

DENNIS SORON

On November 26, 2002, CNN aired a commercial that must have come as quite a surprise to television viewers accustomed to sitting patiently through the usual barrage of flashy, upbeat ads for cars, computers, shampoo, snack food, cellphones, and other consumer items. Sponsored by the Vancouver-based Media Foundation, which also produces the quarterly magazine *Adbusters*, the segment featured a belching pig protruding from a map of North America, inter-spliced with dismal images of overstuffed landfills and crowded, smog-spewing freeways. The accompanying voice-over urged people to reflect seriously upon the implications of their consumerist lifestyles:

> The average North American consumes five times more than a Mexican, ten times more than a Chinese person, and 30 times more than a person in India. We are the most voracious consumers in the world—a world that could die because of the way we North Americans live. Give it a rest.

Presented as part of the campaign for *Adbusters'* annual "International Buy Nothing Day," this "subvertisement" was certainly an unusual thing to see on mainstream television, a medium we have come to expect to be little more than a conduit for commercial messages. As *Adbusters* spokesperson Kalle Lasn subsequently stated in a CNN interview, this ad represented an effort to break through the endless enticements to consume that dominate our current mental environment and to encourage people to realize that "overconsumption is in some sense the mother of all our ecological problems."[1]

While atypical in the context of the commercial mass media, this ad was quite predictable in other respects. Indeed, anti-consumerist organizations and activists have frequently used pig imagery as a way of dramatizing the pathology of contemporary consumer culture. The *Adbusters* website,[2] for instance, makes this announcement:

Only two generations ago, we were a relatively frugal people, living within our means. Today we are the "North American Pig"—bloated with excess, heavily in debt, and out-pigging everyone else in sight. Overconsumption is just the most obvious symptom of a larger sickness: our culture is so empty that it needs to stuff itself to feel full. (quoted in Progler, 1998)

At a broader level, this condemnation of the "swinish" appetites of the consumer masses is symptomatic of a growing consensus within the progressive environmental community: the idea that "the future health of the planet—and thus its capacity to sustain a growing global population—is significantly dependent upon reducing consumption in the affluent societies" (Lodziak, 2000, p. 111). It is also indicative of the idiom in which much contemporary environmental debate has been conducted—moral criticism of the consumerist excess and environmental disregard of ordinary people. From this perspective, environmental damage is attributable primarily to the spread of a "sick" consumer culture that has fostered irresponsible and wasteful personal behaviours and undermined values and psychological traits conducive to frugality, restraint, and respect for the natural world. In contrast, achieving sustainability is seen as largely dependent upon the willingness of individuals to opt out of this culture by reorienting their relationship to material commodities, transforming their values and sources of personal identity, and becoming more mindful in their everyday consumer habits (De Geus, 2003).

Since at least the early 1990s, environmental scientists Michael Brower and Warren Leon (1999) state, "environmental leaders, both in the United States and abroad, have charged that the major sin against the environment that the rich industrial countries commit has been the practice of 'overconsumption'" (p. 8). Unfortunately, they argue, this notion still largely remains "an ill-defined political slogan" that offers few effective paths forward to greater sustainability (p. 8). In this chapter, I engage with the critique of "overconsumption" that has crystallized in recent years among an influential layer of environmental activists and green thinkers. My primary argument is that questions of economic power and social inequality must take a more central role in current debates over the environmental impacts of consumption and the struggle for what Worldwatch Institute president Christopher Flavin (2004) has called "a less consumptive society" (p. xvii). These debates have provided a welcome opportunity to reflect critically upon the role that consumption plays in our everyday lives and the ways in which established patterns of material resource use are leading us towards the brink of environmental disaster. They have also given powerful voice to a variety of legitimate frustrations with consumerist ways of life that are rife with ephemeral commodities yet largely lacking in genuine and durable human satisfaction. In this sense, discussions of overconsumption have advanced a powerful, albeit limited, critique of hyper-commodified ways of life in the advanced capitalist world. Unfortunately, however, by focusing undue attention upon the personal behaviours, values, and psychological motivations of ordinary consumers, they have often also tended to radically simplify the causes of today's ecological crisis, and to dramatically narrow our understanding of how to best confront it.

THE CONSUMPTION JUGGERNAUT

While good grounds exist for challenging the ways environmentalists have sometimes framed the problem of "overconsumption," the dramatic growth in global consumption in previous decades is unquestionably a problem of the utmost significance. As the United Nations Development Programme (UNDP) has underscored (1998), "Runaway growth in consumption in the past fifty years is putting strains on the environment never before seen" (p. 2). During this time, private consumption expenditures at the global level have more than quadrupled, while combined public and private expenditures have grown roughly sixfold (UNDP, 1998, p. 1). Worldwide, per capita consumption of basic goods such as copper, steel, timber, meat, and energy has more than doubled since mid-century, with rates of freshwater use tripling and fossil fuel use more than quintupling in the same period. Such rates of consumption, the UNDP asserts, have been matched by rates of "pollution and waste that exceed the planet's sink capacities to absorb and convert them" (p. 4). Globally, annual carbon dioxide emissions have quadrupled and sulphur dioxide emissions have more than doubled in the past 50 years (UNDP, 1998, pp. 4, 55). Per capita waste in the industrial world alone has approximately tripled in the past 20 to 25 years (p. 4). As Mathis Wackernagel and William Rees have suggested in *Our Ecological Footprint* (1996), an additional 6 to 12 planets would be required to accommodate sustainably the growth in global population, output, and consumption that is anticipated to occur over the next four decades (p. 91).

Although it is possible to debate the precise figures involved in these complex calculations, Betsy Taylor and Dave Tilford (2000) argue that the overall picture is strikingly clear: "Skyrocketing consumption is rapidly depleting the Earth's ecosystems, robbing future generations of vital life-sustaining resources. We are currently using far more of the Earth than the Earth has to offer" (p. 484). As they acknowledge, however, aggregate measures of global consumption fail to highlight adequately the international inequalities that underpin this growing environmental crisis. Indeed, they argue,

> The difference between consumption as practiced in the industrial world and consumption in the developing world is rather astounding: the one fifth of the global population living in the highest-income countries account for 86 percent of private consumption expenditures. The poorest fifth account for a little over 1 percent. (p. 468)

Clearly, the dilemma of overconsumption does not speak to the situation of billions of poor people currently facing serious shortfalls in food, water, shelter, sanitation, health care, education, and other basic consumption needs. Far from enjoying the fruits of the global consumption boom, many poor countries have seen their consumption decline over the past generation. Apart from India and China, per capita consumption expenditures in low-income countries have declined by about 1 per cent annually for the past 15 to 20 years (UNDP, 1998, pp. 47, 50). At the extreme end of the spectrum, the average African household consumes over 20 per cent less today than it did 25 years ago (UNDP, 1998, p. 2).

To their credit, Northern environmentalists have increasingly addressed the interconnections between ecological sustainability and global equity. As Juliet Schor has argued,

> ... [W]hen we talk about the need to cut back consumption and reduce the scale of the global economy in order to develop a more sustainable human relationship to the natural environment, questions of global equity need to be at the forefront of this discussion. One obvious principle of global equity would be that every human being on earth should have the right to an equal share of the global commons. This implies that people in poor countries who pollute far less and degrade the environment far less than is sustainable should be able to increase their use of resources, raise their standards of living, and actually consume more. It also clearly suggests the need for serious reductions in the use of planetary resources by wealthy consumers in the West. (quoted in Soron, 2004)

One strength of the critique of overconsumption that has developed in recent years has been its acknowledgement of the disproportionate responsibility that rich industrial countries must bear for our current environmental crisis. At present, the richest fifth of the global population consume 58 per cent of the world's energy, 65 per cent of electricity, 87 per cent of cars, and 84 per cent of paper (UNDP, 1998, p. 50). The US alone, with roughly 5 per cent of the world's population, consumes one third of its paper, one quarter of its oil, and produces a full 50 per cent of its solid waste. In total, Taylor and Tilford (2000) suggest, a single child born in the US will cause as much environmental damage over the course of his or her lifetime as 13 Brazilians and 35 natives of India (pp. 472, 468).

In many ways, the critical focus on Northern consumption has offered a welcome challenge to earlier tendencies among environmentalists to regard population growth and efforts to achieve rapid economic development in the South as the central obstacles to global ecological sustainability. Looking at issues such as population through the lens of consumption provides a radically new perspective on the problems we now confront. Taking the consumption levels of residents of India as the norm, for instance, the United States currently has a "population" of well over 11 billion people. As the editors of *Confronting Consumption* argue, the 1992 Rio Earth Summit marked an important turning point in global environmental debate in this regard (Princen, Maniates, & Conca, 2002). Here, they argue, Southern activists and government officials succeeded in focusing attention upon unsustainable Northern lifestyles, arguing that "the South's underdevelop-

ment and overpopulation have not been nearly as important for global environmental degradation as the North's overconsumption" (p. 3). In the years since Rio,
they suggest, Northern environmental organizations, activists, and community
groups have taken up this challenge, according an unprecedented amount of effort
to advancing the cause of "sustainable consumption" (UNEP, 2001; OECD, 2002;
Heap & Kent, 2000) and generating countless books, pamphlets, and campaigns
urging Northern consumers towards reducing their consumption and "developing everyday habits which make everyday living less material-intensive" (Sachs,
Reinhard, Manfred, & Behrensmeier, 1998, p. 122).

While environmentalists have often promoted simple, practical, and relatively
unobtrusive lifestyle changes such as biking to work, replacing energy-inefficient
light bulbs, and reducing personal water usage, they have also been infused by a
strong sense of moral purpose (Earthworks Group, 1989; Getis, 1999). As environmental activist and researcher Alan Durning (1992) argues,

> We consumers have an ethical obligation to curb our consumption, since it
> jeopardizes the chances for future generations. Unless we climb down the
> consumption ladder a few rungs, our grandchildren will inherit a planetary
> home impoverished by our affluence—a planet whose climate has been dras-
> tically altered in mere decades, whose air and water are poisoned, whose fer-
> tile soils are worn down, whose living species are decimated in number, and
> whose wild habitats are shrunken and fragmentary. (pp. 136-37)

As it turns out, Durning (1992) suggests, this "obligation" need not be an onerous one to fulfil. Indeed, elevated levels of consumption in the affluent North seem
to bear an often counter-productive relationship to individual and collective well-
being. Indeed, he writes, "the historic rise of the consumer society has been quite
effective in harming the environment, but not in providing people with a fulfilling
life" (p. 36). Self-reported rates of happiness in rich countries have flattened or
declined in the past 50 years even as consumption has ballooned, and these rates
have remained similar to those in much poorer countries (Bond, 2003; Argyle,
1987; Wachtel, 1989). In the same period, the dark side of consumer society has
increasingly come into view: climbing rates of personal debt and bankruptcy; pervasive social alienation and disconnection; the growth of consumption-related
health problems such as heart disease and diabetes; rising levels of depression, anxiety, and other emotional disturbances; job-related stress, chronic "time poverty,"
and so on. Ultimately, Durning (1992) asserts, the responsibility for confronting
this interlinked social and ecological crisis falls upon "us, the consumers" (p. 137).
The choice is ours: we can work to limit our use of ecologically destructive goods,
while cultivating non-material sources of personal happiness, he argues, or else "we
can abrogate our responsibilities and let our life-style ruin the earth" (p. 137).

THERE ARE NOT ENOUGH RICH AND POWERFUL PEOPLE TO CONSUME THE WHOLE WORLD

One notable feature of the established critique of overconsumption is its direct challenge to the belief in "endless economic growth driven by unbridled consumption" that is deeply rooted in the institutions and policies driving social and economic development at the national and international levels (Renner, 2004, p. 96). This challenge has been especially timely in today's political climate, where this "growth fetish" has effectively become a point of consensus across the entire political spectrum (Hamilton, 2004). Indeed, in addressing the perils of overconsumption, environmentalists have often taken issue not only with pro-business forces but also with the left itself, whose traditional struggle for improved material living standards for the general population has often paid little attention to the ecological consequences of continual economic growth. Holding to an overly materialistic conception of progress, Anders Hayden (1999) claims,

> ... much of the left has become too attached in practice to creating more equitable opportunities for consumerist excess, and far too committed to crudely maximizing economic growth, without making a distinction between those activities that ought to grow and those that should be curtailed, as the foundation of a progressive economic alternative. (p. 10)

By focusing too narrowly upon quantitative goals such as industrial expansion and income growth, argues green icon Rudolf Bahro (1984), the left has often neglected the environment and reinforced consumerist norms, assuming that "man [sic] needs everything that capitalism offers him, needs more and ever more" (p. 145). In contrast, as prominent British environmentalist Jonathon Porritt (1985) writes, green politics fundamentally differs from conventional politics on both the left and right in its "belief that quantitative demand must be *reduced*, not expanded" (p. 136).

While such criticisms have provided a useful opportunity to rethink the complex relationship of ecology, economic redistribution, and class politics, and to refocus attention upon the *qualitative*, non-commodified goals of radical struggle, they have also led some environmental activists and thinkers towards a more simplistic position. This position largely denies the relevance of economic power and social inequality within advanced industrial societies, where mass affluence and consumer culture have diffused irresponsible consumption practices widely across the entire population. As Porritt asserts, "thinking green" requires us to dispense with the "redundant polemic of class warfare and the mythical immutability of the left/right divide," and to acknowledge the ways in which we all collude with the ecologically destructive processes of consumer society (quoted in Foster, 2002, p. 104). Instead of indulging in the "old-world" practice of laying blame on the rich and powerful, he suggests, we need to realize that "[a]mong all notional 'classes' of people there are those who exercise their power responsibly in the interest of life on Earth and those who use their power to the detriment of both people and the planet" (Porritt, 1985, p. 226). Thus, within the sphere of personal consumption, a captain of industry may be an exemplary recycler and drinker of shade-grown coffee, whereas a low-wage worker may not. From this perspective, the crucial social antagonism is no longer between capital and labour—both of which are wedded to the goals of unrestrained economic growth and consumption—but between heedless and wasteful consumers and those individuals who have chosen to adopt more ecologically responsible lifestyles.

Indeed, as other thinkers have claimed, consumer society itself has undermined traditional class distinctions by fostering ideological consensus around a shared vision of the "good life" and by furnishing ordinary people with opportunities for frivolous consumption previously reserved for the wealthy elite. As Gary Cross argues in *An All-Consuming Century* (2000), for instance, the ideological victory of consumerism in previous decades has broken down the historic boundary between "elite luxury" and "mass subsistence," creating an "ephemeral commodity culture" that working class people have embraced enthusiastically (pp. 1-5). Similarly, as William Leach states in *Land of Desire* (1993), mass affluence in the post-war era has led to a "democratization of desire," ensuring that all groups are now equally "preoccupied with consumption, with comfort and bodily well-being, with luxury, spending, and acquisition, with more goods this year than last, more next year than this" (p. xiii). In terms reminiscent of a medieval morality play, environmental thinker James Nash denounces our "Sumptuous Society," which he sees as universally overrun by "gluttonous self-indulgence, compulsive inquisitiveness, and ostentatious materialism" (quoted in Hayden, 1999, p. 56). Amidst this orgy of unrestrained consumption, none of us—whatever our status or income—escapes culpability. "All of us in the first world have participated in something of a binge, a half century of unbelievable prosperity and ease," writes Bill McKibben in *The End of Nature* (1999). "We may have had some intuition that it was a binge and the earth couldn't support it, but aside from the easy things … we didn't do much. We didn't turn our lives around to prevent it" (p. 86).

This focus on mass participation in unsustainable consumerist lifestyles has in some cases led to a reconfiguration of the whole language of "class" itself. In recent years, for instance, the notion of the global "consumer class" has become increasingly popular in environmental circles, becoming part of the established vocabulary of organizations such as the United Nations Environment Programme, the Worldwatch Institute, the Sierra Club, and so on (Bentley, 2003; Durning, 1992; Taylor & Tilford, 2000; Gardner, Assadourian, & Sarin, 2004). As Taylor and Tilford (2000) argue,

> To visualize world consumption patterns, it is helpful to divide human population into three distinct classes: the poor, middle class, and the "consumer class." The poorest fifth of the world population—over one billion people—live in abject poverty, surviving on less than a dollar per day. The vast middle class—60 percent of the world population—have most of their basic food,

shelter, and water needs met, live in modest homes with lights, radios, and sometimes a refrigerator and a clothes washer, but own few material possessions and virtually no luxury items.... The remaining 20 percent are the "consumer class." (p. 468)

As an "ecological class," Durning (1992) suggests, this top bracket of global "consumers" is characterized not by its relationship to the means of production, or by relative power or social status, but by an absolute per capita income of over $7500 (US) per year (p. 27). As such, he suggests, this rather expansive class includes "most North Americans, West Europeans, Japanese, Australians, the citizens of Hong Kong, Singapore, and the oil sheikdoms of the Middle East," as well as a sizable portion of the populations of poorer countries (p. 28).

At first glance, this broad categorization would seem to override some important distinctions within the ranks of even the most affluent of consumer societies. By assimilating virtually the entire population of the industrial world into the "consumer class," for instance, it fails to acknowledge adequately the millions of people in it that still face serious material deprivation and unmet basic consumption needs (UNDP, 1998, pp. 2, 51). By creating a picture of generalized consumer excess and luxury spending, it also fails to discern properly the conditions faced by the majority of people in industrial countries whose real incomes and purchasing power have declined steadily since the early 1970s, even as basic survival costs have risen (Gorz, 1999; Offe, 1996). Finally, by creating a "class" so encompassing as to include billionaire CEOs and inner-city single mothers eking out a living on social assistance, it gives little weight to the vast differentials in social status, opportunity, material comfort, political influence, control over life circumstances, and ecologically significant consumption among the world's "consumers."

While acknowledging that huge inequalities of wealth and power exist within the consumer class, Durning (1992) denies that these have much real ecological significance. Judged by global standards, he claims, even the poorest members of this class are active participants in an unprecedentedly wasteful consumer lifestyle—dining on meat and heavily processed and packaged foods, drinking beverages from disposable containers, living in climate-controlled buildings decked out with energy-intensive appliances and filled with superfluous throwaway goods, relying on the private automobile for transportation, and so on (p. 28). Similarly, "the rich"—in spite all of their privileges—are "best taken as a subset of the consumer class, because, in terms of ecological impacts, the greatest disparities are not between the rich and the consumers but between the consumers and the middle-income class" (p. 29). Although they require more money and use more resources, the lifestyles of the rich differ in degree rather than kind from those of others; they are merely the forward edge of a society-wide trend for which all consumers must assume responsibility. In this view, the compulsive drive to consume material goods has become deeply rooted in our collective psyche, binding us all unselfconsciously to a way of life that is both environmentally and personally damaging. As John de Graaf, David Wann, and Thomas H. Naylor write in

Affluenza: the All-Consuming Epidemic (2002), "compulsively, we consume snacks, cigarettes, and electronic games ... somehow oblivious that we are carriers of affluenza—the human disease that strikes Nature like a dozen ongoing hurricanes" (p. 86).

Focusing moral attention upon the end-point of personal consumption, as we have considered, thus challenges any temptation to place inordinate blame for environmental damage upon elites or upon impersonal economic or political processes beyond the individual's control. As celebrated American conservationist Wendell Berry argues in *Sex, Economy, Freedom & Community* (1993), "there are not enough rich and powerful people to consume the whole world; for that, the rich and powerful need the help of countless ordinary people" (quoted in *Quotations on Consumerism*). Those who stubbornly persist in externalizing blame onto governments and wealthy capitalists, he continues, are forgetting something crucial:

> However destructive may be the policies of the government and the methods and products of the corporations, the root of the problem is always found to be in private life. We must learn to see that every problem that concerns us as conservationists always leads straight to the question of how we live. The world is being destroyed, no doubt about it, by the greed of the rich and powerful. It is also being destroyed by popular demand.

Instead of continuing to infantilize ourselves by making plaintive appeals for change to those above us on the socio-economic ladder, Berry believes, we need to take direct personal responsibility for the way we live. This means striving to uproot our insatiable desire for commodities, paring back our consumption, providing for more of our own needs directly through self-production, and acquiring the moral character and practical skills to live much more simply than we now do (Berry, 1989, p. 1986). However necessary such efforts may be, McKibben (1999) suggests, they continually run up against the "inertia of affluence"—our strong psychological resistance to voluntarily relinquishing the status and material comforts to which we've become accustomed (p. 192). Ultimately, however, as psychologist Tim Kasser (2002) asserts, "if we continue to be driven by selfishness and materialism, ecological disaster awaits us" (p. 93).

NOT ONLY CONSUMERS CONSUME

Given the scale of the ecological crisis that we now confront, the moral urgency of Berry, McKibben, and others concerned with the problem of overconsumption is a welcome contrast to the apathy, denial, and expediency that characterize our current political culture. As John Bellamy Foster (2002) asserts, faced with the twin problems of environmental deterioration and public inaction, greens have increasingly been "calling for a moral revolution that would incorporate ecological values into our culture." Unfortunately, he believes,

> ... Behind most appeals to ecological morality there lies the presumption that we live in a society where the morality of the individual is the key to the morality of the society. If people as individuals could simply change their moral stance with respect to nature and alter their behaviour in areas such as propagation, consumption, and the conduct of business, all would be well. (p. 44)

This presumption, as we have seen, is evident in current debates about over-consumption, which have directed their moral judgments mostly towards irresponsible and self-absorbed consumer behaviours. As a consequence, Conrad Lodziak (2002) argues, "the need to reduce consumption is invariably taken to mean that the principal strategy for achieving this is that of urging individuals to consume less" (p. 150). What this individualistic perspective overlooks, he believes, are the various ways in which capitalist imperatives have shaped prevailing consumption patterns, locking people into ecologically destructive ways of life that they have not freely and consciously chosen.

In order to begin to depersonalize and repoliticize our understanding of the problem of overconsumption, we need to first remember that, as Brower and Leon (1999) have put it,

> [P]aradoxically, consumers are not the only ones who consume things, even though discussions of consumption-environment connections have most often focused on "consumer goods" and what individuals consume. Businesses, organizations, and governments also consume things as part of their activities. (p. 14)

This often-neglected domain of "institutional consumption," as Lodziak (2002) labels it, deserves a much greater degree of attention from environmentalists, for it actually "accounts for a far greater proportion of the total volume of goods consumed than the sum total of what is consumed individually and domestically" (p. 153). Public institutions consume a huge volume of resources in building, operating, and maintaining roads, schools, hospitals, airports, harbours, sewage systems, prisons, military systems, and so on. Private businesses also consume enormous amounts of resources, and generate significant pollution and waste, at every stage of the production, distribution, and marketing process. In both arenas, the most environmentally significant "consumption" decisions are determined by the interests and priorities of political and economic elites, largely beyond the direct knowledge or influence of ordinary "consumers."

The issue of water conservation provides one illustrative example of the inadequacy of environmental strategies, which ignore the issue of institutional consumption and focus primarily upon the personal habits of consumers. In recent decades, environmental groups have engaged in countless campaigns to encourage greater conservation of water resources, often urging people to fix leaky faucets in their homes, install low-flow shower heads and water-efficient toilets, reduce wasteful lawn watering, and so on. While encouraging an ethos of environmental responsibility in all of our daily practices is an admirable goal, this focus on direct household usage provides a very limited way of understanding and responding to current patterns of water consumption. At present, Sandra Postel and Amy Vickers (2004) calculate that commercial agriculture and industry account for roughly 92 per cent of global water use, with municipal usage accounting for only 8 per cent (p. 46). In the rich countries of the North, they claim, industry alone is responsible for approximately 59 per cent of freshwater withdrawals, using vast amounts of the public water supply for washing, heating, cooling, processing, and other production processes (p. 60). Indeed, this figure significantly undershoots the true volume used by industry, because companies often tap water directly from their own wells or from nearby rivers and lakes, without metering (pp. 60–61). No matter how sparing consumers may be in their purchasing habits, huge amounts of water are embedded within all of the goods we consume. Under current agricultural methods, for instance, a person who consumes a single 8 ounce piece of beef is also indirectly "consuming" the 25,000 litres of water that went into its production (Postel &Vickers, 2004, p. 54). Of the relatively small amount of water reserved for municipal use within industrial societies, only a portion is devoted to direct household consumption, whereas water system leakage alone can often account for almost 40 per cent of the total supply (p. 56). All of these hidden structural factors are reflected within calculations of "per capita" water usage, but they are beyond the purview of individual consumer decision. Focusing excessive attention on individual or household consumption habits not only obscures the primary source of the problem, it lends credence to regressive "market solutions" such as pre-pay metering that compromise universal citizen access to water and further the commodification of nature.

In spite of Berry's (1989) stated aversion to dividing the world between "guilty producers" and "innocent consumers," the above example suggests that we also need to challenge the distinction between producer and consumer in order to scrutinize the "consumption" practices of producers themselves. It is wrong to think that consumption occurs only at the individual point of final product use. Indeed, as Lodziak (2002) writes, institutional consumption within the capitalist economy entails,

> ... all that is involved in the various stages of producing the final product for consumption (private or public). This includes all that is consumed in producing the means (raw materials, mines, factories, machinery, tools, and so on) or capital goods required for the manufacture of consumer products.... The second form of the institutional consumption of capitalism involves all that is consumed in the various stages involved in the circulation and selling

of goods—advertising, packaging, labelling, warehouses, lorries, offices, shops, and so forth. (p. 154)

The sheer size and ecological significance of this sphere of consumption is difficult to overstate. Lodziak (2002) cites James O'Connor, who calculated that in 1987-88, capital goods[3] alone accounted for 78 per cent of energy use and 88 per cent of all toxic releases in the entire United States (p. 154). According to some estimates, up to 70 per cent of the materials consumed in capitalist economies today are expended within the production process itself, and discarded as waste long before any individual purchaser acquires a final product (Renner, 2004, pp. 101-02). In effect, this means that even very modest acts of personal consumption can unwittingly implicate us in processes that are very environmentally damaging. Newlyweds who exchange rings with each other, for instance, may be acting from non-materialistic motives, and offering each other a small item that will last for decades; and yet, they will also be indirectly involved in a process that has produced roughly 6 tons of toxic mining waste (Gardner et al., 2004, p. 16).

These massive "hidden flows" take place within a privately controlled, profit-oriented production process about which ordinary consumers typically know very little. The commodities that we purchase at the local store arrive on the shelves through a convoluted network of impersonal market relationships that systematically distances us—in both a mental and geographical sense—from the sphere of production and its ecological effects. In the absence of comprehensive labelling schemes, or of public information campaigns to match the ubiquitous influence of commercial advertising, we often lack even the most basic information needed to make ecologically enlightened choices. Even when the appropriate information can be accessed, such choices may not be practically available to us. Beyond the limited issue of consumer awareness, however, is the broader question of economic power. What is significant here is not simply the greater consumption power of "the rich," as Durning and Berry imply, but the power of capital to determine what is produced; how it is produced, packaged, distributed, marketed, and rendered available for consumption; and what environmental costs are externalized onto the public as a whole. Remaining attentive to the effects of this undemocratic power, as Michael Dawson (2003) suggests, can prevent us from simply according ordinary people "all the transferred blame for capitalists' costly, socially irrational actions" (p. 144). Indeed, why should "consumers"—operating with imperfect knowledge and facing all kinds of practical constraints in their everyday lives—assume responsibility for the environmental consequences of an entire economic system over which they have very little democratic control?

One conventional response to this question is that capitalist markets merely "give people what they want," that is, that they are entirely driven by popular demand, and simply respond to the expressed preferences of the sovereign consumer (Friedman & Friedman, 1990). This hyper-liberal perspective exaggerates the autonomy of individual consumers, whose preferences are shaped not only by cultural pressures such as advertising and peer comparison, but by the practical opportunities for satisfying their needs presented to them by the specific social circumstances in which they live. Circumstances such as ours, in which capital exerts a heavy control over the means of daily survival and shapes our media, public spaces, physical environments, and work and leisure opportunities to its own ends, create strong pressures for such needs to take a commodified, materially-intensive form. As Dawson (2003) argues, "consumers" do not necessarily desire to "consume" the objects they use, in the literal sense of destroying them or rendering them unfit for further use (p. 4). Typically, they are merely looking for a practical and socially accessible means of satisfying their needs or desires, and they seek to maximize the pleasure or utility of the goods they acquire for this end. As Dawson warns environmentalists and other progressives, the very act of referring to people as "consumers" reflects a reductive capitalist mentality in which "off-the-job human beings count only as mere money-spending garbage disposals" (pp. 4–5).

While ordinary people do not typically have any in-built desire for "consuming," in the literal sense, and would be amenable to alternative means of meeting their needs were they practically available, capital has a clear stake in maximizing consumption and expanding the commodification of human needs. If public transportation systems, for instance, were improved to the point where they provided people with the quickest, cheapest, and most convenient means of navigating their daily responsibilities, this would bring tremendous benefits to the environment, public health, and the pace and texture of community life. It would also be devastating to the auto industry, whose profits are directly tied in with maintaining socially irrational and environmentally destructive patterns of transportation oriented around the private car. Given the immense productive capacity of capitalism, the prime need of capitalists is to engender high and sustained demand for the commodities they produce. One obvious means of accomplishing this is the multibillion dollar advertising industry, whose relentless "propaganda for commodities" perpetually entices us to consume goods for which we've previously felt little need or desire (Jhally, 1998). Beyond the ideological influence of advertising, capital's monopoly over production ensures that people are not provided with durable, high-quality goods that satisfy their needs efficiently and affordably but with an abundance of ephemeral and often superfluous goods designed for rapid physical, aesthetic, and technical obsolescence. At the political level, as I've argued elsewhere, capital avails itself of its disproportionate power and influence to shape public policy in ways that provide the infrastructure and incentives for profit-yielding private consumption, extend commodification into new spheres, and render people more market dependent by limiting their access to public goods and common resources (Soron, 2005, p. 211). None of these spurs to overconsumption are adequately addressed by environmental perspectives that focus on the values or behaviours of individual consumers in isolation from the wider social arrangements in which they are embedded.

THE SOCIAL EMBEDDEDNESS OF CONSUMPTION

According to Juliet Schor, one key inadequacy of the notion of consumer sovereignty enshrined in neoclassical economics is that it leads to an understanding of consumption "largely stripped of its social dimensions, becoming reduced to the question of goods and the functionality they provide to the individual" (quoted in Soron, 2004). What this individualistic framework overlooks about our consumer choices, as Thomas Princen and his co-editors write in *Confronting Consumption* (2002), is that

> ... far from being autonomous exercises of power by sovereign consumers, such choices in modern political economies are heavily influenced by contextual social forces ... and subject to structural features that often make it convenient, rewarding, even necessary, to increase consumption. Embedding consumption in a larger web of social relations leads us to ask about the influences on consumption choices, including the location of power in structuring those choices. (p. 15)

By challenging the insatiability of consumer wants, questioning the ability of increased consumption to deliver additional human satisfaction, and insisting upon our responsibility for the external effects of our consumption choices, critics of overconsumption have to some extent challenged the assumptions underlying the neoclassical model. In other instances, by morally entreating individuals to change their relationship to goods voluntarily, they have reproduced such assumptions by downplaying the extent to which existing consumption patterns are shaped by social forces and power relations over which we have little personal control (Sanne, 2002).

Resisting such tendencies, Lodziak (2002) has argued that the routinized pressures and practical constraints of everyday life in contemporary capitalist society, far more than the entrancing effect of consumer ideology or hedonistic mass appetites, is what underpins current forms of unsustainable consumption. Once again, the issue of automobile use provides a good illustration here (Soron, 2005, p. 202). Environmentalists are rightly critical of our collective dependency on highly polluting, energy-intensive transportation patterns centred on the private automobile. That said, this dependency is fed and reproduced by a whole set of factors that go far beyond the individual's selfish preference for driving. In many places, particularly rural and suburban areas, public transportation may be virtually non-existent. Or it may simply be far more costly, inconvenient, and time-consuming than car usage, and less adaptable to one's daily work routines and domestic responsibilities. State subsidies for the auto and petroleum industries, combined with chronic underfunding of public services, can perpetuate this imbalance. Commercial sprawl and low-density, rigidly zoned land-use patterns may create distances between home, work, school, hospitals, shopping centres, and other amenities that are too far to manage by foot or by bike, particularly in inclement weather. Inflated property costs in gentrified downtown residential areas and government subsidies for suburban home building may create strong disincentives for people to reduce their commuting distance by moving closer to their workplaces. Neighbourhoods that lack bike paths, sidewalks, and sufficient night-time lighting and are crosscut with multiple-lane roads rimmed with broken glass and other refuse can make alternatives to car travel unsafe and unpleasant.

Taken together, this constellation of social, material, technical, political, and economic incentives and constraints comprises an "infrastructure of consumption" that effectively compels people into making consumption-intensive everyday choices (OECD, 2002; Renner, 2004). In many cases, as Dale Southerton (2004) and his colleagues argue, the pressures and constraints that people in consumer society face are "normative" in nature, that is, related to the everyday demands of "fitting in" to specific social contexts and reference groups and of symbolically establishing one's status and identity (pp. 37–38). The issues at play here go beyond what Taylor and Tilford (2000) identify as our "unexamined faith in personal and spiritual fulfillment achieved via an endless stream of cheap and disposable consumer products" (p. 463). People may, for a wide variety of reasons, comply pragmatically with consumption norms in which they have little personal "faith." Parents wary of commercialism, for instance, may nevertheless buy their children fashionable brand-name goods in order to prevent them from feeling excluded or stigmatized by their peer group at school.

What's more, the fulfilment that people seek may have more to do with their relative social standing than with any intrinsic gratification derived from consumer products themselves. As Juliet Schor (1999), among others, has emphasized, beyond the level of material comfort needed to meet one's basic needs, the pleasure derived from increases in consumption are largely relative rather than absolute. The persistent reality of inequality within consumer society is one of the reasons that people have reported no increase in personal satisfaction after decades in which overall consumption levels have been dramatically ratcheted up. Consumption practices have historically been one of the key sites in which people have struggled to reproduce or elevate their social status symbolically, and this process continues apace today. Indeed, Schor believes that steeply increasing rates of material inequality in the industrial world over the past generation have intensified such competitive pressures, fostering a continual up scaling of consumption norms. Thus, contrary to what Porritt and Berry may claim, class inequality is one of the main drivers of overconsumption and environmental degradation in the world today.

Time is another distributional issue that bears directly upon the problem of overconsumption. Although we may intuitively associate wasteful consumption practices with pampered indolence and leisure, time shortage is perhaps the more important driver of overconsumption in rich Northern societies. In such societies, there is an increasingly broad popular consensus that everyday life has become far too fast-paced, and stressful (Southerton, Warde, & Hand, 2004; Schor, 1992; Southerton & Tomlinson, 2003). This time-squeeze puts a premium upon speed in convenience, creating strong incentives for car and air travel, pre-packaged convenience items, labour-saving appliances, fast food, disposable and single-use goods, and other environmentally damaging products and services. When environmentalists appeal to individuals to cultivate less materially intensive everyday habits, they are effectively asking them to satisfy their needs in a more labour- and time-intensive manner. Cooking one's meals from scratch with various ingredients acquired in bulk requires far more time and effort than microwaving an over-packaged frozen dinner, ordering a pizza, or cruising up to a Burger King drive-through window. At the end of the day, harried and exhausted people will tend to opt for passive, commodified forms of leisure over creative pursuits—such as playing a musical instrument—that can only be cultivated slowly and patiently. Repairing and maintaining clothing, appliances, and other household goods requires more time and developed skills than simply purchasing replacement items.

As these examples suggest, people will need a greater degree of control over the routines and schedules that structure their daily lives if they are to transform their consumption practices in fundamental ways that move beyond the "small" measures that McKibben derides. The current scarcity of time for environmentally friendly self-production practices is particularly evident in the contemporary household. In the past few decades, as Susan Strasser (1982, 1999) has argued, the increasing entry of women into the full-time work force has created a growing labour shortage within the domestic sphere, leading to new time pressures and incentives for the commodification of a wide range of household goods and services previously provided directly by women. In the absence of any effort to address the structural roots of this problem and to cultivate a more egalitarian division of household labour, the call to curb consumption can imply that women should resume unpaid responsibility for meeting domestic needs in an environmentally friendly manner—by hand-washing and sun drying clothes, for instance, or foregoing the use of energy-intensive appliances, convenience items, and so on.

Beyond the home, the routines and time constraints imposed by labour in the paid workforce also tie in directly with the problem of overconsumption. Moral blandishments aside, workers in capitalist society are unavoidably consumers as well. Indeed, as Richard Robbins (1999) argues,

> Those who control the means of production also control the goods that are produced, and so those who labor to produce them must buy them back from those with the means of production. Thus, the severing of persons from the means of production turns them not only into laborers, but into customers of the product of their labour as well. (pp. 88–89)

Within the constraints of a life structured around the routines of alienated labour, people lack the time, the resources, and even the cultivated skills to satisfy their various social and material needs outside of the market in a non-commodified manner. By its very nature, Lodziak (2002) explains, the alienation of labour in capitalist society "requires a dependence on consumer goods. In other words, *we are compelled to consume*" (p. 89). This original state of market dependence is only heightened as people become increasingly deskilled in meeting their own needs directly and as public goods and common resources decline in quality or availability.

As workers are rendered more dependent upon the market for their material survival and self-development, many of their deepest and most pressing needs can remain stubbornly unsatisfied, and this in itself can feed cravings that are acted out within the sphere of consumption. In this category, as Andre Gorz (1967) suggests, are all those "human needs that cannot be expressed in market terms as demands for saleable commodities" (p. 83). These include our need for a healthy environment; for vital collective services; for clean air and water; for free time and opportunities for creative self-expression; for social connection, intimacy, and meaning—needs which all must be addressed socially and collectively rather than through the consumer marketplace. The problem in this case is not, as some critics of overconsumption have argued, that our needs themselves have become warped, but that our social environment creates enormous structural pressures for us to define, express, and satisfy these needs in a commodified and ecologically destructive manner. Thus, as Gorz (1967) asserts, "the nature of capitalism is to constrain the individual to buy back individually, as a consumer, the means of satisfaction of which the society has socially deprived him [sic]" (p. 90).

REPOLITICIZING CONSUMPTION

By placing disproportionate blame for ecological destruction upon consumers' hedonistic propensity for "pigging out," current critiques of overconsumption run the risk of personalizing problems that have systemic roots in capitalist relations of power that, as Foster argues (2002), are innately biased "towards the unlimited commodification of human productive energy, land, and the built environment, and the ecology of the planet itself" (pp. 104–05). This process of personalization is visible in the image of the "North American Pig" itself, which transforms an entire continent—one crosscut with different countries, regions, institutions, political forces, economic interests, classes, and social and cultural groups—into a single swollen creature, writhing and belching in the torpor of greedy indulgence. What this amplified image of consumer gluttony fails to capture are the structural underpinnings of overconsumption in today's "affluent" societies and the abiding inequalities of power with which they are enmeshed. By inserting such factors back into the debate, I have tried to show that we can develop a better sense of the ways in which unsustainable consumption patterns are shaped by the spheres of production and government policy and intertwined with social and material constraints over which ordinary people have little immediate control.

To acknowledge such constraints is by no means to advocate passivity or inaction. Indeed, it merely points to the need for strategies of change that go beyond morally cajoling individuals with "timid calls for personal responsibility and green consumerism," strategies that forthrightly confront the broader social, political, and economic forces that prevent people from meeting their varied needs in less commodified and materially-intensive ways (Maniates, 2002, p. 54). Conventional environmental wisdom today, as Brower and Leon (1999) write, can often leave us feeling that "environmental damage is primarily caused by myriad small actions on the part of individual consumers and that the answer is for individuals to voluntarily change their behaviour in dozens and dozens of ways" (p. 7). As a consequence, they claim, environmentally conscientious people end up not only feeling "guilted" into an onerous lifestyle regimen that has relatively little positive impact but also ignoring "situations where the emphasis must be placed on changing the policies of governments and institutions rather than the habits of consumers" (p. ix). As Michael Maniates (2002) states, consumer choices do have some value, but "control over these choices is constrained, shaped, and framed by institutions and political forces that can be remade only through collective citizen action, as opposed to individual consumer behaviour" (p. 65). In this sense, he believes, those who continue to focus narrowly upon the sphere of personal consumption are only helping to further constrict our already impoverished environmental imaginations, exempt powerful elites from responsibility, and entrench the widespread cynicism about organized political action that has taken root in the neoliberal era. By placing blame for today's environmental crisis upon consumers as aggregated individuals, they are also helping to leave existing structures of power in capitalist society un-scrutinized and to exempt the political and economic elites that inhabit them from proper responsibility. If ordinary people are to assume full responsibility for the environmental consequences of the socio-economic system, then they must acquire full democratic control over that system.

Ultimately, addressing overconsumption as a political problem—one that is intimately linked with prevailing social inequalities, systems of production, government policies, work patterns, time routines, gender norms, social and material infrastructures, and so on—will require us to transcend our very self-identification as "consumers." Indeed, Maniates (2002) argues, it will require "individuals to understand themselves as citizens in a participatory democracy first, working together to change broader policy and larger social institutions, and as consumers second" (p. 47). Although current environmental trends are far from encouraging, signs of hope can perhaps be found among the very masses of people that environmentalists sometimes write off as hopelessly hoodwinked by consumer culture. Indeed, in spite of decades of political inaction in the face of worsening ecological conditions, people throughout the advanced industrial world continue to report high levels of concern for environmental issues. Even in the global heartland of contemporary consumerism, the United States, research has shown that, at the level of personal values, people are concerned strongly with both the environment and the psychological and spiritual emptiness of consumerist lifestyles. In a 1995 study conducted by the Merck Family Fund, for instance, an overwhelming majority of Americans expressed deep dissatisfaction with their culture's greed and materialism, acknowledged their country's disproportionate responsibility for global environmental problems, and admitted that protecting the earth would require "major changes" to their current way of life (Harwood Group, 1995). Simultaneously, however, respondents in this survey also expressed widespread confusion about how such changes could be brought about, feeling that their own scope for agency was mostly confined to small personal actions such as recycling.

This suggests that the crucial struggle today is not to create environmental values from scratch in the venal minds of "consumers," but to ensure that existing yearnings for less commodified ways of life are articulated and expressed in more explicitly political and collective ways. This struggle will entail a thoroughgoing change in "values," but not merely at the level of individual consciousness and personal behaviour. Instead of fostering a narrow moralism about the daily habits of individual consumers while leaving broader economic and political prerogatives un-scrutinized, environmental activists need to strive to make social structures—the very arrangements that shape and constrain individual choice—cultivate and embody ecological and egalitarian values. Instead of simply proselytizing to the consumer masses, they will need to reconnect the struggle for sustainability to practical strategies for institutional change that involve a direct challenge to the amoral priorities of capital. Work time reduction is one strategy for ensuring that future increases in productivity do not simply result in greater output and profit-yielding consumption, but generate the free time needed to cultivate richer sources of identity, deepen social solidarity, and engender more active and participatory forms of democratic life. Reinvigorating the public sphere, by vastly increasing the number and quality of collective goods and services available to citizens, is another means of giving people the practical ability to opt out of wasteful patterns of private consumption. Placing a much greater degree of emphasis upon *producer* as opposed to *consumer* responsibility—by restricting advertising, improving labelling and non-commercial information sources, enforcing sustainable production methods, and extending producer responsibility over the final disposal and recycling of goods—is also a crucial way of ensuring that "consumers" can meet their needs in ecologically responsible ways. Ultimately, as I've suggested above, it is only by achieving a greater degree of popular-democratic control over political and economic life as a whole that we can transform ourselves from ambivalent consumers of the world that exists into active creators of better worlds that might be.

Notes

1. This interview, along with the original "burping pig" ad, can be seen online: <http://www.adbusters.org/metas/eco/bnd/wrapup/kalle.html>.
2. <www.adbusters.com>.
3. That is, goods (such as machinery, tools, buildings, and so on) used in the production of other goods and services.

REFERENCES

A way-cool profit center for your business—The 'Oxy' Bar concept: Making 500% profits is easy! Retrieved April 13, 2005, from <http://www.oxygenstore.net/BottomsUp.htm>.

Acker, J. (1999, June). Old and new boundaries in gender relations. *Mittagvorlesungen, 16*, 33–52.

Adams, M. (2003). *Fire and ice: The United States, Canada and the myth of converging values.* Toronto: Penguin.

Adlung, R. (2000). Services trade liberalization from developed and developing country perspectives. In P. Sauve & R.M. Stern (Eds.), *GATS 2000: New directions in services trade liberalization* (pp. 112–35). Washington: Brookings Institution.

Aglietta, M. (1987). *A theory of capitalist regulation: The US experience.* London: Verso.

Agreement on Trade-Related Aspects of Intellectual Property Rights. (1994). *Annex1C of the Marrakesh Agreement Establishing the World Trade Organization*, signed in Marrakesh, Morocco on 15 April 1994. Retrieved May 25, 2005, from <http://www.wto.org/english/tratop_e/trips_e/t_agm0_e.htm>.

Ahmad, A. (1998, March 13). *Nationalism: Between history and ideology.* Lecture presented at the University of Alberta, Edmonton, Alberta, Canada.

Alexandra, A. (1999, July 14–16). *The commodification of academic knowledge and the Internet.* Paper presented at the first annual Australian Institute of Computer Ethics Conference, Swinburne University of Technology, Lilydale Campus, Melbourne, Australia. Retrieved March 15, 2004, from <http://www.aice.swin.edu.au/events/AICEC99/webabstracts.html>.

Amin, S. (1974). *Accumulation on a world scale: A critique of the theory of underdevelopment.* New York: Monthly Review Press.

An abominable trade. (1995, February 20). *Time Magazine*, p. 49.

Anderson, E.S. (1990). Is women's labour a commodity? *Philosophy and Public Affairs, 19*(1), 71–92.

Andolina, R. (1998, September 24–26). *CONAIE (and others) in the ambiguous spaces of democracy: Positioning for the 1997–8 Asamblea Nacional Constituyente in Ecuador.* Paper prepared for delivery at the 1998 meeting of the Latin American Studies Association, The Palmer House Hilton, Chicago, Illinois.

Andrews, L. & Nelkin, D. (2001). *Body bazaar: The market for human tissue in the biotechnology age.* New York: Crown.

Angell, N. (1913). *The great illusion: A study of the relation of military power to national advantage.* London: G.P. Putnam's Sons.

Argyle, M. (1987). *The psychology of happiness.* New York: Methuen.

Aristotle. (1908). *Aristotle's politics.* (B. Jowett, Trans.) Oxford: Clarendon (Original work dated 330 BC).

Asamblea Nacional Constituyente. (1998). *Constitución Política de la República del Ecuador.* Quito: Pudeleco S.A.

Audley, J. (1997). *Green politics and global trade: NAFTA and the future of environmental politics.* Washington, DC: Georgetown University Press.

Australian Bureau of Statistics. (1975–2005). *Labour force Australia* (Catalogue No. 6202.0). Canberra, Australia: Author.

Australian Bureau of Statistics. (1986). *Labour force Australia: Historical summary 1966 to 1984* (Catalogue No. 6204.0). Canberra, Australia: Author.

Australian Bureau of Statistics. (2000). *Unpaid work and the Australian economy* (Catalogue No. 5240.0). Canberra, Australia: Author.

Australian Bureau of Statistics. (2002). *Time series profiles 2001* (Catalogue No. 2003.0). Canberra, Australia: Author.

Australian Bureau of Statistics. (2003). *Australian social trends 2000* (Catalogue No. 4102.0). Canberra, Australia: Author.

Australian Bureau of Statistics. (2003–2005a). *Australian social trends* (Catalogue No. 4102.0). Canberra, Australia: Author.

Australian Bureau of Statistics. (2003–2005b). *Labour force Australia: Detailed—electronic delivery* [Quarterly] (Catalogue No. 6291.0.55.001). Canberra, Australia: Author.

Ayres, J. (1998). *Defying conventional wisdom: Political movements and popular contention against North American Free Trade.* Toronto: University of Toronto Press.

Bachand, R. (2001). *Les poursuites intentées en vertu du chapitre 11 de l'ALÉNA* (Cahiers de Recherche, Vol. 1, No. 11). Montreal: UQUAM.

Baglole, J. (2002, December 6). Canadian court forbids patents of Harvard's mice. *Wall Street Journal,* p. B6.

Bahro, R. (1984). *From red to green.* London: Verso.

Bakker, K. (2003). From archipelago to network: Urbanization and water privatization in the South. *The Geographical Journal 169*(4), 328–41.

Bakker, K. (2004). *An uncooperative commodity: Privatizing water in England and Wales.* Oxford: Oxford University Press.

Bakker, K., & Cameron, D. (2004). *Good governance in municipal restructuring of water supply: A handbook.* Federation of Canadian Municipalities and Program on Water Issues, Munk Centre for International Studies. Retrieved April 16, 2005, from <http://www.powi.ca/goodgovernance.pdf>.

Bakshi, P., Goodwin, M., Painter, J., & Southern, A. (1995). Gender, race and class in the local welfare state: Moving beyond regulation theory in analyzing the transition from Fordism. *Environment & Planning A, 27*(10), 1539–54.

Barber, B. (1995). *Jihad vs. McWorld.* New York: Times Books.

Barlow, M. (1999, November 26). *The global water crisis and the commodification of world's water supply.* Speech at the Seattle IFG Teach-In. International Forum on Globalization. Retrieved April 16, 2005, from <http://www.ratical.org/co-globalize/ifg112699MB.html>.

Barlow, M., & Clarke, T. (2001). *Global showdown: How the new activists are fighting global corporate rule.* Toronto: Stoddart.

Barlow, M., & Clarke, T. (2002). *Blue gold: The fight to stop the corporate theft of the world's water.* New York: The New Press.

Barnes, T. (2000). Local knowledge. In R.J. Johnston, D. Gregory, G. Pratt, & M. Watts (Eds.), *The dictionary of human geography* (4th ed., pp. 452–453). Malden, MA: Blackwell.

Bartra, A., & Otero, G. (2005). Indian-peasant movements in Mexico: The struggle for land, autonomy and democracy. In S. Moyo & P. Yeros (Eds.), *Reclaiming the land: The resurgence of rural movements in Africa, Asia and Latin America* (pp. 383–410). London: Zed Books.

Batley, R. (1996). Public-private relationships and performance in service provision. *Urban Studies, 33*(4–5), 723–51.

Baxter, J. (1998). Moving towards equality? Questions of change and equality in household work patterns. In M. Gatens & A. Mackinnon (Eds.), *Gender and institutions: Welfare, work and citizenship* (pp. 55–74). Cambridge: Cambridge University Press.

Baxter, J. (2002). Patterns of change and stability in the gender division of labour in Australia, 1986–1997. *Journal of Sociology, 38*(4), 399–424.

Beck, U. (2000). The cosmopolitan perspective: Sociology of the second age of modernity. *British Journal of Sociology, 51*(1), 79–105.

Beer, M. (1929). *A history of British socialism.* London: G. Bell & Sons.

Bellinghausen, H. (2002, December). Guerre sournoise dans la forêt lacandonne. *Le monde diplomatique, 585,* 14.

Bellinghausen, H. (2003, January 2). Más de 20 mil indígenas preguntan al presidente Vicente Fox dónde está la paz. *La Jornada.* Retrieved 2 January 2003, from: <http://www.jornada.unam.mx/003n1pol.php?origen=index.html>.

Bello, W. (2002). *Deglobalization: Ideas for a new world economy.* London: Zed Books.

Bello, W. (2003, Fall). The economics of Empire. *New Labor Forum* [Online version]. Retrieved June 13, 2005, from <http://qcpages.qc.edu/newlaborforum/html/12_3article9.html>.

Bello, W. (2004). The re-emergence of balance of power politics. *YONIP! Yes, Observe National Independence & Peace.* Retrieved January 18, 2005, from <http://www.yonip.com/main/articles/reemergence_of_balance.html>.

Bentley, M. (2003). *Sustainable consumption: Ethics, national indices and international relations.* Doctoral dissertation, American Graduate School of International Relations, Paris.

Berman, E.H. (1998). The entrepreneurial university: Macro and micro perspectives from the United States. In J. Currie & J. Newson (Eds.), *Universities and globalization: Critical perspectives* (pp. 225–249). Thousand Oaks: Sage.

Berman, M. (1981). *The reenchantment of the world.* Ithaca: Cornell University Press.

Berry, W. (1986). *The unsettling of America.* San Francisco: Sierra Club Books.

Berry, W. (1989). *What are people for?* San Francisco: North Point Press.

Berton, P. (1990). *The Great Depression, 1929–1939.* Toronto: McClelland & Stewart.

Betz, H.G., & Johnson, C. (2004). Against the current—stemming the tide: the nostalgic ideology of the contemporary radical populist right. *Journal of Political Ideologies, 9*(3), 311–27.

Birchfield, V., & Freybert-Inan, A. (2004). Constructing opposition in the age of globalization: The potential of ATTAC. *Globalizations, 1*(2), 278–304.

Bittman, M., & Jocelyn, P. (1997). *The double life of the family: Myth, hope and experience.* Sydney: Allen and Unwin.

Blockade creates black-market boom for kidneys. (1996, September 1). *Edmonton Journal,* p. F4.

Blumstein, J.F. (1992). The case for commerce in organ transplantation. *Transplantation Proceedings, 24*(5), 2190–97.

Blunden, A. (1999). Knowledge for sale. *Andy Blunden's Homepage.* Retrieved April 14, 2004, from <http://home.mira.net/~andy/works/knowage.htm>.

NOT FOR SALE

Body parts pedlar. (2002, October 18). *Toronto Sun*, p. 1.

Boli-Bennet, J. (1980). Global integration and the universal increase of state dominance 1910–1970. In A. Bergesen (Ed.), *Studies of the Modern World System* (pp. 77–108). New York: Academic Press.

Bond, M. (2003, October 4). The pursuit of happiness. *New Scientist*, pp. 40–47.

Bond, P. (2000). Defunding the fund, running on the bank. *Monthly Review*. Retrieved April 13, 2005, from <http://www.findarticles.com/p/articles/mi_m1132/is_3_52/ai_63858959>.

Bond, P. (2002a, September-December). Principles, strategies and tactics of decommodification in South Africa. *Links, 22.* Retrieved May 25, 2005, from <http://www.dsp.org.au/links/back/issue22/Bond.htm>.

Bond, P. (2002b). *Unsustainable South Africa: Environment, development and social protest.* London: Merlin Press.

Bond, P. (2005). Strategies for social justice movements from Southern Africa to the United States. *Foreign Policy in Focus.* Retrieved January 20, 2005, from <www.fpif.org>.

Borland, J., Gregory, B., & Sheehan, P. (2001). Inequality and economic change. In J. Borland, B. Gregory, & P. Sheehan (Eds.), *Work rich, work poor: Inequality and economic change in Australia* (pp. 1–20). Melbourne: Centre for Strategic Studies, Victoria University.

Boswell, T., & Chase-Dunn, C. (2000). *The spiral of capitalism and socialism: Toward global democracy.* Boulder, CO: Lynne Rienner.

Bothwell, R., & Kilbourn, W. (1979). *C.D. Howe: A biography.* Toronto: McClelland and Stewart.

Bowles, S. (1982). The post-Keynesian capital-labor stalemate. *Socialist Review, 12*(5), 45–71.

Bowles, S., & Gintis, H. (1986). *Democracy and capitalism: Property, community and the contradictions of modern social thought.* New York: Basic Books.

Boyer, R., & Drache, D. (Eds.). (1996). *States against markets.* London: Routledge.

Bratt, C. (1993, June; 1994, November). *Interviews by Gordon Laxer.* Bratt was the Director of European Affairs at the Swedish Employers' Federation (SAF) in Stockholm.

Brecher, J., Costello, T., & Smith, B. (2000). *Globalization from below: The power of solidarity.* Cambridge, MA: South End Press.

Broad, R. (2004). The Washington consensus meets the global backlash: Shifting debates and policies. *Globalizations, 1,* 129–54.

Broomhill, R., & Sharp, R. (1999). Restructuring our lives: Engendering debates about social and economic policies in South Australia. In J. Spoehr (Ed.), *Beyond the contract state: Policies for social and economic renewal in South Australia* (pp. 132–155). Adelaide: Wakefield Press.

Broomhill, R. (2001). Neoliberal globalism and the local state: a regulation approach. *Journal of Australian Political Economy, 48,* 115–40.

Broomhill, R., & Sharp, R. (2004). The changing male breadwinner model in Australia: A new gender order? *Labour & Industry, 15*(2), 1–24.

Brower, M., & Leon, W. (1999). *The consumer's guide to effective environmental choices: Practical advice from the Union of Concerned Scientists.* New York: Three Rivers Press.

Brown, J.R. (2000, December 1). Privatizing the university—the new tragedy of the commons. *Science, 290,* pp. 1701–02.

Bruntland, G. (Ed.). (1987). *Our common future: The World Commission on environment and development.* Oxford: Oxford University Press.

Brunvald, J. H. (1993). *The baby train and other lusty urban legends.* New York: W.W. Norton.

Brysk, A. (2000). *From tribal village to global village: Indian rights and international relations in Latin America.* Stanford: Stanford University Press.

Bryson, L. (2001, December). Motherhood and gender relations: Where to in the twenty-first century? *Just Policy, 24,* 12–23.

Buchbinder, H., & Newson, J. (1991, Spring-Summer). Social knowledge and market knowledge: Universities in the information age. *The Gannet Centre Journal,* pp. 17–30.

Budds, J., & McGranahan, G. (2003). Are the debates on water privatization missing the point? Experiences from Africa, Asia, and Latin America. *Environment and Urbanization, 15*(2), 87–113.

Burguete, C., & Mayor, A. (Eds.). (2000). *Indigenous autonomy in Mexico* (pp. 24–52). Copenhagen: International Work Group for Indigenous Affairs.

Business Communications Company. (2003). *The market for tissue and organ transplantation.* Retrieved December 6, 2004, from <http://www.ecnexxt.com>.

Canada. Royal Commission on Reproductive Technologies (1993). *Proceed with care: Final report of the Royal Commission on New Reproductive Technologies.* Ottawa: Government of Canada.

Canadian Dimension. (1995). Think nationally act locally. *Canadian Dimension, 29*(3), 4.

Canadian Gallup Polls. (1980). *Canadians speak out.* Toronto: McNamara Press.

Canadian Organ Replacement Register. (1996). *1994 Annual report.* Ottawa: Canadian Institute for Health Information.

Canadian Organ Replacement Register. (2003). *Preliminary report 2002.* Ottawa: Canadian Institute for Health Information.

Cano, A. (2005, April 23). Ecuador: la rebelión de los forajidos. *La Jornada* (Mexico City). Retrieved April 25, 2005, from <http://www.jornada.unam.mx/2005/abr05/050423/044n1mun.php>.

Carlsen, L. (2004). Conservation or privatization? Biodiversity, the global market and the Mesoamerican Biological Corridor. In G. Otero (Ed.), *Mexico in transition: Neoliberal globalism, civil society and the state* (pp. 52–71). London: Zed Books.

Cass, B. (1998). The social policy context. In P. Smyth & B. Cass (Eds.), *Contesting the Australian way: States, markets and civil society* (pp. 38–54). Cambridge: Cambridge University Press.

Castañeda, J. (1993). *Utopia unarmed: The Latin American left after the Cold War.* New York: Knopf.

Castañeda, J. (2004, June 19). George W. Bush and America's neglected hemisphere. *Daily Times.* Retrieved May 26, 2005, from <www.dailytimes.com.pk/default.asp?page=story_19-6-2004_pg3_7>.

Castells, M. (1997). *The power of identity.* Oxford: Blackwell.

Castles, F. (1985). *The working class and welfare: Reflections on the political development of the welfare state in Australia and New Zealand, 1890–1980.* Wellington: Allen & Unwin.

Castles, F.G. (1989). *Australian public policy and economic vulnerability.* Sydney: Allen & Unwin.

Celis Callejas, F. (2005, April 3). El movimiento que no aguantó más. *Masiosare* [Political Supplement of *La Jornada*]. Retrieved April 10, 2005, from <http//www//jornada.unam.mx/2005/abr05/050403/mas-celis.html>.

Centro de Derechos Humanos Fray Bartolomé de Las Casas. (1998). *Acteal: Entre el Duelo y la Lucha.* San Cristóbal, Chiapas: Author.

Chand, V.K. (2001). *Mexico's political awakening.* Notre Dame: University of Notre Dame Press.

Chase-Dunn, C. (1989). *Global formation: Structures of the world-economy.* Oxford: Basil Blackwell.

Chase-Dunn, C. (1990). Resistance to imperialism: Semiperipheral actors. *Review, 13*(1), 1–31.

Chase-Dunn, C. (2004, June 23). *Social evolution and the future of world society*. Paper presented to the Future of World Society Symposium, University of Zurich, Switzerland.

Chase-Dunn, C., & Hall, T.D. (1997). *Rise and demise: Comparing world-systems*. Boulder, CO: Westview Press.

Childress, J.F. (1992). The body as property: Some philosophical reflections. *Transplantation Proceedings, 24*(5), 2143–48.

Church, E. (1998, July 21). Authors "blur" old rules of business. *Globe and Mail*, p. B13.

Clark, E.A. (2000). Academia in the service of industry: The Ag Biotech Model. In J.L. Turk (Ed.), *The corporate campus: Commercialization and the dangers to Canada's colleges and universities* (pp. 69–86). Toronto: James Lorimer and Company.

Clough, S.B. (1952). *Economic history of Europe*. Boston: D.C. Heath.

Cobb, C., Halstead, T., & Rowe, J. (1995, October). If the GDP is up, why is America down? *The Atlantic Monthly*, pp. 59–78.

Collins, G.M. (1991). History of organ preservation. In M.G. Phillips (Ed.), *UNOS: organ procurement, preservation and distribution in transplantation* (pp. 101–03). Richmond, VA: UNOS.

Comaroff, J., & Comaroff, J.L. (1999). Occult economies and the violence of abstraction: Notes from the South African postcolony. *American Ethnologist, 26*(2), 147–79.

Comité Clandestino Revolucionario Indigena del Ejercito Zapatista de Liberación Naciona. (CCRI-EZLN). (2005, June 29, 30, July 1). Sexta Declaración de la Selva Lacandona. *La Jornada*. Retrieved September 26, 2005, from <http://www.jornada.unam.mx/>.

Committee on Economic, Social and Cultural Rights (CESCR). (2002, November 26). CESCR adopts general comment on right to water [Press release]. Geneva: Author.

Conca, K. (2000). The WTO and the undermining of global environmental governance. *Review of International Political Economy, 3*(2), 484–94.

Confederación de Nacionalidades Indígenas del Ecuador (CONAIE). (2004a). El movimiento indígena no se ha dejado liquidar. *Press Bulletin*. Retrieved January 26, 2005, from <http://conaie.org/?q=node/28&PHPSESSID=61c22aadb3ac57c3542e5811b163e904>.

Confederación de Nacionalidades Indígenas del Ecuador (CONAIE). (2004b). *Manifiesto de la Conaie al país*. II Congreso de las Nacionalidades y Pueblos Indígenas del Ecuador. Retrieved January 27, 2005, from <http://conaie.org/?q=node/29&PHPSESSID=621b1875 cab986ce58387ebb5e8bc3e1>.

Connell, B.(1987). *Gender and power*. Cambridge: Polity Press.

Conway, Janet. (2004). Citizenship in a time of Empire: The World Social Forum as a new public space. *Citizenship Studies, 8*(4), 367–81.

Conway, John. (1994). *The West: The history of a region in confederation* (2nd ed.). Toronto: Lorimer.

Cooke, B., & Kothari, U. (2002). *Participation: the new tyranny*. London: Zed Books.

Correa, G. (2001, February 25). El objetivo de Fox, una paz sin cambios. *Proceso, 1269*, 20–22.

Corrigan, P., & Sayer, D. (1985). *The great arch: English state formation as cultural revolution*. Oxford: Basil Blackwell.

Counce, W.M., Patrick, C.H., & Phillips, M.G. (1991). Embalming the organ and tissue donor. In M.G. Phillips (Ed.), *UNOS: organ procurement, preservation and distribution in transplantation* (pp. 209–12). Richmond, VA: UNOS.

Cox, R.W. (1987). *Production, power, and world order: Social forces in the making of history*. New York: Columbia University Press.

Creger, J.H., Guindon, V.G., & Ferree, D.M. (1991). Transportation of organs. In M.G. Phillips (Ed.), *UNOS: organ procurement, preservation and distribution in transplantation* (pp. 145–49). Richmond, VA: UNOS.

Crompton, R. (1999). The decline of the male breadwinner: Explanations and interpretations. In R. Crompton (Ed.), *Restructuring gender relations and employment: The decline of the male breadwinner* (pp. 1–25). Oxford: Oxford University Press.

Cross, G. (2000). *An all-consuming century: Why commercialism won in modern America.* New York: Columbia University Press.

Crozier, M., Huntington, S.P., & Watanuki, J. (1975). *The crisis of democracy.* New York: New York University Press.

Cunningham, P.M. (1988). The adult educator and social responsibility. In R.G. Brockett (Ed.), *Ethical issues in adult education* (pp. 133–45). New York: Teachers College Press.

Cunningham, P.M. (1993). *Let's get real: A critical look at the practice of adult education.* Keynote address presented at the fifty-first annual meeting of the Mountain Plains Adult Education Association, Albuquerque, New Mexico. Retrieved April 14, 2005, from <http://www.nl.edu/academics/cas/ace/resources/PhyllisCunningham_insight.cfm>.

Daar, A.S. (1992). Rewarded gifting. *Transplantation Proceedings, 24*(5), 2207–11.

Daly, H. (1994). *Farewell speech upon his resignation as Senior Economist in the Environment Department of the World Bank.* Retrieved June 13, 2005, from <http://www.whirled-bank.org/ourwords/daly.html>.

Dávalos, P. (2000, February). *Publicación Mensual del Instituto Científico de Culturas Indígenas, 2*(11). Retrieved April 2, 2002, from <http://icci.nativeweb.org/boletin/feb2000/davalos.html>.

Dawson, M. (2003). *The consumer trap: Big business marketing in American life.* Chicago: University of Illinois Press.

De Cecco, M. (1974). *Money and empire: The international gold standard, 1890–1914.* London: Basil Blackwell.

De Geus, M. (2003). *The end of over-consumption: Towards a lifestyle of moderation and self-restraint.* Utrecht: International Books.

De Graaf, J., Wann, D., & Naylor, T.H. (2002). *Affluenza: The all-consuming epidemic.* San Francisco: Berrett-Koehler.

DePalma, A. (2002, March 1). WTO pact would set accounting rules. *New York Times* [Late edition-final], p. W1.

Desai, L.M. (2000, September 21). *The WTO: The test case for globalisation.* Presentation to the ninth Comparative Politics Conference, Politics in a Global Economy, University of Bergen, Norway.

Desperate Iraqis sell their kidneys. (1993, November 27). *Edmonton Journal,* p. A10.

Desperate man buys kidney in India. (1995, January 7). *Edmonton Journal,* p. A8.

Destituye el Congreso de Ecuador a Lucio Gutiérrez tras revuelta social. (2005, April 21). *La Jornada.* Retrieved April 25, 2005, from <http://www.jornada.unam.mx/imprimir.php?fecha=20050421&nota=029n1mun.php>.

Díaz Polanco, H. (1997). *Indigenous peoples in Latin America: The quest for self-determination.* Boulder, CO: Westview Press.

Dixon, K. (1998). *Les Evangélistes du Marché.* Paris: Raisons d'Agir Éditions.

Doherty-Delorme, D. (1999). The corporate takeover of our universities and colleges. *Education, Limited, 1*(4), 11–19. Ottawa: The Canadian Centre for Policy Alternatives.

Draft Treaty to Share the Genetic Commons. (2002). *World Social Forum, Porto Alegre.* Retrieved May 25, 2005, from <http://www.ukabc.org/genetic_commons_treaty.htm#c>.

NOT FOR SALE

Drohan, M. (2000, September 25). Gruesome tales show Nigeria's desperate state. *Globe and Mail*, p. A1.

Dumoulin, D. (2002, June). *Les collines bleues du Chiapas: La conservation de la nature entre autoritarisme, autonomies et chantage écologique*. Contribution to the Conférence Démocratisation et Conflits Écologiques, IHEAL, Paris.

Durning, A. (1992). *How much is enough? The consumer society and the future of the earth*. New York: W.W. Norton.

Earthworks Group. (1989). *50 simple things you can do to save the Earth*. Berkeley, CA: Earthworks Press.

Egan, K. (1996). Forging new alliances in Ecuador's Amazon. *SAIS Review, 16*(2), 123–42.

Egypt holds inquiry on sale of body parts. (1999, March 28). *Guardian Weekly*, p. 5.

Eisendrath, C.R. (1992). Used body parts: buy, sell or swap?. *Transplantation Proceedings, 24*(5), 2212–14.

Eisenstein, Z. (1996, Fall). Stop stomping on the rest of us: Retrieving publicness from the privatization of the globe. *Indiana Journal of Global Legal Studies, 4*(1), 59–96.

Ejército Zapatista de Liberación Nacional (EZLN). (1994). Today we say: Enough is enough. *First declaration of the Lacandon Jungle*. Retrieved May 28, 2003, from <http://www.ezln.org/documentos/1994/199312xx.en.htm>.

Ekpere, J.A. (2000). The OAU model law and Africa's common position on the TRIPs review process. *Draft Paper*. Retrieved June 10, 2005, from <http://www.ictsd.org/dlogue/2001-07-30/Ekpere.pdf>.

Esping-Andersen, G. (1985). *Politics against markets: The social democratic road to power*. Princeton: Princeton University Press.

Esping-Andersen, G. (1990). *The three worlds of welfare capitalism*. Cambridge: Polity Press.

Esping-Andersen, G. (1999). *Social foundations of post industrial economies*. New York: Oxford University Press.

Esping-Andersen, G., Gallie, D., Hemerijck, A., & Myles, J. (Eds.). (2002). *Why we need a new welfare state*. New York: Oxford University Press.

Estache, A., & Rossi, C. (2002). How different is the efficiency of public and private water companies in Asia? *World Bank Economic Review, 16*(1), 139–48.

Esteva, G. (2000). Comer o comernos: el drama en el campo. *Agravios a la Nación México*. Fundación Rosenbluth: Galileo Ediciones.

European Renal Association-European Dialysis and Transplant Association. (1996). *Annual reports, 1975–94*. London: ERA-EDTA Registry.

European Transplant Coordinators Organization. (2004, March). Definitive data of international transplant activity, IRODAT 2003. *Organs and Tissues, 2*, 79–82.

Eurotransplant Statistics. (2003). *Transplantation Statistics by Country*. Retrieved December 6, 2004, from <http://www.eurotransplant.nl/statistics/netherlands99.htm>.

Evans, R.W. (1992). Need, demand, and supply in organ transplantation. *Transplantation Proceedings, 24*(5), 2152–54.

Evernden, N. (1991). *The natural alien: Humankind and the environment*. Toronto: University of Toronto Press.

Falconer, T. (2001). *Watchdogs and gadflies: Activism from marginal to mainstream*. Toronto: Penguin.

Falk, R. (2001). Humane governance and the environment: Overcoming neoliberalism. In B. Gleeson & N. Low (Eds.), *Governing for the environment: Global problems, ethics and democracy* (pp. 221–36). New York: Palgrave.

Fine, S. (2001, April 5). The tuition's okay, but don't expect a prof. *Globe and Mail*, pp. A1, A12.

Finkel, M. (2001a, May 27). Complications. *New York Times Magazine*, pp. 26–33, 40, 52, 59.

Finkel, M. (2001b, June 3). This little kidney went to market. *Edmonton Journal*, p. E3.

Flavin, C. (2004). Preface. *State of the World 2004* (pp. xvii–xix). New York: W.W. Norton.

Foster, J.B. (2002). *Ecology against capitalism*. New York: Monthly Review Press.

Fox, J. (1996). How does Civil Society thicken? The political construction of social capital in rural Mexico. *World Development 24*(6), 1089–1103.

Fox, R.C., & Swazey, J.P. (1992). *Spare parts: Organ replacement in American society*. Oxford: Oxford University Press.

Frank, A.G. (1967). *Capitalism and underdevelopment in Latin America*. New York: Monthly Review Press.

Fraser, D. (1973). *The evolution of the British Welfare State: A history of social policy since the Industrial Revolution*. London: Macmillan.

Freire, P. (1996). *Pedagogy of the oppressed*. New York: Continuum.

Friedman, M., & Friedman, R. (1990). *Free to choose*. London: Secker & Warburg.

Friedman, T.L. (1999). *The Lexus and the olive tree*. New York: Farrar, Strauss and Giroux.

FWJ Advertizing. (2001, March 13). Correspondence with informed business leaders.

Gamble, A. (1988). *The free economy and the strong state: The politics of Thatcherism*. Durham: Duke University Press.

Gardner, G., Assadourian, E., & Sarin, R. (2004). The state of consumption today. *State of the World 2004* (pp. 3–21). New York: W.W. Norton.

Geisinger, A. (1999). Sustainable development and the domination of nature: Spreading the seed of the western ideology of nature. *Boston College Environmental Affairs Law Review*, *27*(1), 43–74.

George, S. (1988). *A fate worse than debt*. London: Penguin Books.

Germany. Bundestag Study Commission. (2002). *Globalization of the world economy— Challenges and answers* [Short version of the final report]. Berlin: 14th Legislative Session of the German Bundestag.

Getis, J. (1999). *You can make a difference* (2nd ed.). Boston: WCB McGraw-Hill.

Gil, G. (2005, January 28). Gordon Laxer's notes on speech presented at the 'América do Sul: Integração, soberania e desenvolvimento' session, World Social Forum, Porto Alegre, Brasil.

Gilbreth, C. & Otero, G. (2001, July). Democratization in Mexico: The Zapatista uprising and civil society. *Latin American Perspectives, 28*(4), 7–29.

Gleick, P. (2000). Is there a human right to water? *The world's water 2000–2001* (pp. 1–17). Washington: Island Press.

Glick, R. & Rose, K. (1999). Contagion and trade: Why are currency crises regional? *Journal of International Money and Finance, 18* (4), 603–17.

GlobeScan. (2004). *Poll of 35 countries finds 30 prefer Kerry, 3 Bush*. Retrieved September 8, 2004, from www.GlobeScan.com.

Goldberg, K. (2001). Corporate elite rules BC. *Canadian Dimension, 35*(4), 3.

Goodman, J. (2003, October 5). *Nationalism, globalism and neoliberalism in Australia*. Draft paper presented at the Globalism and its Challengers conference, Bergen, Norway.

Gorz, A. (1967). *Strategy for labour: A radical proposal*. Boston: Beacon Press.

Gorz, A. (1999). *Reclaiming work: Beyond the wage-based society*. Cambridge: Polity Press.

248

Goubert, J.P. (1986). *The conquest of water*. London: Polity Press.

Grant, G. (1965). *Lament for a nation*. Toronto: McClelland & Stewart.

Gregg, P. (1950). *A social and economic history of Britain: 1760–1972*. London: Harrap.

Gregory, R.G., & Hunter, B. (1995). *The macro economy and the growth of ghettos and urban poverty in Australia* (Discussion Papers, No. 325). Canberra: ANU Centre for Economic Policy Research.

Gret, M., & Sintomer, Y. (2005). *The Porto Alegre experiment—learning lessons for better democracy*. London: Zed Books.

Grusky, S. (2001). Privatization tidal wave: IMF/World Bank water policies and the price paid by the poor. *Multinational Monitor, 22*(9), 14–23.

Guthman, J. (2004). *Agrarian dreams: The paradox of organic farming in California*. Berkeley: University of California Press.

Gutiérrez-Haces, T. (2002). Territoires en Mondialisation: le chapitre 11 de l'ALENA et l'espace local au Mexique. In M. Azuelos, M.E. Cosío-Zavala, & J.M. Lacroix (Eds.), *Intégration dans les Amériques dix ans d'ALENA*. Paris: Presses Sorbonne Nouvelle.

Gutiérrez-Haces, T. (2004, December). La inversión extranjera directa en el TLCAN. *Economia Unam, 3*, 30–53.

Haass, R. (2000, November 11). *Imperial America*. Paper presented at the Atlanta conference, Puerto Rico. Retrieved May 26, 2005, from <www.brook.edu/dybdocroot/views/articles/haass/2000imperial.htm>.

Half-dead convict in China stripped of skin, organs. (2001, June 28). *Edmonton Journal*, p. A3.

Hamilton, C. (2004). *Growth fetish*. London: Pluto Press.

Hannah, L. (1992). The economic consequences of the state ownership of industry. In R. Floud & D. McCloskey (Eds.), *The economic history of Britain since 1700* (pp. 168–194). Cambridge: Cambridge University Press.

Hardin, G. (1968, December 13). The tragedy of the commons. *Science, 162*(3859), 1243–1248.

Harding, A. (1997). The suffering middle: Trends in income inequality in Australia 1982 to 1993–94. *Australian Economic Review, 30*(4), 341–58.

Hardt, M., & Negri, A. (2000). *Empire*. Cambridge, MA: Harvard University Press.

Harrison, K. (1996). *Passing the buck: Federalism and Canadian environmental policy*. Vancouver: UBC Press.

Hartridge, D. (1997, January). What the general agreement on trade in services can do. *Opening markets for banking worldwide: The WTO general agreement on trade in services*. London: British Invisibles Conference.

Harvey, N. (2002, December 28). PPP y derechos indígenas. *La Jornada*. Retrieved December 28, 2002, from <http://www.jornada.unam.mx/2002/dic02/021228/013a1pol.php?origen=opinion.html>.

Harwood Group. (1995). *Yearning for balance: Views of Americans on consumption, materialism, and the environment*. Takoma Park, MD: Merck Family Fund.

Hassan, J. (1998). *A history of water in modern England and Wales*. Manchester: Manchester University Press.

Hayden, A. (1999). *Sharing the work, sparing the planet: Work time, consumption, & ecology*. Toronto: Between the Lines.

Heap, B., & Kent, J. (2000). *Toward sustainable consumption—a European perspective*. London: The Royal Society.

Heeter, C.P. (1998). *Written testimony of Charles P. Heeter Jr. [partner, Office of Government Affairs] before the United States International Trade Commission, General Agreement on*

Trade in Services (Investigation No. 332–385). Washington: International Trade Commission.

Hegel. G.F.W. (1952). *Philosophy of right.* (T.M. Knox, Trans.). Oxford: Clarendon Press. (Original work published in 1821.)

Hennessy, R. (2001). *Profit and pleasure: Sexual identities in late capitalism.* New York: Routledge.

Henríquez, E., & Aponte, D. (2000, December 2). Ordena Fox el retiro de 53 retenes en tres zonas de Chiapas. *La Jornada.* Retrieved December 3, 2000, from <http://www.jornada. unam.mx/2000/dic00/001202/026n1pol.html>.

Hernández Navarro, L., & Herrera, R.V. (Eds.). (1998). *Acuerdos de San Andrés.* Mexico City: Ediciones Era.

Hill, L.H. (1998). From global consciousness to social action: An examination of adult education theory. *Proceedings from the annual meeting of the Adult Education Resource Council.* Retrieved April 15, 2004, from <http://www.edst.educ.ubc.ca/aerc/1998/hill.htm>.

Hobsbawm, E. (1991). *Nations and nationalisms since 1780.* Cambridge: Cambridge University Press.

Hobsbawm, E. (1994). *Age of extremes: The short twentieth century, 1914–1991.* London: Abacus.

Hoffmann, R.M., & Belzer, F.O. (1991). Organ preservation: Kidney, liver, pancreas. In M.G. Phillips (Ed.), *UNOS: organ procurement, preservation and distribution in transplantation* (pp. 105–09). Richmond, VA: UNOS.

Hopkins, T.K., & Wallerstein. I. (1977). Patterns of development in the modern world system. *Review, 1*(2), 111–46.

Hornborg, A. (2001). *The Power of the machine.* Walnut Creek: Altamira Press.

Human Rights Watch. (1997). *Implausible deniability: State responsibility for rural violence in Mexico.* New York: Human Rights Watch.

Humphries, J. (1998). Towards a family-friendly economics. *New Political Economy, 3*(2), 223–40.

Huntington, S. (2004, Spring). Dead souls, the denationalization of the American elite. *National Interest, 75,* 5–18.

Hurtig, M. (2002). *The vanishing country.* Toronto: M&S.

Ingold, T. (2000). *The perception of the environment.* London: Routledge.

International Forum on Globalization. (2002). *Alternatives to economic globalization.* Vermont: Berrett-Koehler.

Ironmonger, D. (1996). Counting outputs, inputs and caring labour: estimating gross household product. *Feminist Economics, 2*(3), 37–64.

Jeffrey, B. (1999). *Hard right turn: The new face of neo-conservatism in Canada.* Toronto: Harper Collins.

Jessop, B. (1994). Post-Fordism and the state. In A. Amin (Ed.), *Post-Fordism: A reader* (pp. 251–79). Oxford: Blackwell.

Jhally, S. (Director). (1998). *Advertising and the end of the world* [Motion picture]. Northampton, MA: Media Education Foundation.

Jimenez, M. (2002, March 29). Europe's poorest sell their kidneys. *National Post,* pp. A1, A12.

Johnston, J. (2000). Pedagogical guerrillas, armed democrats, and revolutionary counterpublics: Examining paradox in the Zapatista uprising in Chiapas Mexico. *Theory and Society, 29,* 463–505.

Johnston, J., & Laxer, G. (2003, February). Solidarity in the age of globalization: Lessons from the anti-MAI and Zapatista struggles. *Theory and Society, 31*, 1–53.

Johnstone, N., & Wood, L. (Eds.). (2001). *Private firms and public water: Realising social and environmental objectives in developing countries.* London: Edward Elgar.

Kahan, B.D. (Ed.). (1988). *Cyclosporine: applications in autoimmune disease.* London: Grune and Stratton.

Kant, I. (1979). *Lectures on ethics.* (L. Infield, Trans.). London: Methuen. (Original work published in 1780.)

Kasser, T. (2002). *The high price of materialism.* Cambridge, MA: The MIT Press.

Kearney, M., & Varese, S. (1995). Latin America's indigenous peoples: Changing identities and forms of resistance. In R.L. Harris & S. Halebsky (Eds.), *Capital, power, and inequality in Latin America* (pp. 207–31). Boulder: Westview Press.

Keynes, J.M. (1932–33). National self-sufficiency. *Yale Review, 22*, 761–63.

Kimbrell, A. (1993). *The human body shop: The engineering and the marketing of life.* San Francisco: Harper and Row.

Kloppenburg, J. Jr., Lezberg, S., De Master, K., Stevenson, G.W., & Hendrickson, J. (2000, Summer). Tasting food, tasting sustainability: Defining the attributes of an alternative food system with competent, ordinary people. *Human Organization, 59*(2), 177–86.

Knijn, T., & Ostner, I. (2002). Commodification and de-commodification. In B. Hobson, J. Lewis, & B. Siim (Eds.), *Contested concepts in gender and social politics* (pp. 141–69). Cheltenham, UK: Edward Elgar.

Kobrin, S. (1982, Fall). Trends in forced divestment of foreign affiliates, 1960–1979. *Center for Transnational Corporations Reporter, 13.*

Kofman, E., & Youngs, G. (2003). *Globalization: Theory and practice* (2nd ed.). London: Continuum.

Kondratiev, N. (1998). *The works of Nikolai D. Kondratiev* (N. Makasheva, W. Samuels, & V. Barnett, Eds.). London: Pickering and Chatto.

Kozloff, N. (2005). *Evidence suggests Venezuela's Chavez is following through on his rhetoric.* Retrieved March 28, 2005, from <www.VHeadline.com>.

Krajnc, A. (2000). Wither Ontario's environment? Neoconservatism and the decline of the environment ministry. *Canadian Public Policy, 26*(1), 111–27.

Krajnc, A., & Weis, T. (2000). The new politics of bloodsport in Ontario. *Canadian Dimension, 34*(5), 42–45.

Kuyek, D. (2001, March). Intellectual property rights: Ultimate control in R&D in Asia. *GRAIN Briefings.* Retrieved August 22, 2005, from, <http://www.grain.org/briefings/?id=35>.

Kuznets, S. (1967). *Secular movements in Production and Prices: Their nature and their bearing upon cyclical fluctuations.* Boston: Riverside Press. (Original work published in 1930.)

Kymlicka, W., & Norman, W. (2000). Citizenship in culturally diverse societies: Issues, contexts, and concepts. In W. Kymlicka & W. Norman (Eds.), *Citizenship in diverse societies* (pp. 1–41). Oxford: Oxford University Press.

Lachman, R. (1987). *From Manor to market: Structural change in England, 1530–1640.* Madison: University of Wisconsin Press.

Lairson, T.D., & Skidmore, D. (2003). *International political economy: The struggle for power and wealth.* Toronto: Nelson Thomson.

Land, W., & Cohen, B. (1992). Postmortem and living organ donation in Europe: Transplant laws and activities. *Transplantation Proceedings, 24*(5), 2165–67.

Laxer, G. (1995). Opposition to continental integration: Sweden and Canada. *Review of Constitutional Studies, 2*(2), 342–95.

Laxer, G. (2001). The movement that dare not speak its name: The return of left nationalism/internationalism. *Alternatives, 26*, 1–32.

Laxer, G. (2003, January/February). Stop rejecting sovereignty: Confronting the anti-globalization movement. *Canadian Dimension, 37*(1), 29–31.

Le Bot, Y. (1997). *Subcomandante Marcos: El sueño Zapatista*. Barcelona: Plaza & Janes.

Leach, W. (1993). *Land of desire: merchants, power, and the rise of a new American culture*. New York: Pantheon Books.

Leborgne, D., & Lipietz, A. (1988). New technologies, new modes of regulation: some spatial implications. *Environment & Planning D: Society and Space, 6*, 263–80.

Leys, C. (2003). *Market-Driven politics: Neoliberal democracy and the public interest*. London: Verso.

Li, T. (2002) Engaging simplifications: Community based resource management, market processes and state agendas in Upland Southeast Asia. *World Development, 30*(2), 265–83.

Local Futures. (2001). *Local knowledge: Women and the knowledge economy*. Retrieved April 15, 2004, from <http://www.localfutures.com/article.asp?aid=31>.

Lodziak, C. (2002). *The myth of consumerism*. London: Pluto Press.

LOTIS Committee. (2002). *The case for liberalising trade in services*. London: International Financial Services.

Louçã, F. (1999). Nikolai Kondratiev and the early consensus and dissensions about history and statistics. *History of Political Economy, 31*(1), 169–205.

Low, N. (1995). Regulation theory, global competition among cities and capital embeddedness. *Urban Policy and Research, 13*(4), 205–25.

Lukacs, G. (1971). *History and class consciousness* (R. Livingstone, Trans.). London: Merlin Books. (Original work published in 1920/1967.)

Luxemburg, R. (1976). *The national question: Selected writings by Rosa Luxemburg* (H.B. Davis, Ed.). New York: Monthly Review Press.

Lynch, C. (1998). Social movements and the problem of globalization. *Alternatives, 23*, 149–73.

Macas, L. (1991). *El levantamiento indígena visto por sus protagonistas*. Quito: Instituto Científico de Culturas Indígenas.

Macas, L. (2005, January 14). *Somos millones de hombres y mujeres*. CONAIE inaugural presidential speech delivered January 14, 2005. Retrieved January 26, 2005, from <http://conaie.org/?q=node/40&PHPSESSID=23b96d555768d7d1634690aaf00537f9>.

MacDonald, P. (2000). Gender equity, social institutions and the future of fertility. *Journal of Population Research, 17*(1), 1–6.

Macpherson, C.B. (1977). *The life and times of liberal democracy*. Oxford: Oxford University Press.

Makela, F. (2001). The intrusion of big business into academia's ivory tower. *CAUT Bulletin, 48*(4), A11.

Mandel, E. (1980). *Long waves of capitalist development: The Marxist interpretation*. London: Cambridge University Press.

Mander, J., & Goldsmith, E. (Eds.). (1996). *The case against the global economy: And for a turn toward the local*. San Francisco: Sierra Club Books.

Maniates, M. (2002). Individualization: Plant a tree, buy a bike, save the world? In T. Princen, M. Maniates, & K. Conca (Eds.), *Confronting consumption* (pp. 43–66). Cambridge, MA: The MIT Press.

Mann, H. (2001). *Private rights, public problems: A guide to NAFTA's controversial chapter on investor rights*. Winnipeg: International Institute for Sustainable Development and World Wildlife Fund US.

Marchak, P. (1998). Environment and resource protection: Does NAFTA make a difference? *Environment and Development, 11*(2), 133–54.

Marshall, T.H. (1950). *Citizenship and social class*. Cambridge: Cambridge University Press.

Martinez-Alier, J. (1987). *Ecological economics: Energy, environment and society*. Oxford: Blackwell.

Marx, K. (1952). *Wage labour and capital*. Moscow: Progress.

Marx, K. (1973). Kritik des Gothaer Programms. In K. Marx & F. Engels (Eds.), *Werke Band 19* (pp. 13–32). Berlin: Dietz Verlag.

Marx, K. (1976). *Capital, Volume 1* (B. Fowkes, Trans.). Harmondsworth: Penguin Books. (Original work published in 1887.)

Marx, K. (1977). *Das Kapital, 1. Band*. Berlin: Dietz Verlag. (Original work published in 1887.)

Marx, K., & Engels, F. (1978) Die deutsche ideologie. *Werke Band 3*. Berlin: Dietz Verlag.

Maturana, H.H., & Varela, F.J. (1987). *The tree of knowledge: The biological roots of human understanding*. Boston: Shambhala.

McCaughan, E. (1997). *Reinventing revolution*. Boulder, CO: Westview Press.

McCullough, P. (1993). *Brain dead, brain absent, brain donors: Human subjects or human objects?* Toronto: John Wiley and Sons.

McDonald, D.A. (2002). No money, no service: South Africa's poorest citizens lose out under attempts to recover service costs for water and power. *Alternatives, 28*(2), 16–20.

McDowell, L. (1991). Life without father and Ford: The new gender order of post-Fordism. *Transactions of the Institute of British Geographers, 16*(4), 400–19.

McGuinness, T., & Thomas, D. (1997). The diversification strategies of the privatised WaSCs in England and Wales: a resource-based view. *Utility Policy, 6*(4), 325–39.

McInnes, C. (2001a, October 11). Group slashing red tape dominated by business, labour chief says. *Vancouver Sun*, pp. B1, B5.

McInnes, C. (2001b, October 17). Liberal red tape cull to be secret process. *Vancouver Sun*, p. B6.

McKibben, B. (1999). *The end of nature*. Toronto: Anchor Books.

McMurtry, J. (1998). *Unequal freedoms: The global market as an ethical system*. Toronto: Garamond.

McMurtry, J. (1999). *The cancer stage of capitalism*. London: Pluto Press.

McMurtry, J. (2001, July-December). The commodity Cul-de-Sac. *Socialist Studies Bulletin, 65*, 5–21.

McNally, D. (1981, Autumn). Staple theory as commodity fetishism: Marx, Innis and Canadian political economy. *Studies in Political Economy, 6*, 35–63.

McNally, D. (1993). *Against the market: Political economy, market socialism and the Marxist critique*. New York: Verso.

McNally, D. (2001). *Bodies of meaning: Studies on language, labour and liberation*. Albany: State University of New York Press.

McNally, D. (2002). *Another world is possible: Globalization and anti-capitalism*. Winnipeg: Arbeiter Ring.

Merchant, C. (1982). *The death of nature*. New York: Harper and Row.

Meyer, B. (1990). The power of money: Politics, occult forces and Pentecostalism in Ghana. *African Studies Review, 41*(3), 15–37.

Meyer, B. (1995). Delivered from the powers of darkness: Confessions of satanic riches in Christian Ghana. *Africa, 65*(2), 236–55.

Mezirow, J. (1995). Transformation theory of adult learning. In M.R. Welton (Ed.), *Defense of the lifeworld* (pp. 39–70). Albany: State University of New York Press.

Mijeski, K.J., & Beck, S.H. (1998, September 24–26). *Mainstreaming the indigenous movement in Ecuador: The electoral strategy.* Paper presented at the XXI International Congress of the Latin American Studies Association, Chicago.

Miles, A. (1996). Adult education for global social change: Feminism and women's movement. In P. Wangoola & F. Youngman (Eds.), *Towards a transformative political economy of adult education: Theoretical and practical challenges* (pp. 277–92). Dekalb, IL: LEPS Press, Northern Illinois University.

Miliband, R. (1995). *Socialism for a sceptical age.* New York: Verso.

Miller, P. (1997). From Locke to Gaia: environmental ethics and Canadian forest policy. In A. Wellington, A. Greenbaum, & W. Cragg (Eds.), *Canadian issues in environmental ethics* (pp. 50–66). Peterborough: Broadview Press.

Mitchell, R.A., & Shafer, N. (1994). *New money for healthy communities.* Tucson: Thomas H. Greco, Jr.

Mittelman, J.H. (1996). The dynamics of globalization. In J.H. Mittelman (Ed.), *Globalization: Critical reflections: Vol. 9. International political economy yearbook.* London: Lynne Rienner.

Monckton, S. (2005, January 19). Latin America: Cuba and Venezuela strengthen solidarity. *Green Left Weekly.* Retrieved June 6, 2005, from http://www.greenleft.org.au/back/2005/611/611p18.htm.

Morris, D. (1996). Communities: Building authority, responsibility, and capacity. In J. Mander & E. Goldsmith (Eds.), *The case against the global economy* (pp. 434–445). London: Earthscan.

Morrow, R.A., &. Torres, C.A. (1995). *Social theory and education: a critique of theories of social and cultural reproduction.* Albany: State University of New York Press.

Murphy, J. (2003). Reply to Humphrey McQueen. *Labour & Industry, 13*(3), 99–103.

National Film Board of Canada. (1993). *The body parts business* [Motion picture]. Ottawa: National Film Board, No. 9193 089.

Naughton, J. (2001, May 3–9). Well webucated? *Guardian Weekly,* p. 24.

Newson, J. (1994). Subordinating democracy: The effects of fiscal retrenchment and university-business partnerships on knowledge creation and knowledge dissemination in universities. *Higher Education, 27,* 141–61.

Newson, J. (1998). The corporate-linked university: From social project to market force. *Canadian Journal of Communications, 23,* 107–24.

Nisbet, R. (1986). *Conservatism.* Minneapolis: University of Minnesota Press.

Noble, D.F. (2000, April 15). Comeback of an education racket. *Le Monde Diplomatique.*

Nolan, M. (2003). The high tide of a labor market system: the Australasian male breadwinner model. *Labour & Industry, 13*(3), 73–92.

Noske, B. (1997). *Beyond boundaries: Humans and animals.* Montreal: Black Rose Books.

Offe, C. (1984). *Contradictions of the welfare state* (J. Keane, Ed.). Cambridge: MIT Press.

Offe, C. (1996). *Modernity and the state.* Cambridge: Polity Press.

O'Hare, D. (1999, August 5). *Testimony before the Subcommittee on Trade of the House Committee on Ways and Means Hearing on the United States negotiating objectives for the WTO Seattle.* Presented at the Ministerial meeting, Washington.

Okri, B. (1992). *The famished road.* London: Vintage Books.

Olivera, O., & Lewis, T. (2004). *Cochabamba: Water rebellion in Bolivia*. Cambridge, MA: South End Press.

O'Reilly, J., & Spee, C. (1998). The future of regulation of work and welfare: time for a revised social and gender contract? *European Journal of Industrial Relations*, 4(3), 259–81.

Organ Procurement and Transplantation Network. (2002). *Annual Report*. Retrieved October 15, 2003, from <http://www.optn.org/data/annualReport.asp>.

Organ thugs may have removed man's eyes. (1995, November 25). *Edmonton Journal*, p. A10.

Organ transplants. (1996, Fall). *Time Magazine* (Special Issue), p. 56–59.

Organization for Economic Co-Operation and Development (OECD). (2002, June). *Towards sustainable consumption: An economic conceptual framework*. Paris: Environment Directorate.

Organization of African Unity. (2000). *African model legislation—for the protection of the rights of local communities, farmers and breeders, and for the regulation of access to biological resources, formally endorsed*. Retrieved May 25, 2005, from <http://www.grain.org/brl/?docid=798&lawid=2132>.

Organs removed on eve of Chinese executions, group says. (1994, August 29). *Edmonton Journal*, p. A6.

Orloff, A.S. (1993). Gender and the social rights of citizenship: The comparative analysis of gender relations and welfare states. *American Sociological Review*, 58(3), 303–28.

Otero, G. (1995). Mexico's political future(s) in a globalizing economy. *Canadian Review of Sociology and Anthropology*, 32(3), 319–43.

Otero, G. (1999). *Farewell to the peasantry? Political class formation in rural Mexico*. Boulder, CO: Westview Press.

Otero, G. (2004a). Global economy, local politics: Indigenous struggles, citizenship and democracy. *Canadian Journal of Political Science*, 37(2), 325–46.

Otero, G. (2004b). *Mexico in transition: Neoliberal globalism, the state and civil society*. London: Zed Books.

Otero, G., & Jugenitz, H. (2003). Challenging national borders from within: The political-class formation of indigenous peasants in Latin America. *Canadian Review of Sociology and Anthropology*, 40(5), 503–24.

Overbeek, H. (2002). Neoliberalism and the regulation of global labor mobility. *The Annals of the American Academy of Political and Social Science*, 581(1), 74–90.

Panitch, L., & Gindin, S. (2004). Global capitalism and American Empire. *Socialist Register*, 1–42.

Panitch, L., & Leys, C. (2003). *Socialist register 2004: The new imperial challenge*. London: Merlin.

Panitchpakdi, S. (2002, February 5). WTO services negotiations 2002: A Business-Government Dialogue on U.S. Trade Expansion Objectives. *Speech to the US Coalition of Service Industries*. Washington: U.S. Department of Commerce.

Pappas, N. (2001). Family income inequality. In J. Borland, B. Gregory, & P. Sheehan (Eds.), *Work rich, work poor: Inequality and economic change in Australia* (pp. 21–39). Melbourne: Centre for Strategic Studies, Victoria University.

Patomäki, H., & Teivainen, T. (2004). The World Social Forum: An open space or a movement of movements? *Theory, Culture & Society*, 21(6), 145–54.

Patrick, C.H., Phillips, M.G., & Diethelm, A.G. (1991). Donor nephrectomy. In M.G. Phillips (Ed.), *UNOS: organ procurement, preservation and distribution in transplantation* (pp. 53–76). Richmond, VA: UNOS.

Peck, J., & Tickell, A. (1994). Searching for a new institutional fix: the "after-Fordist crisis and the global-local disorder". In A. Amin (Ed.), *Post-Fordism: A reader* (pp. 280–315). Oxford: Blackwell.

Peck, J., & Tickell, A. (1995). The social regulation of uneven development: "regulation deficit", England's South East, and the collapse of Thatcherism. *Environment and Planning A*, 27(1), 15–40.

Petras, J., & Veltmeyer, H. (2001). *Globalization unmasked: Imperialism in the 21st century.* Halifax: Fernwood Books.

Petrella, R. (1998). *Le Bien Commun. Eloge de la solidarité* (Cahiers Libres). Lausanne: Editions Page Deux.

Petrella, R. (2001). *The water manifesto.* London: Zed Books.

Pfau-Effinger, B. (1998). Culture or structure as explanations for differences in part-time work in Germany, Finland and the Netherlands? In. J. O'Reilly & C. Fagan (Eds.), *Part-time prospects: An international comparison of part-time work in Europe, North America and the Pacific Rim* (pp. 177–96). London: Routledge.

Pigem, J. (2002, September). Barcoding Life. *New Internationalist, 349*, p. 26.

Pirates Ahoy! (2002, September). *New Internationalist, 349*, p. 25.

Pocock, B. (2003). *The work/life collision.* Sydney: Federation Press.

Polanyi, K. (1957). *The great transformation: The political and economic origins of our time.* Boston: Beacon Hill. (Original work published in 1944.)

Polanyi, K. (1968). *Primitive, archaic and modern economies.* Boston: Beacon Press.

Polster, C. (1996). Dismantling the liberal university: The state's new approach to academic research. In B. Brecher, O. Fleischmann, & J. Halliday (Eds.), *The university in a liberal state* (pp. 106–21). Brookfield: Avebury.

Polster, C. (2000). The future of the liberal university in the era of the global knowledge grab. *Higher Education, 39*, 19–41.

Porritt, J. (1985). *Seeing green: The politics of ecology explained.* New York: Basil Blackwell.

Postel, S., & Vickers, A. (2004). Boosting water productivity. *State of the World 2004* (pp. 46–65). New York: W.W. Norton.

Pozarnik, J. (2005). *Historical process will give Chavez new Venezuelan socialism concrete form.* Retrieved May 13, 2005, from <www.headline.com/readnews.asp?id=34098>.

Prebisch, R. (1971). *Change and development—Latin America's great task.* New York: Praeger.

Priest, L. (2002, November 16). Boss gets organ from domestic. *Globe and Mail*, p. A1.

Princen, T., Maniates, M., & Conca, K. (2002). Confronting consumption. In T. Princen, M. Maniates, & K. Conca (Eds.), *Confronting consumption* (pp. 1–20). Cambridge, MA: The MIT Press.

Probert, B. (1996). The riddle of women's work. *Arena Magazine, 23*, 39–45.

Probert, B. (2002). "Grateful slaves" or "self-made women": A matter of choice or policy? *Australian Feminist Studies, 37*, 7–18.

Progler, J.A. (1998). Urging the "North American Pig" to cut consumption. *Muslimedia*. Retrieved April 30, 2005, from <http://www.muslimedia.com/archives/features98/northpig.htm>.

Project for the New American Century (PNAC). (2000). *Rebuilding America's defenses: Strategy, forces and resources for a new century.* Washington, DC: Author.

Prud'homme, J.F. (1998). Interest representation and the party system in Mexico. In P.D. Oxhorn & G. Ducatenzeiler (Eds.). *What kind of democracy? What kind of market? Latin America in the age of neoliberalism* (pp. 169–192). University Park: Pennsylvania State University Press.

Public Citizen. (2001). *NAFTA chapter 11 Investor-to-States cases: Bankrupting Democracy.* New York: Public Citizen.

Quotations on Consumerism / Overconsumption. *Recycling Program—University of St. Thomas.* Retrieved May 15, 2005, from <http://www.stthomas.edu/recycle/consume.htm>.

Radin, M.J. (1996). *Contested commodities: The trouble with trade in sex, children, body parts, and other things.* Cambridge, MA: Harvard University Press.

Raiskums, B.W. (2001). *Principles and principals.* Anchorage: PWR & Associates.

Reid, H., & Taylor, B. (2000). Embodying ecological citizenship: Rethinking the politics of grassroots globalization in the United States. *Alternatives, 25,* 439–66.

Renner, M. (2004). Moving toward a less consumptive economy. *State of the World 2004* (pp. 96–119). New York: W.W. Norton.

Reporter killed over organ trade, says dad. (1996, October 4). *Edmonton Journal,* p. A5.

Ribeiro, S. (2003, January 25). *Biopiracy.* Workshop presented at the 3rd World Social Forum, Porto Alegre, Brazil.

Rickman, A. (2002, February 8). *Interview with Deputy Director of Sierra Club of Canada.*

Rifkin, J. (1998). *Le siècle biotech.* Paris: Éditions la Découverte et Syros.

Rinehart, J. (1996). *The tyranny of work: Alienation and the labour process* (3rd ed.). Toronto: Harcourt Brace.

Robbins, R.H. (1999). *Global problems and the culture of capitalism.* Boston: Allyn & Bacon.

Robbins, R.H. (2005). *Global problems and the culture of capitalism* (3rd ed.). Toronto: Pearson.

Ruiz Hernández, M. (2000). The plural national indigenous assembly for autonomy (ANIPA): The process of creating a national legislative proposal for autonomy. In C. Burguete & A. Mayor (Eds.), *Indigenous autonomy in Mexico* (pp. 24–52). Copenhagen: International Work Group for Indigenous Affairs.

Rural Advancement Foundation International (RAFI). (2000, November 2). Call to Dialogue or Call 911? *RAFI Geno-Type.* Retrieved May 25, 2005, from <www.etcgroup.org/documents/geno_call911.pdf>.

Sachs, W., Reinhard, L., Manfred, L., & Behrensmeier, R. (1998). *Greening the North* (T. Nevill, Trans.). New York: Zed Books.

Sahlins, M. (1972). *Stone age economics.* Chicago: Aldine.

Sanne, C. (2002). Willing consumers—or locked-in? Policies for sustainable consumption. *Ecological Economics, 42,* 273–87.

Saunders, D. (2002, October 30). For-profit US schools sell off their textbooks. *Globe and Mail,* p. A1.

Sauve, P., & Wilkie, C. (2000). Investment liberalization in GATS. In P. Sauve & R.M. Stern (Eds.), *GATS 2000: New Directions in Services Trade Liberalization* (pp. 331–63). Washington: Brookings Institution.

Scheper-Hughes, N. (1998). The new cannibalism. *New Internationalist, 300,* 14–17.

Scheper-Hughes, N. (2000). *Postmodern cannibalism: Black market trade of human organs.* Toronto: Information Access.

Schor, J. (1992). *The overworked American: the unexpected decline of leisure.* London: Basic Books.

Schor, J. (1999). *The overspent American: Why we want what we don't need.* New York: Harper Collins.

Schumpeter, J. (1939). *Business cycles: A theoretical, historical and statistical analysis of the capitalist process* (Vols. 1–2). New York: McGraw-Hill.

Sciabarra, C.M. (1980, May). Government and the railroads during World War I: Political capitalism and the death of enterprise. *Historian: The Undergraduate Journal of Research and Scholarship, 20*, 31–45. Retrieved May 20, 2005, from <http://www.libertarian.co.uk/lapubs/histn/histn045.htm>.

Sells, R.A. (1992). The case against buying organs and a futures market in transplants. *Transplantation Proceedings, 24*(5), 2198–2202.

Selverston-Scher, M. (2001). *Ethnopolitics in Ecuador: Indigenous rights and the strengthening of democracy.* Miami: North-South Center Press.

Senituli, L. (2002, September). The gene hunters. *New Internationalist, 349*, p. 13–14.

Shaker, E. (1999). Higher education, limited: Private money, private agendas. *Education, Limited, 1*(4), i–xx. Ottawa: The Canadian Centre for Policy Alternatives.

Shaver, S. (2002). Gender, welfare, regimes and agency. *Social Politics, 9*(2), 203–11.

Shirley, M. (2002). *Thirsting for efficiency: The economics and politics of urban water system reform.* Oxford: Elsevier Press.

Shiva, V. (1997). Economic globalization, ecological feminism, and sustainable development. *Canadian Woman Studies, 17*(2), 22–27.

Shiva, V. (2002). *Water wars: Privatization, pollution and profit.* London: Pluto Press.

Shot to order for organ transplants. (1998, March 8). *Edmonton Journal*, p. F5.

Shrybman, S. (1997, May). *An environment guide to the World Trade Organization.* Ottawa: Canadian Alliance on Trade and Environment.

Silva, G., Tynan, N., & Yilmaz, Y. (1998). Private participation in the water and sewerage Sector—Recent Trends. *Public Policy for the Private Sector* (Note 147, pp. 1–8). Washington, DC: World Bank Group.

Simpson, A.W.B. (1986). *A history of the land law* (2nd ed.). Oxford: Oxford University Press.

Singer, D. (1999). *Whose millennium? Theirs or ours?* New York: Monthly Review Press.

Sklair, L. (2001). *The transnational capitalist class.* Malden: Blackwell.

Sleeman, J.F. (1953). *British public utilities.* London: Sir Isaac Pitman & Sons.

Smith, A. (1994) *The wealth of nations* (E. Cannon, Ed.) New York: Random House. (Original work published in 1776.)

Smith, P.J., & Smythe, E. (1999). Globalization, citizenship and technology: The MAI meets the Internet. *Canadian Foreign Policy, 7*(2), 83–105.

Smyth, P. (1998). Remaking the Australian way: the Keynesian compromise. In P. Smyth & B. Cass (Eds.), *Contesting the Australian way: States, markets and civil society* (pp. 81–93). Cambridge: Cambridge University Press.

Soron, D. (2004). The politics of consumption: an interview with Juliet Schor. *Aurora Online.* Retrieved August 22, 2005, from <http://aurora.icaap.org/2004Interviews/JulietSchor.html>.

Soron, D. (2005, Spring). Death by consumption. *Labour / le Travail, 55*, 197–212.

Southerton, D. & Tomlinson, M. (2003). *Pressed for time—the differential impacts of a "time squeeze"* (CRIC Discussion Paper, No. 60). Manchester: University of Manchester.

Southerton, D., Warde, A., & Hand, M. (2004). The limited autonomy of the consumer: Implications for sustainable consumption. In D. Southerton, H. Chappells, & B. Van Vliet (Eds.), *Sustainable consumption: The implications of changing infrastructures of provision* (pp. 32–48). Northampton, MA: Edward Elgar.

Starr, A. (2000). *Naming the enemy: Anti-corporate movements confront globalization.* London: Zed Books.

Statesmen's year-book (1913). New York: St. Martin's Press.

Stavenhagen, R. (2000). Towards the right to autonomy in Mexico. In C. Burguete & A. Mayor (Eds.), *Indigenous autonomy in Mexico* (pp. 10–21). Copenhagen: International Work Group for Indigenous Affairs.

Sterling, S.R. (1990). Towards an ecological worldview. In J.R. Engel & J.G. Engel (Eds.), *Ethics of environment and development: Global challenge, international response* (pp. 77–86). Tucson: The University of Arizona Press.

Stern, S. (1987). *Resistance, rebellion, and consciousness in the Andean peasant world, 18th to 20th Centuries.* Madison: University of Wisconsin Press.

Strasser, S. (1982). *Never done: A history of American housework.* New York: Pantheon Books.

Strasser, S. (1999). Epilogue: From Walden to Wal-Mart: consumers and their critics. In M. Brower & W. Leon (Eds.), *The consumer's guide to effective environmental choices: Practical advice from the Union of Concerned Scientists* (pp. 179–203). New York: Three Rivers Press.

Suter, C. (1992). *Debt cycles in the world-economy: Foreign loans, financial crises and debt settlements, 1820–1990.* Boulder, CO: Westview.

Swenarchuk, M. (1988, February 29). *Environmental impacts of the Canada-U.S. Free Trade Agreement.* Prepared for The Standing Committee on Finance and Economic Affairs, Canadian Environmental Law Association.

Swenarchuk, M. (1998). The MAI and the environment. In A. Jackson & M. Sanger (Eds.), *Dismantling democracy: The Multilateral Agreement on Investment (MAI) and its impact* (pp. 120–37). Ottawa: The Canadian Centre for Policy Alternatives and James Lorimer.

Swift, R. (2002). *The no-nonsense guide to democracy.* Toronto: Between the Lines.

Taussig, M. (1980). *The devil and commodity: Fetishism in South America.* Chapel Hill: University of North Carolina Press.

Taylor, B., & Tilford, D. (2000). Why consumption matters. In J.B. Schor & D.B. Holt, *The consumer society reader* (pp. 463–487). New York: The New Press.

Taylor, C. (2002). Modern social imaginaries. *Public Culture, 14*(1), 91–124.

Taylor, W. B. (2000). Patterns and variety in Mexican village uprisings. In J.E. Kicza (Ed.), *The Indian in Latin American history* (Rev. ed., pp. 157–89). Wilmington: Scholarly Resources.

Teeple, G. (1995). *Globalization and the decline of social reform.* Toronto: Garamond Press.

Tello, C., & Cordera, R. (1985). *La Disputa por la Nación.* Mexico: Siglo XXI.

Therborn, G. (1984, Spring). Classes and states: Welfare state developments, 1881–1981. *Studies in political economy, 13*, 7–41.

Thompson, E.P. (1991). *Customs in common.* New York: The New Press.

Thrift, N. (1994). Commodification. In R.J. Johnston, D. Gregory, G. Pratt, & M. Watts (Eds.), *The dictionary of human geography* (3rd ed., pp. 78–79). Malden, MA: Blackwell.

Toner, G. (1997). Environment Canada's continuing roller coaster ride. In G. Swimmer (Ed.), *How Ottawa spends, 1996–97: Life under the knife* (pp. 99–132). Ottawa: Carleton University Press.

Traynor, K. (2002, February 14). *Interview with environmental staff at the Canadian Environmental Law Association.*

Turcotte, J.G. (1992). Supply, demand, and ethics of organ procurement: The medical perspective. *Transplantation Proceedings, 24*(5), 2140–42.

Ungerson, C. (1997). Social politics and the commodification of care. *Social Politics, 4*(3), 362–81.

United Kingdom. Department of Trade and Industry. (2002, October 10). *Liberalising trade in services: Summary of requests made to EC/UK.* Retrieved May 3, 2005, from <http://www.dti.gov.uk/ewt/gats1.pdf?nourl=www.dti.gov.uk/%2520publications/pdflink/&pdfpdfload=02%252F1403>.

United Nations Development Programme (UNDP). (1998). *Human Development Report 1998*. New York: Oxford University Press.

United Nations Environmental Programme (UNEP). (2001). *Consumption opportunities: Strategies for change*. Paris: UNEP.

United Nations Environmental Programme. Secretariat of the Convention on Biological Diversity. (1992, June 5). *Convention on Biological Diversity, Rio de Janeiro*. Retrieved May 25, 2005, from <http://www.sdinfo.gc.ca/docs/en/biodiversity/Default.cfm>.

United Network for Organ Sharing (UNOS). (1996a). *Number of U.S. transplants by organ and donor type, 1988–95 document*. Richmond: UNOS.

United Network for Organ Sharing (UNOS). (1996b). *Organ: Heart—number of transplants performed, 1968–1987 document*. Richmond: UNOS.

United States. CIA. (2005). *The world fact book*. Updated February 10. Retrieved February 27, 2005, from <http://www.odci.gov/cia/publications/factbook/fields/2051.html>. [no pagination]

United States. General Accounting Office. (2002). *Water infrastructure: Information on financing, capital planning, and privatization* (GAO-02-764). Washington: Author.

United States. House Committee on Energy and Commerce. Subcommittee on Health and the Environment. (1984). *Hearing on National Organ Transplant Act* (HR. 4080). 98th Congress.

Vanek, M. (1996). *Nedalo se tady dychat*. Prague: Maxdorf.

Verdery, K. (1998). Property and power in Transylvania's decollectivization. In C. Hann (Ed.), *Property relations* (pp. 160–80). Cambridge: Cambridge University Press.

Wachtel, P. (1989). *The poverty of affluence*. Philadelphia: New Society.

Wackernagel, M., & Rees, W. (1996). *Our ecological footprint: Reducing human impact on the earth*. Gabriola Island: New Society.

Wallerstein, I. (1979). *The capitalist world economy*. Cambridge: Cambridge University Press.

Warde, I. (2001, March). For sale: US academic integrity. *Le Monde Diplomatique*, p. 13.

Wearne, P. (1996). *Return of the Indian: Conquest and revival in the Americas*. London: Cassell and Latin America Bureau.

Weber, P.G., & Heinrichs, D.F. (1991). Coordination of single and multiple organ recovery. In M.G. Phillips (Ed.), *UNOS: organ procurement, preservation and distribution in transplantation* (pp. 151–57). Richmond, VA: UNOS.

Weis, T., & Krajnc, A. (1999). Greenwashing Ontario's lands for life: Why some environmental groups are complicit in the Tory's disastrous plan. *Canadian Dimension*, 33(6), 34–38.

Weisbrot, M. (2001, September/October). Tricks of trade: The only thing "free" about it is the free ride it gives giant corporations. *Sierra*, pp. 64–70, 84–85.

Weisskopf, T.E., Bowles, S., & Gordon, D. (1985). Two views of capitalist stagnation: Underconsumption and challenges to capitalist control. *Science and Society*, 49(3), 259–86.

Wesselius, E. (2002a). *Behind GATS 2000: Corporate power at work* (The World Trade Organisation Series, No. 4). Amsterdam: Transnational Institute.

Wesselius, E. (2002b). *Liberalisation of trade in services: Corporate power at work* (GATSWATCH Briefing Paper). Amsterdam: Corporate Europe Observatory.

Williams, C.C., & Windebank, J. (2003). The slow advance and uneven penetration of commodification. *International Journal of Urban and Regional Research*, 27(2), 250–64.

Wilpert, G. (2004, September 15). A historic date for Venezuela, Latin America and the left, *ZNet*, pp. 1–7.

Winfield, M.S. (2002). Environmental policy and federalism. In H. Bakvis & G. Skogstad (Eds.), *Canadian federalism: Performance, effectiveness and legitimacy* (pp. 124–37). Don Mills, ON: Oxford University Press.

Winpenny, J. (1994). *Managing Water as an Economic Resource.* London: Routledge.

Winpenny, J. (2003). *Report of the World Panel on Financing Infrastructure.* France: World Water Council.

Wojciechowski, J.A. (2001). *Ecology of knowledge.* Washington: The Council for Research in Values and Philosophy.

Wolf, J.S. (1991). Brief history of transplantation. In M.G. Phillips (Ed.), *UNOS: organ procurement, preservation and distribution in transplantation* (pp. 5–6). Richmond, VA: UNOS.

Wood, E.M. (1999a). *The origin of capitalism.* New York: Monthly Review Press.

Wood, E.M. (1999b). The politics of capitalism. *Monthly Review, 51*(4), 12–26.

Wood, E.M. (2002, August-September). Keyword: Capitalism. *New Socialist, 37.* Retrieved April 13, 2005, from <http://newsocialist.org/magazine/37.html>.

Wooden, M. (2001). The growth of "unpaid" working time. *Economic Papers, 20*(1), 29–44.

Woodhouse, H. (2003, February 1–4). Strengthening Saskatchewan communities through education. *Saskatchewan Notes, 2*(3), Canadian Centre for Policy Alternatives—SK.

World Bank. (2002). *Globalization, growth, and poverty: Building an inclusive world economy.* New York: Oxford University Press.

World Commission on Environment and Development (Brundtland Commission). (1987). *Our common future.* Oxford: Oxford University Press.

World Trade Organization. (1994). *General Agreement on Trade in Services.* Retrieved April 4, 2005, from <http://www.wto.org/english/docs_e/legal_e/26-gats.pdf>.

World Trade Organization. (1998a, September 18). *Health and social services: Background note by the secretariat* (WTO Document Symbol: S/C/W/50). WTO Council for Trade in Services.

World Trade Organization. (1998b, November 12). *Report of the meeting held on 14 October 1998* (WTO Document Symbol: S/C/M/30). WTO Council for Trade in Services.

World Trade Organization. (1998c). Services GATS (Section 6). *WTO—A Training Package.* Retrieved April 15, 2005, from <http://www.wto.org/English/thewto_e/whatis_e/eol/e/default.htm>.

World Trade Organization. (1999a, February 9). *Recent developments in services trade—Overview and assessment* (WTO Document Symbol: S/C/W/94). WTO Council for Trade in Services.

World Trade Organization. (1999b, August 5). *Preparations for the 1999 ministerial conference* (WTO Document Symbol: S/C/W/119). WTO Council for Trade in Services.

World Trade Organization. (2000, December 22). *Special session on Communication from the European communities and their member states—GATS 2000: Construction and Related Engineering Services* (WTO Document Symbol: S/CSS/W/36). WTO Council for Trade in Services.

World Trade Organization. (2001a, March 28).*Guidelines for the scheduling of specific commitments under the general agreement on trade in services* (WTO Document Symbol: S/L/92). WTO Council for Trade in Services.

World Trade Organization. (2001b, June 22). *Special Session: Report of the meeting held on 14 to 17 May 2001* (WTO Document Symbol: S/CSS/M/9). WTO Council for Trade in Services.

World Trade Organization. (2002, July 12). *Examples of measures to be addressed by disciplines under GATS article VI.4—Informal Note by the Secretariat* (WTO Document Symbol: JOB(01)/62/Rev.2). WTO Working Party on Domestic Regulation.

World Trade Organization. (2004, November 10). *United States-measures affecting the cross-border supply of gambling and betting services: Report of the panel* (WTO Document Symbol: WT/DS285/R).

World Trade Organization. (2005a, January 14). *Measures affecting the cross-border supply of gambling and betting services: Appellant submission of the United States.* Retrieved April 4, 2005, from <http://www.ustr.gov/Trade_Agreements/Monitoring_Enforcement/ Dispute_Settlement/WTO/Section_Index.html>.

World Trade Organization. (2005b, April 7). *Measures affecting the cross-border supply of gambling and betting services: Report of the Appellate Body* (WTO Document Symbol: WT/DS285/AB/R).

Wright, E.O. (2005, March 4–6). *Basic income as a socialist project.* Paper presented at the fourth congress of the U.S. Basic Income Guarantee Network (USBIG Congress), New York, NY.

WuDunn, S. (1997, May 18). Japan split by debate over organ transplants. *Edmonton Journal*, p. F5.

Yashar, D. (1998). Contesting citizenship: Indigenous movements and democracy in Latin America. *Comparative Politics, 31*, 23–42.

Yashar, D. (1999). Democracy, indigenous movements, and the postliberal challenge in Latin America. *World Politics, 52*(1), 76–104.

Zakaria, F. (1995). Back to the future: 1914–1991 after history's detour. *National Review, 47*(23), 54–55.

Zamosc, L. (1994). Agrarian protest and the Indian movement in the Ecuadorian Highlands. *Latin American Research Review, 29*(3), 37–68.

Zumwalt, J.P. (1996). *Pressure Politics and Free Trade: Influence of the Services Industry on the Uruguay Round.* Washington: National Defense University, National War College.

NOTES ON CONTRIBUTORS

KAREN BAKKER is Assistant Professor in the Department of Geography, University of British Columbia. Her publications on water privatization include a book (*An Uncooperative Commodity: Privatizing Water in England and Wales*, Oxford University Press), numerous academic articles, and reports for Environment Canada and the Federation of Canadian Municipalities. Current work focuses on the impacts of both state and private sector neglect of water supply for urban poor in the South—the subject of her contribution to the UNDP's Human Development Report for 2006. She is currently editing a book on water governance in Canada (UBC Press forthcoming).

RAY BROOMHILL is Associate Professor within the Australian Institute for Social Research at the University of Adelaide. His research interests are in Australian political economy, gender studies, and public policy, and he is currently researching the impact of global restructuring on working experiences and gender relations in Australia.

ELLEN GOULD is a Vancouver-based consultant to consumer groups, municipal governments, professional associations, and the Harrison School of Law, Georgetown University on the impacts of international trade agreements. Her published reports include "Trade Treaties and Alcohol Advertising," *Journal of Public Health Policy* 26, no. 3 (2005); *International Trade Agreements: An Update* (Richmond, BC: Union of BC Municipalities, July 2004); "Implications of the GATS Negotiations for Consumers," *Transatlantic Consumer Dialogue* (June 2004); "Trade Liberalization and Its Impacts on Alcohol Policy," *Johns Hopkins University SAIS Journal* (Winter–Spring 2002).

DR. TERESA GUTIÉRREZ-HACES is a researcher at the Instituto de Investigaciones Económicas and Professor of Political Science at the Universidad Nacional Autónoma de México (UNAM). She heads the project "The U.S. Foreign Economic Policy towards Mexico and Canada." She has a PhD in Political Science from the Sorbonne in Paris. Since 1989, she has been actively researching and publishing on the debate on Free

Trade and Protectionism as well as NAFTA's impact on the three North American countries.

TREVOR W. HARRISON is Professor of Sociology at the University of Lethbridge and former Research Director of Parkland Institute. He is the author or editor of six books on Canadian society and politics, including *Of Passionate Intensity: Right-Wing Populism and the Reform Party of Canada* (1995), *Requiem for a Lightweight: Stockwell Day and Image Politics* (2002), and *The Return of the Trojan Horse: Alberta and the New World (Dis)Order* (2005), and is a frequent public commentator on political events in the province and nationally.

HEIDI JUGENITZ completed an MA in Latin American Studies at Tulane University exploring the Ecuadorian indigenous movement, and she is now working on a PhD in International Development Studies at Tulane University. She has worked for three years in Africa at the UN World Health Organization, Africa Branch.

ANITA KRAJNC is Assistant Professor in Political Studies at Queen's University. Her research and teaching focuses on how the labour and environmental movements are changing their strategies and tactics in the face of neo-liberal globalization.

GORDON LAXER is a political economist at the University of Alberta. He is the author, editor, or co-editor of four books including *Open for Business: The Roots of Foreign Ownership in Canada* (1989), *The Trojan Horse: Alberta and the Future of Canada* (1995), and *Global Civil Society and its Limits* (2003). Laxer's current research is on the US Empire and its challengers from popular-democratic internationalist nationalisms, globalism and globalization, Canadian society, development and underdevelopment, and energy security. Laxer is a public intellectual and the Director and co-founder of Parkland Institute, a non-corporate institute that does research for the public good. He was principal investigator of the SSHRC-funded *Globalism and its Challengers* Project (2000–2006).

DAVID MCNALLY is Professor of Political Science at York University in Toronto, Ontario. His research interests span radical political economy, political theory, Marxism, radical theories of language and culture, globalization, and global justice movements. His books include *Another World is Possible: Globalization and Anti-Capitalism* (2002), *Bodies of Meaning: Studies on Language, Labor and Liberation* (2000), *Against the Market: Political Economy, Market Socialism and the Marxist Critique* (1993), and *Political Economy and the Rise of Capitalism* (1990).

BIRGIT MÜLLER is a senior researcher at the LAIOS-CNRS in Paris. Her current research focus is on biotechnology in the international arena and in the everyday world of food producers. Her books include *Toward an Alternative Culture of Work* (Westview Press 1991), *Political and Institutional Change in Post-Communist Eastern Europe* (CSA

1999), *Disenchantment with the Market Economy: East Germans and Western Capitalism after 1989* (Berghahn Books 2006).

GERARDO OTERO is Director of Latin American Studies and Professor of sociology at Simon Fraser University. He is the editor of *Neoliberalism Revisited: Economic Restructuring and Mexico's Political Future* (Westview 1996) and *Mexico in Transition: Neoliberal Globalism, the State and Civil Society* (Zed Books 2004) and author of *Farewell to the Peasantry? Political Class Formation in Rural Mexico* (Westview 1999). His new edited book, *Food for the Few: Neoliberal Globalism and the Biotechnology Revolution in Latin America* is forthcoming with The University of Texas Press. His current research is about states and agrarian movements.

RHONDA SHARP is Professor of Economics in the Hawke Research Institute at the University of South Australia. She is an internationally recognized scholar in the area of feminist economics. Her research has straddled the interrelated areas of economics, political economy, gender studies, and public policy.

DENNIS SORON is Assistant Professor in the Sociology Department at Brock University in St. Catharines, Ontario. His teaching and research interests include social theory, cultural studies, the political economy of consumption, social movements, and the intersection of labour and environmental politics.

JENNIFER SUMNER is Assistant Professor in the Adult Education and Community Development Program at the Ontario Institute for Studies in Education at the University of Toronto. Her research interests include adult education and lifelong learning, critical pedagogy, knowledge production, sustainability and globalization, rural communities, the organic farming movement, and the civil commons. She is the author of *Sustainability and the Civil Commons: Rural Communities in the Age of Globalization* (University of Toronto Press 2005).